FOODS & FLAVORS FROM NEPAL

FOODS & FLAVORS FROM NEPAL

Jyoti Pathak

HIPPOCRENE BOOKS, INC.
NEW YORK

Also by Jyoti Pathak
Taste of Nepal

Book design by Acme Klong Design and K & P Publishing.

For further information, contact:
HIPPOCRENE BOOKS, INC.
171 Madison Avenue
New York, NY 10016
www.hippocrenebooks.com

ISBN: 978-0-7818-1437-9

Cataloging-in-Publication Data available from the Library of Congress.

Printed in the United States of America.

DEDICATION

This cookbook is dedicated to my late mother, Kiran Kumari Pandey (1928-2021), for being the most dedicated and loving mother in the world who always believed in me and taught me everything in life, including the depth of Nepali cooking and the hope it will be enjoyed by the rest of the world. Her spirit never left me while working on this book.

ACKNOWLEDGEMENTS / DHANYABAAD

Thanks to my husband, Kamal D. Pathak, for great support and encouragement in testing every dish over and over until I was satisfied with the result. Thanks also to my three children, Rachana, Sapana, and Parag, my son-in-law Prabhat, and my daughter-in-law Ruma for their invaluable advice and guidance whenever I was lost. A special appreciation to my oldest daughter, Rachana for instilling self-discipline in me until the completion of the project by assisting in research and editing.

Thanks to my publishing team at Hippocrene Books, with deepest appreciation to my most helpful editor, Priti C. Gress, for responding to my questions and queries so promptly while I worked on this project and Barbara Keane-Pigeon, managing editor, for the final editing with great attention to details and her valuable advice. Thank you for helping to fulfill my dreams of a cookbook with photos.

CONTENTS

PREFACE
BHUMIKA

have been humbled to receive overwhelmingly positive feedback from the readers of my first cookbook, *Taste of Nepal*, over the last twelve years. That first book was my attempt to introduce Nepal's unique culinary heritage, cultural insights, ingredients, festivals, and lifestyles to people all around the world and readers were fascinated by the diverse culinary heritage of Nepal. Although the recipes were easy to follow, there were no pictures and no cultural commentary and some of my readers requested more information. One wrote to me, "The book has an impressive range of recipes, a vast amount of background information on the history, geography and culture of your beautiful country and more, but without pictures we are kind of hesitant to try some recipes." This is when I knew I had to write this cookbook, *Foods and Flavors from Nepal*.

Inspired by my readers' comments, in 2011, I grabbed a camera and started to take photos of my dishes, ingredients, meal preparations, and vegetables grown in my backyard garden. I sought to highlight Nepal's unique cultural heritage, cuisines, regional foods, recipes, festivals, lifestyles, and my personal travel stories. I also created a blog called "Taste of Nepal" that quickly grew in popularity. After more than 110 blog posts, readers kept me motivated by asking intriguing questions and posting commentary. Many people started to cook Nepali food and the feedback was encouraging. My readers shared their attempts to cook new dishes and asked where to find certain ingredients. I proudly shared information about my home country and cultural upbringing.

In the beginning of 2021, the publisher of Hippocrene Books approached me with the idea of updating my first cookbook with photos as she saw an intense interest in Nepali cooking and culture. Thus this new cookbook was born which includes recipes from the original book along with some new recipes, photographs, and cultural commentary. It is also inspired by the Nepali diaspora. Since writing my first book, many second generation Nepalese have shared their attempts to create Nepali cooking with me. Some of them made dishes with non-Nepali friends and thereby spread our unique Nepali cuisine across the globe. When I heard stories that their copy of *Taste of Nepal* was stained with spices and oil, I felt gratified.

Over the years I have visited Nepal to pursue my research on Nepali dishes, ingredients, regional foods, and traditional methods of cooking. I have taken thousands of photographs of Nepali vegetable markets, street food stalls, rice and buckwheat fields, food and festivals, in both Kathmandu and in more rural areas. With my camera, I captured everything I saw and felt. My daily morning visits to the Ason markets in Kathmandu were rewarding to learn about fresh vegetables. Some vendors would recognize me and tell me all about the fruits and vegetables they had just picked. My friends and family shared their cooking techniques and secrets to enhance the flavor of Nepali cuisine. Some of these photographs now appear in this book.

Visitors and tourists who have spent time in Nepal have come to understand the virtues and diversity of Nepali food. Many tell me that they appreciate the fresh and healthy aspect of our food. Some friends have told me that although they no longer reside in Nepal, they still eat traditional food from their home country. They say that their beloved simple "*daal-bhaat-tarkaari*" (lentil-rice-vegetable) combination meal is the "best diet to stay healthy" and the only food they crave every day.

Since my first book, I have observed that like most cuisines, the winds of globalization have led to an interesting fusion of cooking ideas. Recipes are constantly changing and modernizing with the times. As the size of the Nepali diaspora expands, new Nepali restaurants, food trucks, and food delivery services are opening up in many large cities. Some of these restaurants even sell "street food" similar to the delicious snacks I ate in Kathmandu. For instance, I've attended *momo* (Nepali-style stuffed dumplings) tastings here in the U.S. When I first came to the U.S. years ago, there were very few Nepali ingredients and spices available in stores. Now, they are available online and even in some local Nepali stores. These changes are a pleasant surprise, that has made Nepali food more accessible.

When I first started my journey over twelve years ago, there were not many Nepali cookbooks. These days, many people learn about Nepali cuisine from the Internet and YouTube. It is now possible to learn about Nepali cuisine through blogs, online videos, or even discussion forums. Although people increasingly turn to the Internet, good old-fashioned cookbooks remain a valuable reference and something many cooks cherish. I hope this cookbook will give Nepali food lovers the opportunity to expand their culinary horizons or refresh and re-create dishes they have loved. With photographs and new and revised recipes, my goal is to encourage more people to try their hand at preparing Nepali dishes. As always, I am eager to hear your feedback and suggestions.

—Jyoti Pandey Pathak

WELCOME TO NEPAL!
SWAAGAT CHHA!

Nepal is known for its Himalayan peaks, stunning landscapes, Hindu and Buddhist religious monuments, white-water rafting, bird-watching, safaris, and green vegetation. It is equally famous for its rich cultural traditions, unique cuisines, and year-round festivals. More than one hundred ethnic groups live in Nepal, each with their own distinct foods, customs, and traditions. The greate/st attraction for many visitors is the welcoming hospitality of the Nepali people.

Nepal is a landlocked country bordered by Tibet on the north and India to the east, west, and south. It is the birthplace of Buddha. Although Nepal is a small country, it contains the greatest variation in altitude on earth, from the lowlands of the Tarai in the south to the world's tallest mountain, Mt. Everest (29,028 feet). The length of the country is 550 miles from east to west and it averages 125 miles from north to south. Nepal can be roughly divided into three geographic areas: the high Himalayan region, the mountain region, and the Tarai region, each with its own distinct customs, history, economy, and environment. These different landscapes have shaped the culinary traditions of Nepal's more than twenty-nine million people. Hinduism and Buddhism live side-by-side and these traditions have blended in some instances to the point where you cannot separate one from the other. Nepal's official language is Nepali (related to Sanskrit) and it is written in Devanagari script. Tourism is one of Nepal's main industries and visitors can experience this diverse, rich country through its festivals and celebrations.

For centuries Nepal had relatively little contact with the rest of the world. Because of this isolation, Nepali foods and traditions were not influenced by foreign ingredients, resulting in a unique culinary culture. After 1950, when Nepal opened its borders to the outside world, its cuisine, especially in the capital of Kathmandu, was increasingly influenced by the culinary traditions of neighboring areas. Nepali food evolved to incorporate Indian, Chinese, and Tibetan influences. Modern Nepali cooking, foods, and eating habits have also been shaped by exposure to many Western influences, a process that has been facilitated by Nepal's popularity as a tourist destination. However, in rural villages, cooking has stayed close to its traditional roots, and in some areas, villagers still cook the same food their ancestor have made for centuries.

Given Nepal's vast geographic and cultural diversity, it is difficult to generalize about what constitutes Nepali cuisine. It is, however, characterized by its simplicity, lightness, and health-fulness. A typical meal uses only the freshest local ingredients, minimal fat, and an artful combination of herbs and spices. Meat, poultry, and fish are served only occasionally, mostly during celebrations. Nepali cuisine varies by region, but most meals consist of some form of rice or other grain accompanied by dried beans, lentils, peas, and fresh vegetables. In the mountain regions, local staples include *sattu* or *tsaampa* (roasted flour), *thukpa* (noodle soup with vegetables), yak cheese, and boiled potatoes with salted yak butter tea. In the rural and hilly regions where there is a scarcity of rice, Nepalese typically consume a simple meal of cornmeal, buckwheat, barley grain, or millet porridge (*dhindo*), usually accompanied by some kind of pickle and *gundruk* (fermented dried leafy vegetables). Culinary influences from the northern part of Nepal include fermented bamboo shoots (*taamaa*), salted and pickled radish (*sinki*), sun-dried fish, yak meat (*sukeko maachaa, sukuti*), and various preserved vegetables that are pickled, fermented, or sun-dried (*gundruk, sinki* and *achaar*). *Momos* (bite-size stuffed dumplings) are another common dish that has roots in the north. *Sukuti* (dehydrated meat) is common in the hilly areas where there is a harsher climate with less favorable growing conditions.

Other Nepali dishes are inspired by the indigenous Newari culture that exists largely in the Kathmandu Valley. Newari meat dishes often are made with buffalo meat. Some typical Newari meat dishes include *chowelaa* (grilled and spiced meat), *kachilaa* (marinated, spiced raw ground meat), *takhaa* (jellied meat soup), *bhuttan* (boiled and fried organ meat), *haku chowelaa* (broiled meat with spices), *swan puka* (batter-filled lungs), and *momochaa* (meat-filled dumplings). Other dishes include *kwaanti* (sprouted eight-bean soup), *chataamari* (rice flour bread), *woh* (lentil patties), *laakhaa-mari* (ceremonial sweet bread), *yoh-mari* (stuffed steamed rice bread), *samay-baji set* (pressed rice flakes with meat, vegetables, soybeans, and boiled-fried eggs), and *juju dhau* (sweetened yogurt). Homemade alcohol, *ailaa* and *thwon*, is prepared during festival times or celebration.

A common meal in many areas of Nepal is "*Daal-Bhaat-Tarkaari*" (Lentil-Rice-Vegetable). There are at least a dozen variations of this staple combination, and each has a different taste and flavor. The rice is usually boiled and accompanied by *daal* (lentil soup), which is prepared from dried beans, lentils, or peas. Vegetables are the third component of this staple meal. A variety of fresh vegetables and many leafy greens pre-dominate Nepali meals and are cooked according to regions and seasons. Most vegetables are cultivated, but some are gathered in the wild such as fern tips, bamboo shoots, and even nettle greens. Nepali spicing is mild and subtle with a moderate use of oil, but meals are often accompanied by a side dish of spicy pickles. *Daal-Bhaat-Tarkaari* is artfully presented on flat, compartmentalized plates called *khande thaal*. It might also be served on a round platter made from brass, steel, or copper with accompanying bowls. The rice and bread are placed directly on the plate or in the largest compartment, while vegetables and lentils are placed in the individual bowls or in the smaller compartments. This way one can taste each dish individually, or mix them according to preference. A single plate of rice is rarely enough to satisfy most Nepalese, and is almost always followed by a second, and in many cases, a third helping.

Nepali food is often associated with Indian or Tibetan food, or a combination of both, but it has its own distinct flavors and textures. North Indian spices provide bold flavors in sauces and condiments and cumin, coriander, black pepper, turmeric, red and green chilies, garlic, and fresh ginger are seen in both cuisines. However, the two most authentic Nepali spices, *jimbu* (Nepali aromatic leaf garlic) and *timmur* (Nepal pepper), are not seen in Indian cooking. I would say Nepali food is neither Tibetan nor North-Eastern Indian, but has a unique taste of its own.

This book is an attempt to showcase the art of Nepali cooking and make Nepali cuisine available to a wider audience. Home-cooked Nepali meals are neither difficult nor complicated. As is true for all cuisines, traditional cooking methods are vanishing due to fast foods and quick shortcuts. Food is always changing and evolving, but it is useful to document the culinary traditions of the past before they are completely forgotten. Cooking is an art and should be pleasurable. Beginners should not worry about making mistakes. Cooking is not like a math chart. If your dish turns out different than what you expected, you can easily repair it with a pinch of this and a pinch of that. It is a learning process. I hope the recipes and cultural insights in this book will help you to broaden your culinary horizons. Welcome to my kitchen!

A GUIDE TO CUSTOMS AND ETIQUETTE IN NEPALI DINING

Here are a few basics about Nepali dining etiquette to better understand the country and culture:

- The joint family system, where the father, mother, married sons and their spouses and children all live together, is still widespread in Nepal. During meals, family members gather on the kitchen floor, sitting cross-legged, on a low wooden stall or mat (*pirka* or *chakati*). Some modern families use western-style tables and chairs. Dining together is a joyful occasion. Customs are deeply ingrained and food taboos are taken seriously.

- When you are in a Nepali kitchen, shoes are taken off due to religious reasons and hygiene.

- To begin the meal, family members offer a small amount of food to their gods and ancestors and bow their heads to express gratitude for the food provided.

- Usually the food is first served to the eldest or most respected family members or friends. All dishes are served together at the same time, usually by a female member of the family. If you desire a second helping, you don't serve yourself. Dishes are not passed around. Rather, the cook or hostess spoons the prepared food onto your plate. They keep an eye on who needs what, and make sure that everyone eats well by repeatedly offering more food. Men and children often dine first, followed by women.

- Before and after eating, water is provided to wash hands, rinse the mouth, and gargle.

- Traditionally, Nepalese eat with their right hand, as the left hand is considered unsanitary. Western influences have introduced silverware, but some Nepalese are still convinced that food tastes better with their hands. Eating with one's hands forms a connection between the texture and temperature of food, improves digestion, and prevents overeating. Eating this way has its own etiquette: use only the right hand and just the tips of the fingers to mix the rice with vegetables, leaving the palm perfectly clean.

- It is common to make noisy slurping sounds while eating or drinking.

- Leftover food is called *baasi-khaana* and is traditionally given to animals as a gesture of kindness to all living things.

- In many orthodox Hindu homes, *maacha-maasu* (meat and fish) may not be mixed or served together. There is no scientific reason for this that I know of, but logically speaking (and this is just my opinion), our forefathers probably thought that it would be improper to mix two kinds of protein for digestion.

- Some religious people with orthodox views avoid eating food cooked by others but will accept food like fruits, milk, and vegetables.

- In the Nepali language, *jutho* refers to tasting food from a cooking pot with a stirring spoon or eating food from someone else's plate or sipping water from other people's glass, and doing so is considered impure and makes food polluted or inedible. This is one of the most important food taboos in Nepal and observing it is a sign of respect.

- Although Nepal is one of the poorest countries in the world, it is known as one of the most hospitable countries. Guests are always looked upon as gods and Nepalese consider it an honor to welcome visitors, including strangers and passersby, and treat them with kindness and courtesy. From the rich to the poor, Nepalese always offer guests some kind of food and beverage.

- Food is a constant topic of conversation in Nepal. No meal is complete without an extended discussion about food, such as how it is cooked, how it is served, and ruminating about recently enjoyed meals. It is also common to talk about one's health, weight loss or gain, and which foods treat various ailments.

- Dining in restaurants is not common. Most people eat at home, and a lot of time is spent preparing family meals. Entertaining is always done at home and the most authentic dishes are always found in individual homes.

- Culinary traditions and recipes are passed down by word-of-mouth from mother to daughter or daughter-in-law, or from grandmothers and aunts over time, with each generation adding their own special touches. Young girls learn to cook by watching and helping in the kitchen. Nepali cooks are not accustomed to measuring devices and cooking is mostly guided by basic principles and common sense, like most culinary traditions. There are no set rules that one has to follow.

Chapter 1

NEPAL'S CULINARY CULTURE

Food and Nepali Festivals

Nepal may be a small country but it has rich cultures, customs, and traditions—there are possibly more festivals celebrated in Nepal than anywhere else in the world. If you look at a Nepali calendar, there is a festival almost every month throughout the year. Nepali festivals are a wonderful time for relatives and friends to gather and food is an essential part of any Nepali celebration. The majority of Nepali festivals are celebrated according to the lunar calendar and some last for days. For religious festivals, Nepalese offer foods to various deities to get blessed. These sacred foods are then deemed auspicious and are shared with friends and neighbors. Nepal is a land of various cultures, religions, and ethnic groups and each group follows their own distinct customs. This section only lists select major festivals and their foods.

Paddy Plantation Day Festival
Rastriya Dhaan Diwas / Dahi Cheuraa Day

Nepalis celebrate the 15th day of the Nepali calendar, *Ashad Pandra (Bikram Sambat)*, as *Rastriya Dhan Diwas* (June 29) or Paddy Plantation Day Festival. On this day, farmers plant green rice seedlings by hand in the fields, sing traditional *asare* folk songs, and dance and play in the muddy fields.

Rice is the most important crop in Nepal and more than two-thirds of farmers living in rural areas depend on agriculture for their livelihoods. Many farmers in rural Nepal do not have an adequate irrigation system so the monsoon rains are critical. The annual "*Rastriya Dhan Diwas*" is important in farmers' lives as the monsoon rain soaks the rice fields and makes it easier to plant the seedlings.

After planting, the farmers and their families get together to enjoy a feast of *dahi-cheuraa*, seasonal fruits, *saandheko aloo* (a potato dish), other ceremonial foods, and homemade local rice beer. The *Rastriya Dhan Diwas* festival, sometimes called the *Dahi-Cheura* festival, is not limited to farmers and their families only, it is celebrated all over Nepal with enthusiasm to welcome the monsoon season.

CHEURAA

Cheuraa, chewraa, or *bajee* are pressed, pounded, or flattened rice flakes. They are prepared from soaked or parboiled rice grains that have been flattened by large heavy rollers into flat flakes. They are dehydrated and the finished product is ready-to-eat rice flakes. The old-fashioned method of pounding the grains in a heavy wooden mortar with a pole still exists in many villages, and is preferred by many, although it is slowly being replaced by machines. It is a popular food item in Nepal because it can be consumed without further cooking, stores well, is easy to carry, and is light and healthy.

DAHI-CHEURAA

Dahi-Cheuraa is a mixture of yogurt and flattened rice. When *cheuraa* flakes absorb the moisture of yogurt, they become soft and delicious. This mixture provides a burst of energy, does not cause bloating, and keeps farmers full for a long time. It is also easy to digest and has nutritional value for worn-out farmers.

Winter Festival
Maaghe Sankranti

Maaghe Sankranti, also called *Makar Sankranti*, is one of the most important and auspicious religious festivals in Nepal. It is celebrated on the first day of *Maagh* (on Nepali calendar *Bikram Sambat*), which falls in January. Nepalese celebrate the festival to mark the end of winter and the onset of spring when the temperatures get warmer and the days get longer.

Devotees wake up early often before sunrise and take ritual baths in holy rivers, while singing devotional songs and offering water to Surya (sun god). According to some beliefs, the bath is to purify the self and soul. After the bath, these devotees visit different temples and offer flowers, sacred foods, and light incense.

During this winter festival, Nepalese often visit their elder relatives, friends, and family, where they receive and give blessings. Like all Nepali festivals, food plays a major role during *Maaghe Sankranti*, also known as "*gheu-chaaku-tarul-pidaalu khane din*" (translation: "a day to eat sweets made from molasses, clarified butter, and root vegetables"). Family members get together and prepare special feasts. Traditional foods eaten during this festival include *Kaalo Daal Khichadi*, a one-pot meal cooked by combining rice, black gram daal, and spices and enjoyed with a generous serving of *gheu* and paired with sautéed green leafy vegetables (*gheu*, also spelled ghee, is a clarified butter made clear by heating and removing the sediment of milk solids). Other food items that make *Maaghe Sankranti* special are *sakhar-khanda* (sweet potatoes), *pidaalu* (taro roots), and *tarul* (yam). Sweet potatoes and taro are generally boiled and served in slices. Yams are delicious first boiled and then stir-fried with spices or made into a curry. The special favorites of the festival are *Til ko Laddu* (Sesame Seed Balls), *Tilauri* (bite-size chewy sesame candy), and *Chaakus*. *Til ko Laddu* are delicious, nutty round sweets prepared from toasted white sesame seeds, jaggery, and shredded coconut. *Chaakus* are retreated molasses patties in different sizes and shapes and are usually bought at markets. They are a sugary treat and the most important *Maaghe Sankranti* food.

The foods eaten during this festival are geared towards warming up the body during a cold winter, good nourishment, a lifetime free of disease, and purification of one's body. It is such a colorful, vibrant, and exciting time of the year in Nepal and the festival is celebrated with happiness, harmony, and warmth. During the festive time, you will see people queue up in the markets to buy root vegetables of all different sizes, shapes, and textures. Two weeks before the festival starts, people head to the market to stock up on food items such as *chaaku* patties in different sizes and shapes, semi-solid jaggery in plastic bags, sesame seed candy, and other food items.

Sacred Thread Festival
Janai Purnima

Janai Purnima is a festival of sacred thread, which is celebrated all over the country on the full moon day of Shrawan month (Nepali calendar *Bikram Sambat*) which falls in the month of August. It is one of the most important Hindu festivals. On this day, observers first take a ritual bath in the river to purify themselves, and then visit different temples. On this auspicious day, Hindu men renew their *janai*, which is a sacred white thread they wear. The priest chants mantras and performs the ritual of changing the old janai to a new thread. On this day, the family priest also ties a sacred yellow thread around the wrists of the entire family and gives blessings. There is a belief that wearing sacred thread brings good luck, protection from disease, safety, and bliss in life. Nepalese who reside in the Southern Terai area celebrate *Raksha Bandan* on this auspicious day. It is a festival to celebrate brother-sister day where sisters tie *rakhi* around the wrists of their brothers and wish them a long life and protection from disease.

There is no festival complete without a family gathering and a feast. On this day, a special dish called *Kwaanti, Quantee,* or *Biraula* is prepared and served with other ceremonial dishes. *Kwaanti* is a delicious stew-like soup prepared from a colorful array of mixed sprouted beans. Traditionally, the sprouts are prepared with a combination of nine different types of colorful beans: urad beans, mung beans, green peas, soybeans, black-eyed peas, chickpeas, kidney beans, fava beans, and field peas. The beans are washed, soaked overnight, and left to sprout in a warm place. This wholesome soup is highly nutritious and usually eaten with steamed rice. Today, *Kwaanti* is cooked regularly in many Nepali households, and one does not have to wait for festival time to enjoy it.

Dashain / Bijaya Dashami Festival

Dashain, *Badadashain* or *Bijaya Dashami* is a 15-day-long national (religious) festival of Nepal. It is the longest and the most auspicious and joyous festival in the Nepali annual calendar, celebrated by Nepali people throughout the globe. It is not only the longest festival of the country, but it is also the one that is most anticipated. The festival falls around October-November, starting from the bright lunar fortnight and ending on the day of the full moon. *Dashain* symbolizes the victory of good over evil. The goddess Durga is worshipped in all her manifestations throughout the country. *Dashain* time is a national holiday in Nepal and all government offices, educational institutions, banks, post offices, and some embassies are closed during Dashain.

Dashain is all about family gatherings, feasts, reunions, and cultural, social, and religious exchanges. It is a busy time of travel as people return to their villages. Many families clean, paint, and decorate their houses for these family reunions. It is a time to fly kites from the *kausi* (roof top), and a time to play *kauda* (cowrie shell game) and *taas* (card games). Swings made of bamboo are constructed for children and adults to enjoy all over the towns and villages. During this period, you will see people throughout Nepal in a festive mood. The streets are bustling with street vendors and store windows are decorated with *Dashain* themes and playing auspicious *mangal dhun*. The streets are lively and colorful and children are dressed in their new clothes and shoes. Women adorn themselves with jewelry and colorful traditional outfits.

The first day of the festival is called *Ghatasthaapanaa*, where Nepali Hindu households sow barley seeds in their *Pooja Kotha* (prayer room) and observe the seeds germinate and grow into beautiful shoots, called golden *Jamaraa*.

The tenth and main day of the *Dashain* festival (*Dashami*) is considered very important and auspicious. On that day, a special thick red paste called *acheeta ko raato tikaa* is prepared by mixing bright red vermillion powder, plain yogurt, and white rice grain. The elders of the family, parents, or relatives give this *tikaa* to junior and younger relatives who come for their blessings. The *tikaa* is applied in the middle of the forehead gently by using the tip of three fingers. Great care is taken to make a perfect round-shaped *tikaa* and to make sure it sticks on the forehead for the entire day. The red color of *tikaa* signifies "shakti" (strength). It is believed to bring spiritual wisdom, good health, peace and prosperity in one's life. It also symbolizes good luck, happiness, and healing. After applying *tikaa*, the golden-yellow shoots called *jamaraa*, are carefully placed over the head or tucked behind the ear of recipients. Some people chant Sanskrit Vedic *slokas* or give *aashirbaad* blessings while applying the *tikaa*. The following is the most common *slokas*: "*Om Jayanti Mangala Kaali Bhadra Kali Kapalini.*" Along with the *achheta ko raato tikaa* and *jamaraa*, people receive *dakshinaa*, which is blessed money for good luck.

After the ceremony, a big feast is prepared with great enthusiasm and delight. The importance of food is expressed by saying "*Dashain Aayoo, Khaula Piula,*" which literally translates to "*Dashain* is here, will eat and drink (feasting time)." After the important religious rites are performed, a number of goats, water buffalos, ducks, and chicken are sacrificed and offered to deities. A great feast is prepared with *prashad ko maasu* (blessed meat) along with other celebrated dishes that are eaten and distributed among friends, relatives, and neighbors. For many families this may be one of the few occasions during the year that they are able to eat meat. Meat is the major component of this festival. The meat is bone-in curried meat *pakku*, cooked with a delicate mixture of herbs and spices to make a gravy called *maasu ko kabob* that tastes even better the next day. Meats are also made into *sekuwaa* (roast), *saandheko* (marinated and made into salad-like dish), *bhutuwaa* (fried), *bari* (meatballs), or *jhol maasu* (soupy meat dish). All parts of the butchered animal are utilized, including the liver, intestines, brain, kidney, tongue, tripe, and blood.

A typical *Dashain thaali* consists of rice *pulau* (festive rice), meat dish, *maas ko bara* (urad bean fritters), different kinds of bean dishes, fried or curried vegetables, *cauli-alu* (cauliflower and potato medley), *kankro ko achaar* and *mula ko achaar* (pickled cucumber or radish), *sel-roti* (rice bread), *poori* (puffed bread). To end the meal, yogurt, *sikarni*, and various traditional sweet dishes are served.

Tihaar Festival

The five-day-long festival of *Tihaar* is the second biggest and most colorful festival in Nepal, and comes two weeks after *Dashain/Bijaya Dashami* between the months of October/November every year. During *Tihaar*, Laxmi, the goddess of wealth and prosperity, is worshipped. People clean their houses and decorate them with small clay oil lamps that are lit and placed in doorways, windows, and stairs to welcome the goddess. On this day, almost all government offices, educational institutions, banks and other public buildings are closed. *Tihaar* is celebrated with enthusiasm and happiness. Entire neighborhoods—the houses, streets, store fronts, and other public places—are all lit with lights and clay lamps, and decorated with marigold flower garlands. It is the festival of triumphs of good over evil, light over darkness, and knowledge over ignorance. In addition to worshipping Laxmi, special ceremonies are performed to worship animals. They are called *kaag tihaar* (crows), *kukkur tihaar* (dogs), and *gai tihaar* (cows). The five-day festival also celebrates *Bhai-Tikaa* (Brother-Sister Day), *Bhintunaa* (Newari New Year), *Mha Puja* (worship of self), and *Chhath Puja* (festival devoted to Surya, god of energy).

Feasts are an important part of any celebration, and *Tihaar* is a festival of sweet treats, and many delicately flavored sweets are prepared with various ingredients and flavorings. They are shared and exchanged with family, friends, and neighbors to celebrate the joyous occasion.

When I think of a *Tihaar* feast, it always includes *Sel-Roti* (Sweet Rice Flatbread), *Anarsaa* (fried rice cookies topped with sesame seeds), *Fini Roti* (layered pastry especially made for the festivals), *Aalu-Achaar* (spicy potato salad), *Poori* (puffed bread), *Juju Dhau* (creamy yogurt from Bhaktapur), and other freshly made sweets. The traditional *Tihaar* evening meal is *Daal-Bhaat*, and vegetables are prepared in a number of ways along with other celebratory food items.

Sel-Roti (*page 147*) is always prepared during Nepali religious festivals and for other special occasions such as weddings, birthdays, and family celebrations. It is also prepared as a sacred food for the gods (*naivedya*) and offered ritualistically to deities. *Sel-roti* along with other festive foods such as *laddu* and *peda* is distributed among friends and family as a *prashad* (blessed food).

In the narrow streets of Kathmandu, Patan, and the Bhaktapur area, you will see many century-old local sweet shops filled with a variety of traditional sweets. The *Haluwai Pasale* (sweet maker) and his staff are busy stretching and designing the dough into perfectly beautiful sweet bread. The most popular traditional Newari Mari sweets are *Laakhaa-Mari* bread. They arc a flaky-crunchy textured delicious cookie-bread. The dough is hand rolled, made into a beautiful design, deep-fried, and glazed with a light icing to create a translucent satiny finish.

Brother-Sister Day / Bhai-Tikaa

Bhai-Tikaa is the fifth and last day of the *Tihaar* festival and is observed to honor brothers by sisters. On this auspicious day, sisters begin the ceremony by offering special prayers, flowers, and fruits to deities, then apply *saptarangi tikaa* (seven-colored *tikaa*) on their brothers' foreheads. Then they place a garland made of three different kinds of flowers, *sayapatri, makhamali,* and *dubo* (marigold, globe amaranth, holy grass) around their brother's neck to wish them happiness, longevity, and prosperity. The brothers, in return, offer gifts to their sisters and pledge to protect and take care of them throughout their lives. Nepali traditions are deep-rooted and symbolize the bond, love, and respect for family and community.

After the end of the *Bhai-Tikaa* ceremony, sisters treat their brothers with their favorite food cooked specially for them. A special *Bhai-Tikaa* tray is prepared and decorated with several different varieties of dry fruits, nuts, fresh seasonal fruits, and traditional Nepali sweets. A typical *Bhai-Tika* sweets are *Anarsaa Roti*, which is sweet rice flour patties (cookies) topped with poppy seeds or sesame seeds. The rice dough is hand stretched into circles and deep fried, giving the cookies a crisp texture, and poppy seeds provide a pleasant nutty flavor. For a Nepali feast, *Sel-Roti* (Sweet Rice Flatbread, page 147) is a must item. A large quantity of *Sel-Roti* is cooked and then accompanies other traditional food items. *Khajuri* and *Fini Roti*, a flaky fried cookie, are other favorites along with *Peda* (round patties made from slowly simmered milk) and *Laddu* (sweet balls made from different flour, page 285). During this auspicious time, *Haluwai Pasale* (sweet makers) make a large quantity of assorted festive sweets. These festive sweets are more decorative than everyday treats and are often infused with cardamom, food coloring, and many other fancy ingredients.

Indra Jatra Festival and Samay Baji Food Offering

The eight-day long religious festival of *Indra Jatra* is celebrated according to the lunar calendar between the months of August/September. This festival honors Indra, the god of rain. It is also the long-awaited festival when the living goddess Kumari is carried in a *rath* (chariot) accompanied by musical bands around the narrow streets of Kathmandu. As the chariot is pulled through old Kathmandu, thousands of devotees wait to get a glimpse of the goddess and her blessings. People anxiously wait to see *Lakhay*, the dance of demons (masked dancers dressed in a costume) in the streets.

Indra Jatra is one of the liveliest religious festivals in Nepal, celebrated with much enthusiasm. A spectacular display of ritual food tower offerings, *Samay Baji*, is created and displayed in front of many temples. The sacred food is offered to the goddesses Kumari, Shree Ganesh, Seto, and Kalo Bhairab. After the offering, the food is considered *Prashad* (blessed by the deities). The *Prashad* will be shared and distributed and represents good luck, prosperity, fortune, health, and longevity.

To create the food tower, a large amount of *cheura* (pressed rice flakes) is placed in the auspicious site, then it is decorated with meat, vegetables, legumes, and sweet dishes. All the foods are selected according to traditions and customs. The ritual food tower consists of flattened rice flakes (*cheura* or *baji*), puffed rice (*samaya, swaya baji*), spiced black soybeans, julienned and fried fresh ginger rhizomes (*palu, aduwa*), marinated grilled meat (*chowella*), dried fish fried in oil (*sanya, sidra-maacha*), boiled-fried eggs, fresh fruits, lentil patties (*baara, woh*), several varieties of Newari mari breads, and alcohol (*ailaa*). Sometimes a smoked whole fish is placed on top of the *Samay Baji*

tower, which symbolizes good luck and fortune for the coming years ahead. *Laakha-mari*, the ceremonial Newari bread in different shapes and sizes are also placed in some display. Sometimes red clay containers of *Juju Dhau* (king of yogurt) and delicious creamy yogurt from Bhaktapur are placed around the display. A little red clay container of *rakshee* (local liquor), *jaad* (local beer), *chhang* or *thon* (a milky white, tart, slightly sweet liquor made from fermented rice) is placed around the *Samay Baji* display.

During this festival, hundreds of devotees come to the auspicious site with food items as an offering to the deities or just to pray. They offer money, traditional sweets, such as *anarsa-roti* (sweet rice patties with poppy seeds), *khajuri* (Nepali cookies), *khaaja* (flaked flour bread), *ladoo* (sweet chickpea balls), dry fruits, and other sweets and place them around the *Samay Baji*. There are numerous award-winning, creative displays of *Samay Baji* all over areas of Kathmandu, Bhaktapur, and Patan. It is really a festival of culinary art. There is also always traditional devotional music playing during the festival.

Today, *Samay Baji* is made regularly in many Newari households—one does not have to wait for the *Indra Jatra* festival to enjoy it. *Samay Baji* is served at many religious functions as a *Sagun* food. *Sagun* is a ceremony that involves presentation of auspicious food items, flowers, fruits, and sweets offered for good luck and best wishes. The auspicious foods are given during family celebrations, birthdays, weddings, or when someone is going away for a long journey. These days, a *Samay Baji* platter is served as a starter food in many restaurants or as a light lunch. The most popular food items are *cheuraa* (flattened rice), grilled and marinated meat, boiled-fried eggs, fried soybeans, julienned ginger, lentil patties, potato salad, bean dishes, small fried fish, and homemade wine.

Rice Feeding Ceremony
Paasne / Annaprashana

The century-old tradition of *Paasne* or *Annaprashana* is a rice-feeding ceremony for when infants are first fed rice, usually when they reach the age of six months old. The word *Annaprashana* in Sanskrit literally translates to "grain initiation." The *Paasne* ceremony is a time of joy, when a fam-

ily comes together to usher the baby from infancy to childhood and enjoy a sumptuous feast. It is the first important ceremony in a baby's life as they are introduced to solid foods which signifies change in the child's life. The day and time of the *Paasne* is usually chosen by an astrologer, and family and friends are invited to celebrate. On *Paasne* day, the child is dressed in a traditional outfit, the auspicious yellow-colored *tikaa* is drawn on his/her forehead, and *dubo ko mala* (garland made from holy grass) is put around the baby's neck. The baby sits on his/her aunt's lap seated on the floor. A special *kheer* (sweetened rice pudding) is prepared and given to the baby with blessings. Each family member feeds the baby a taste of rice and gives blessings with gifts.

Apart from *kheer*, eighty-four different varieties of dishes called *Chaurasi Benjan* are prepared. This includes fresh fruits, dry-fruits and nuts, several vegetable dishes, a variety of meat dishes, dried fish and fish preparations, boiled eggs, sel-roti, lentil patties, and ceremonial sweets. A giant, attractive *tapari* is made, which is a woven leaf plate, made by stitching several fresh saal leaves together. A large quantity of cooked rice is placed in the center of the leaf plate. Then the *Chaurasi Benjan* foods are placed in small plates along with floral offerings, and ritual objects are placed around the large decorative *tapari*. Some families also add the decorated head of a goat and flowers to their *Paasne* displays. A lot of attention is paid to decorate the food spread for this occasion that is then laid out in front of the baby.

Ceremony for Ancestors
Shraadh

Shraadh, also spelled *Shraddha*, or *Sraddha* is a ceremony performed to honor one's deceased parents and pay homage to their ancestors. It is performed yearly by sons or grandsons to ensure that the souls of their ancestors rest in peace. Usually, the eldest male performs the *puja* ceremony and others participate in rituals that are performed by the family priest. During this time, families give gifts of food, clothes, and *dakshina* (money) to the priest who performs the rituals. Close relatives come to the house and participate in the rituals and eat the food prepared for *Shraadh*. The food offerings are cooked at home, ensuring they are *chokho* (pure and fresh). Tasting the food during the preparation is not allowed. A special dish, *kheer* (rice pudding), is prepared and served to the priest along with other food. *Shraadh* food items are simple vegetarian foods and no alcohol is allowed. Usually, this consists of buttered rice, *Aalu ko Achaar* (Spicy Potato Salad), *Paalungo ko Saag* (Sautéed Spinach Achaar), *Phulaura* (round fritters made from urad daal), various *achaars*, fresh fruits, yogurt, and sweets made of milk, clarified butter (*gheu*), and sugar (*peda, laddu, jeri*).

Malekhu ko Maachaa
(Malekhu Fried Fish)

Sampling delicious, freshly caught fried fish of Malekhu. Cooking and eating Nepali food is a discovery of the culture in this fascinating Himalayan country. Malekhu, Dhading, is a scenic, sleepy, little village located about halfway between Kathmandu and Pokhara. It is a pleasant 3-hour drive from Kathmandu on the Prithivi Highway which overlooks the Trishuli River. We passed through rural villages and got a snapshot of a gaau-ghar (rural village) lifestyle while surrounded by breathtaking vistas of the river and the mountains.

Malekhu is famous for its just-caught fresh fish, which may be served deep-fried, smoked, or curried with Nepali spices by a number of road-side restaurants, all served with zero pretense. Buses usually stop at Malekhu for lunch breaks and travelers enjoy shopping for fried fish, smoked river fish on wooden skewers, and locally grown fruits, vegetables, beans, lentils, and peas. We had heard that if you have never tried Malekhu ko Maachaa, you are missing out on a special treat of Nepal so we were looking foward to eating here.

We made a quick stopover at Malekhu Bazaar on our way to Manakaamanaa Devi Temple from Kathmandu. It was hard to select which roadside restaurant to go to. Every single one of them had an abundant supply of freshly-caught fish. We had our choice of deep-fried or smoked fish, fried crawfish, sun-dried fish on a wooden skewer, or curried fish, something to please everyone in our group. We finally selected a restaurant

that had many varieties of deep-fried fish. We asked the pretty woman who wore a green Nepali cholo (blouse) if we could have Malekhu ko Maachaa and if it would be possible to fry our order in fresh new oil. She smiled and replied, "Gladly hajur, I can cook the fish any way you like and create a special dish for you." She told us that the fish was caught in the morning from the Trisuli River. Our sampling of Nepali hospitality started here! We sat at a roughly made wooden table and watched her cook for us.

First, she discarded the previously used oil, and then poured enough new oil to fill two inches in a large Nepali cast-iron karaahi (wok-shaped frying pan). A karaahi is one of the most indispensable cooking utensils in Nepali kitchens. It is made of heavy cast-iron and can withstand high cooking temperatures. It also absorbs heat quickly and distributes it evenly, making it one of the best utensils to fry fish over a wood-burning stove. To make "spicy fried fish Nepali style" she had already marinated the fish with salt, ground turmeric, ginger-garlic paste, ground cumin, ground mustard, chili paste, lemon juice, egg, and flour. The oil was heated until faintly smoking over a chulo (a wood-fed stove). Working with six or seven marinated fish at a time, she deep-fried the fish in a single layer, turning occasionally, until golden brown and crispy outside but moist inside. She drained the excess oil in the jhaajar (large slotted spoon) and transferred the fish onto a stainless-steel plate. The intoxicating aroma of freshly fried fish filled the air. The fried fish is eaten whole with head, tail, and bones, which provide a somewhat unexpectedly pleasant soft crunch.

The best memories of this area started here—we absolutely loved the Malekhu ko Maachaa! We savored every bite of the fish which was served with golbheda ko achaar (tomato chutney) and spicy potato patties. After finishing this platter, we were ready for more fried fish and jinghe maachaa (crayfish or crawfish). It was truly a memorable village dining experience and reminded me of a folk dohari song titled, "Malekhu maa bhet - Malekhu ko taaja maachaa khaanu hos hai!" (Translation – "Let's meet at Malekhu and eat fresh fish!")

After our lunch, we toured the other road-side stalls that were well stocked with dried fish sukuti, dried beans, lentils, and peas along with fresh vegetables. Another beautiful young woman who held a hand-held Nepali taraaju (measuring device) was selling locally grown vegetables. She asked us, "Malekhu ko taajaa-mitho maachaa khanu bhayo te?" ("Did you try delicious and fresh fish from Malekhu?"). (See recipe for Maleku Fried Fish on page 215.)

This photo shows a traditional way of making maachaa ko sukuti (dried fish). First, several small fish are artfully woven onto bamboo skewers. They are placed in an upright position, or on top of the wood-fired stove then dehydrated until the moisture has evaporated and the fish has dried to touch. The fish skewer is removed and the fish hung to air-dry further in natural sun rays.

The Magic of Making Sutkeri ko Ausedhi
Postpartum Super Confectionery Prepared for Nursing Mothers

Sutkeri ko Ausedhi, sutkeri masalaa, mishri paakh, battissa ko paakh/pokhunaa washaw, or *mishri pakh jwalaa* is a nutritious, delicious, and sweet medicinal confectionery that has been prepared in Nepal for centuries. The word "*sutkeri*" is used to describe the rest required for a mother after she gives birth to a baby. "*Ausedhi*" refers to specially prepared medicinal food. According to ancient customs, the new mothers are given *sutkeri ko ausedhi* along with other nutritious foods after the eleventh day of childbirth. It is the ultimate dietary supplement to help recover from childbirth, to boost energy, and to encourage milk production for a lactating mother.

Sutkeri ko Ausedhi is made by mixing several herbs and spices, clarified butter, edible gum, *khuwaa* (thickened and concentrated milk products), rock sugar, ground nuts, seeds, and dry fruits. Other important ingredients include *battisaa* powder (page 23) and *jesthalangwagi churna* powder (page 23), a medicinal plant mixture consisting of thirty-two different herbal plants. The mixture is cooked until it reaches a fudge-like consistency, somewhat chewy, rich, and sweet. This delicious and nutritious postpartum super food is typically eaten one to two tablespoons at a time, in the morning and evening along with a glass of warm milk.

Old traditions and customs are a part of everyday life in Nepal. Pregnancy, childbirth, and post-postpartum care is taken seriously and is called *sutkeri ko syahaar* in Nepali. New mothers are not allowed to work or lift any heavy objects. They are relieved of all household responsibilities, and are encouraged to stay indoors for at least four to six weeks to have complete rest and recovery. Furthermore, cultural beliefs dictate that a mother may not go out and be exposed to wind, cold air, or rain, which in Nepali is called "*cheeso laaglaa.*" This custom helps new mothers heal and restore their health as they are nurtured. Usually, older family members or an experienced helper is assigned to take care of a new mother, to prepare food, and to take care of the newborn. The new mother and baby are given a warm mustard oil massage right after delivery to speed up postpartum healing. In some families, the mother and her newborn get a full body massage two to three times a day. Elder relatives often remind new mothers by saying, "*Sutkeri maa syahaar ne gare, jeu bigrincha*" ("If one does not take care of the body during the postpartum period it could lead to serious illness later in life; if nourishing food is not eaten, one can suffer from back pain, premature aging, joint pain, and digestive disorder.")

In addition to complete rest, certain postpartum diets are prepared using traditional recipes that have been passed down through generations. These recipes include a broth-soup made from any variety of meat served with buttered rice (*gheu haaleko ko bhaat re maasu ko ras*) that helps speed up recovery. Another common and ultimate *sutkeri* food is ajowan soup as it helps boost a mother's milk supply, and is known to alleviate gas pain. Some people even add goat leg bones to the soup to make it more nutritious. Another popular meal served right after delivery is *gheu-chaaku-bhaat* (buttered rice with brown sugar). Other foods include boiled milk with honey, lentil soups, fresh vegetables cooked with minimum spices, and fresh fruits. Heavily spiced foods, chilies, caffeine, deep-fried foods, sour foods, and ice-cold foods are avoided.

When my daughter gave birth to her first child, I was determined to figure out how to make medicinal food the authentic way! I called my friends and family for their recipes for *Sutkeri ko Ausedhi*. Many of them were not sure about the proper proportions, and they told me "*alikiti*," or a little bit more or less, with a hand gesture. One cousin remembered her mother-in-law added a generous amount of soaked fenugreek seeds. She preferred not to grind the seeds because the soaking process softened the spice. Another friend told me not to grind the dry nuts into powder, but instead to chop the nuts halfway for a better texture. Others use fennel seeds sparingly. I found each family had their own selection of ingredients and their own preferred method of cooking, which had been passed down from their grandmothers, mothers, and other family members. There are actually no set rules for this recipe. After experimenting, the following is my version of *Sutkeri ko Ausedhi* that I grew up eating in childhood, when my younger siblings were born.

SUTKERI KO AUSEDHI

1 cup fenugreek seeds
½ cup ajowan seeds
2 cups fennel seeds
3 cups clarified butter (gheu), divided
1½ cups edible gum (available online)
2½ cups whole raw almonds
1 cup raw pistachios
1 cup raw cashews
1 cup pecans
1½ cups shelled walnuts
1 cup unsweetened coconut chips
1 cup raisins
2½ cups dried dates
Seeds of 15 cardamom pods, finely ground

Seeds of 10 black cardamom pods, finely
   ground
1 tablespoon ground cinnamon
1 teaspoon ground cloves
5 small whole nutmegs, finely ground
1 cup pumpkin seeds or melon seeds, plus
   ½ cup for decorating top
3½ cups granulated sugar (or sugar crystal)

Ayurvedic Ingredients (available to purchase
   at Nepali, Indian and on-line stores)
1 cup Battisaa powder
½ cup Jesthalangwadi powder
7 to 8 cups milk khuwaa

In a medium saucepan, combine fenugreek seeds, ajowan seeds, and fennel seeds with enough water to cover, and bring to a boil over high heat. Reduce heat to medium-low, cover pan, and continue cooking until seeds are soft, about 10 minutes. Remove from heat and drain, reserving the seeds. When cooled, place the seeds in a food processor or blender and process adding up to ½ cup water to make a semi-thick puree. You may want to do this in two batches if needed. Transfer the puree to a bowl and reserve.

Heat 1 cup clarified butter in a medium saucepan over medium-low heat and add the edible gum and fry until it puffs up, stirring constantly. With a slotted spoon, transfer the gum to paper towels to drain and set aside.

In the same pan, fry the almonds in the clarified butter, stirring constantly, until they start to get browned and toasted through. Using a slotted spoon, transfer to paper towels to drain. Similarly in the same pan, fry, one by one, the pistachios, cashews, pecans, walnuts, coconut chips, raisins, and dates until toasted through. Remove each immediately and drain. (Be careful that the nuts and fruits don't start to burn as they will continue to cook after being removed from the heat.) Once all have cooled, for best texture chop the nuts and fruit by hand into small pieces, or you can use a food processor. Place all in a bowl and set aside.

In a separate large saucepan, heat the remaining 2 cups clarified butter over medium-high heat and add the *Battisaa* powder and *Jesthalangwadi* powder and stir until well mixed. Mix in the ground fenugreek, ajowan, and fennel seed mixture and the *khuwaa*, and cook until the liquid has almost evaporated.

Add nut mixture and mix well. Add ground cardamon, black cardamom, cinnamon, cloves, nutmeg, and pumpkins seeds and mix well. Cook, stirring from time to time, until the mixture has thickened and reduced, about 25 minutes.

Stir in sugar and continue cooking, stirring and scraping the sides of the pan, until the mixture begins to pull away from the sides of the pan to create a thick solid mass. At this stage, butter starts separating from the pan.

Mix in 1 cup of fried gum and stir well. Remove the *sutkeri ko ausedhi* from the heat and transfer onto a serving tray and let it cool completely. Sprinkle with the melon or pumpkin seeds and remaining fried gum.

WHAT IS BATTISAA POWDER?

This is a powdered mixture of thirty-two *Ayurvedic* herbs and spices suited for pregnant and lactating women. It is widely believed in Nepal that *battisaa* powder contains beneficial or curative effects for women who have experienced excessive bleeding, pain in their lower abdomen, and miscarriage. The proportions of the herbs and spices in the *battisaa* mixture used in *Sutkeri ko Ausedhi* varies from family to family. Here is a list of ingredients in Nepali and English:

Amalaa (gooseberry), *Arjun (terminalia arjuna)*, *Ashwogandha* (winter celery), *Baayubidanga (embelia)*, *Barro (terminalia bellirica)*, *Bel* (Bengal quince), *Bhringaraaj* (trailing eclipta), *Daalchinee* (cinnamon), *Gurjo* (heart shaped moonseed), *Gokhur* (calthrops), *Harro (chebulic myrobolon)*, *Jethi madhu* (licorice), *Jira* (cumin), *Jwaanu* (ajowan), *Kaafal* (bay berry), *Kaauso* (common cowitch), *Kachur* (east India arrowroot), *Koiraalo* (mountain ebony, bauhinia), *Kurilo* (wild asparagus), *Majitho* (madder), *Marich* (black pepper), *Naagakeshar* (iron wood tree), *Naagarmoothe (cyperus scariosus)*, *Paasaanved* (rockfoil), *Pipalaa* (long pepper), *Punarnavaa* (spreading hog wood), *Sataawar* (wild asparagus), *Shankhapuspee* (butterfly pea), *Simal* (red cotton tree), *Sutho* (ginger), *Tej pat (Indian cassia lignea)*, *Thulo okhati (astilbe rivularis bush)*.

WHAT IS JESTHALANGWADI POWDER?

Jesthalangwadi is another type of powder made by mixing different medicinal and herbal plants often used to prepare medicinal *Sutkeri ko ausedhi*. Here is a list of the ingredients in Nepali and English:

Alainchi (black cardamom), *Ashwogandhaa* (winter cherry), *Bhringaraj* (trailing edipta), *Chandan-shreekhanda* (sandalwood), *Jaifal, Jaaipatree* (nutmeg), *Jatamashi* (spikenard), *Thulo piplaa* (Java pepper), *Krishna Jirak* (black Niger), *Kush* (sacrificial grass), *Marich* (black pepper), *Mungrelo* (black cumin), *Nilo Kamal* (blue water lily), *Rukh Keshar* (iron wood tree, bark, leaves, flower), *Sukumel* (green cardamom)

(Source: Research paper Food Science, Nepal - Acharya, Kharel, Bhandari)

Roadside Tea Vendors
Chiya Pasal

Chiya (pronounced *chee-yah*) or milky tea is the most widely consumed hot beverage in Nepal, where it is enjoyed throughout the day, starting in the early morning until after dinner. Some people drink tea instead of eating breakfast, followed by an early lunch.

Last year, when I was walking with my son, Parag, near the Nardevi area of Kathmandu, on our way to a shopping center, I heard a lady calling us, "*Namaste didi, taato, taato chiya khaanos.*" This translates to "Greetings! Come and enjoy the hot tea." She was a *chiya pasale* (tea vendor) inviting us to try her piping hot, freshly made tea. If you have ever traveled to Nepal or are familiar with Nepali customs, Nepali often refer to an elder or someone they respect using the word "*didi*" which means "sister." The tea vendor was calling me *didi* as a form of respect.

We accepted her invitation and sat on a small wooden bench next to her. Her large aluminum tea kettle was simmering on a portable gas stove. She poured the strained tea into a small glass and served us. The warm, delicious tea was comforting and refreshing. We chatted and listened to the conversations around the bench of other customers, who shared stories, gossip, and political news. An older man wearing a Nepali *bhaadgaule topi* (handwoven black cap) sitting next to us told us that his *chiya* had to be the same shade of his skin (which meant a little brown, not milky white), strong, and flavorful. He also said if you boil the tea leaves with water and sugar in it, the tea stays hot longer. Another smiling lady with neatly braided long hair was dipping *Nebico* biscuits into her tea glass, finding comfort and rest before the day's chores.

Tea drinking is a national obsession in Nepal. Sipping a steaming glass of milky tea slowly and chatting with others is an enjoyable pastime. Each morning, tea vendors prepare big pots of fresh tea. When the first batch is finished, another batch is made. Nepali tea is naturally cooked with milk, sugar, loose black tea, and water. The tea vendor combines all the ingredients in a kettle and boils the mixture on a stovetop until it reaches just the right color and flavor or desired consistency. The tea vendor has to keep a sharp eye to ensure the pot does not overflow. Sometimes they add fresh ginger slices, cinnamon sticks, and cloves to make a spicy and strong tea. I rarely found cardamom used in their tea, perhaps because of the high cost of the spice. The tea is usually strained directly into small glasses before serving. The tea stalls run from dawn to dusk, and a small glass of tea is a very affordable 20 to 30 Nepali rupees.

These days, tea bags have become more popular in Nepal, but I still prefer loose black tea for

its richer flavor, color, and usually lower price. Tea is grown mainly in the eastern parts of Nepal and Nepali tea is now exported all over the world.

During a trekking adventure with my daughter, Rachana, to Pokhara-Jomsom-Muktinath trail in Nepal, we drank countless cups of steaming and flavorful tea. The tea provided a quick burst of energy and gave us a chance to rest our legs. A hot pot of steaming tea was always ready at our stops at roadside tea vendors or teahouses. At one stop, the tea vendor showed me how he prepared the delicious tea. He used loose, broken black tea leaves and boiled them with water, milk, and sugar until it reached just the right color and flavor. He then strained it through a thin cloth and served it steaming hot.

POKHARA BAZAAR TEA

Makes 4 servings

3 cups whole or low-fat milk	8 whole black peppercorns
¼ cup sugar or adjust to taste	3 tablespoons loose black tea (preferably
1½ teaspoons minced fresh ginger	strong, full-bodied, Nepali tea)

In a medium-size saucepan, combine the milk, sugar, ginger, peppercorns, tea, and 6 cups of water and bring to a boil over medium-high heat. Reduce the heat to medium-low and continue to simmer until the tea becomes light brown. Strain the tea directly into individual cups and serve immediately.

The Role of Rice in Nepali Culture
Akshataa ko tikaa, Akshataa ko raato tikaa

One could say that life starts with rice and ends with rice in Nepal. Not only is rice used as nourishment, it is integral in Nepali traditions, ceremonies, rituals, festivals, and religious observances. Rice is present in all stages of life including pregnancy, birth, a child's first grain ceremony, marriage, and death.

Many Nepalese consider rice grains to be sacred. Some Hindu devotees start their day with a visit to their neighborhood temples and shrines at dawn. As offerings they bring a small copper or silver tray with *akshataa* (an uncooked and unbroken rice grain used in ritualistic worship to bring protection, energy, and prosperity to the devotee), vermilion powder, flowers, and incense known as *poojaa saamagri*.

Annapurna, the goddess of prosperity and abundance whose name literally translates as "grain" (*anna*) and "prosperity" (*purna*), is worshipped to promote a bountiful harvest. Throwing out or wasting food is considered disrespectful to Annapurna, the goddess of grain. As children, we were often reminded of the common Nepali saying, "*Anna le saraap-chha*," which translates as, "If you waste the rice grain in your present life, the goddess will curse you and in your next life you will suffer from starvation."

On many religious occasions, *akshataa ko tikaa* is prepared with uncooked rice grains, red vermilion powder, and yogurt mixed into a paste. This paste is applied to the forehead at family blessings and given to travelers for good luck. On the tenth day of *Dashain*, an important religious festival in Nepal (also called *Tikaa* Day, page 11), the family elders give *akshata ko rato tikaa* (red rice paste) as a blessing of good health, happiness, and prosperity. In certain parts of Nepal, they use white rice *tikaa*, without color (*seto akshata ko tika*), and widows are given yellow *tikaa* (*pahelo akshata ko tikaa*).

A Hindu religious ceremony known as the rice-feeding ceremony, *Paasne* or *Annaprashana*, is performed when a child reaches six months of age. During this *Paasne* ceremony, a child is fed rice as his or her first solid food, and this represents knowledge, wisdom, and purity (*see page 16*).

Rice also plays an important part in Nepali Hindu marriage ceremonies. For example, a groom's party is welcomed with a sprinkling of unhusked puffed rice (*laavaa*). A sacred flame is lit to start the wedding and an offering of puffed rice, raw rice, and rice mixed with butter is added to the fire for purity, fertility, and prosperity. For the bride's welcoming ceremony, rice grains are placed across the doorway of her husband's home. As she enters the house, she steps in seven small piles of rice to promote prosperity, positive energy, and happiness for her new family. Following the bride's welcoming ceremony, the bride and her mother-in-law play a ceremonial game called *paathi bharne*. This is the placing of white rice in a *paathi* which is a metal container for measurement of grains. In some families, the bride must serve rice when she moves into the groom's house.

Rice plays a role during mourning periods as well, as plain boiled rice is one of the few foods that can be consumed by the next of kin during the first thirteen days.

Rice flour is also used for religious occasions. Rice flour is mixed with water to form a thin paste that is used to draw intricate religious symbols called *aipan* on the ground. During the *Laxmi Pooja* festival during *Tihaar*, small footprints are drawn with rice paste at the entrance of many households, on the stairs, and all over the house to welcome the goddess of wealth and prosperity and ask her to bless the family with good luck. Rice and rice flour are also used to prepare sacred offerings (*naivedya*) for deities and consumed as blessed food (*prashaad*).

Finally, even some customary Nepali greetings have to do with rice. For instance, a common greeting is "*Bhanchha garnu bhayo?*" (in Nepali) or "*Jane dhuna la?*" (in Newari) ("Have you had your rice?" or "Have you finished your meal?") This is the first question asked regardless of the time of day and establishes care and concern for the other's well-being. An invitation to dinner would be, "*Aaja bhaat khaanaaunus,*" which means, "Come over for a rice dinner."

My husband and I were raised in households where rice was served two or three times a day. Although he has lived outside Nepal longer than in the country, he takes rice seriously. If he does not eat rice with dinner, it is as if no meal has been eaten at all. To give an example of what a large role rice plays in many Nepali households in Kathmandu, when I was growing up in Kathmandu, breakfast often started with soothing, nutritious, creamy rice porridge (*jaulo*) early in the morning. Lunch eaten before heading to school or work consisted of rice, lentils, and vegetables. Snacks eaten throughout the day contained pressed rice flakes or rice flour. Supper was freshly cooked rice accompanied by lentils, gravy-based or fried vegetables, and perhaps a small quantity of meat or fish with pickle and chutney.

Daals
The Wonderful World of Dried Beans, Lentils, and Peas

Daals need little introduction in Nepali cuisine and no Nepali meal would be complete without them. The term *daal* is used to include any dried legumes, such as lentils, beans, and peas. There are many forms of daal available, such as whole, split with skin, split without skin, or ground into flour. Each variety is cooked in its own way. For example, daal that is split without skin cooks much faster than whole daal. The simple *musuro ko daal* (split red or pink lentils without skin) and *pahelo mung ko daal* (split yellow mung beans) are the easiest and quickest cooking daals.

Daals are either cooked by themselves or combined with vegetables, rice, and other ingredients. When cooked daal is paired with rice, the meal is called *daal-bhaat*, which is eaten throughout Nepal. A bowl of rice and daal is a warm, soothing comfort food. Daals are prized for their high protein content and are one of the primary proteins in a Nepali vegetarian diet.

Daal is also the name given to the cooked versions of daals. In general, Nepalese prefer thinner daal and typically cook it to a soup-like consistency rather than thicker porridge-like forms of it, making it suitable to eat over boiled rice.

Daals are very easy to cook and do not require any special skills. There are just two simple steps: First, simmer them with spices until the lentils disintegrate into a soft puree. Then, temper or fry some spices in clarified butter or oil and add for extra flavor. The main spices used are asafetida, cumin,

DAAL-BHAT FOR FUEL & ENERGY

Tourism is one of the main industries in Nepal. According to the Nepal Tourism Board 197,191 foreign visitors visited Nepal in 2019 to trek, mountain climb, visit world heritage sites, and to experience Nepal's diverse cultures, festivities, and spirituality. These days, if you walk down any street in Kathmandu where souvenir shops are located, you will see a standard t-shirt printed with "Daal-bhat power 24 hour" (translation: "rice with lentils give energy 24 hours"). There is truth to this slogan. Warm *daal-bhat* is a nutritious popular dish for many tourists who visit Nepal for trekking. This traditional dish is served two times a day with variation. The combination meal is delicious, well balanced, and a great source of lasting energy. Before a climbing trip, local Nepali porters eat a large quantity of rice-lentils, which serves as fuel and energy to help their strenuous climb. While trekking, porters often joke that the distance they travel can be measured by the amount of rice-lentils they consume—to reach the lower hills, one needs to eat "*due maanaa daal-bhat*" (translation: 2 cups rice-lentils), while a more challenging hill requires "*teen maanaa daal-bhat*" (translation: 3 cups rice-lentils).

jimbu, mustard seeds, cloves, cinnamon, bay leaves, and dried red chilies. Some recipes also call for frying onions, garlic, ginger, and tomatoes in oil and adding toward the end of the cooking process.

Daals can be prepared one or two days in advance and stored covered in the refrigerator. It can be reheated by simmering gently with additional water. It is a versatile food; you can make it highly spicy or mild according to your taste, as the daals absorb the flavors of other ingredients that they are cooked with. Daals double in volume with cooking, and when cooled the mixture thickens, but you can add water to make it thinner. These days, many people cook daals in a pressure cooker to speed up the cooking time.

Dried legumes can also be cooked in many other ways. For example, they are soaked, pureed, made into fried snacks and breads, sprouted, or made into sweet dishes. Or they can be mixed with chopped vegetables and made into *meusaura-titaura* (dried nuggets).

Jimbu and timmur for sale at a Nepali market. A local measuring device called an ek maanaa, adhaa maanaa, *or* chauthai maanaa *is displayed. One* maanaa *is equal to roughly one cup. The metal handy tool is used to measure spices, rice, lentils and other grains.*

Jimbu and Timmur:
Two of Nepal's Most Authentic Spices

Jimbu

Jimbu (pronounced *jim-bu*), is a dried, aromatic, perennial herb that is virtually unknown outside the Himalayan region. It is also known as *jhikucha* in the Newari language and *jamboo/faran* in Uttarakhand, India. In scientific journals, *jimbu* is called *Allium Hypsistum Stearn* and belongs to the *Amaryllidaceae* family.

Local villagers and their family members sometimes need to travel several hours to the wild areas of the mountain regions where jimbu has been growing in abundance for centuries. These villagers carefully hand-pick the green and tender foliage. Although they collect both the flowering and non-flowering parts of the plant, many of them believe the best flavors come from the buds that are not fully opened. Harvest is conducted between July and September.

After collection, green jimbu is spread on dry mats in well-ventilated covered shady areas. The harvesters believe that drying in direct sunlight makes poor quality jimbu, without color and flavor. The herb is dried for several days until all the moisture has evaporated. This is the most traditional, simplest, and least expensive way of preserving the herb in the remote areas.

The flavor of the herb is weakened or nearly lost during the drying process. Jimbu loses its green color and starts to look like brownish dried grass. By the time it hits Nepali markets, jimbu is commonly sold in dried strands. The herb has a distinct flavor which is somewhat similar to garlic or shallots. Although the distinct aroma of the herb is nearly lost during the drying process, it can be brought back to maximum flavor by browning it in hot oil until fully fragrant. Generally, a small pinch of jimbu is sufficient to flavor a dish and it should be used with discretion. It is generally not used in its raw form.

Nepalis have a remarkable fondness for this herb and they use it as a tempering spice (*jhanae masalaa*) to flavor daals, stir-fried vegetables, salads, and pickles. The aromatic herb also adds flavor to preserved pickles (*achaars*). Traditionally, jimbu is fried in clarified butter (*gheu*) or mustard oil to maximize its flavor and the infused oil is poured into a prepared dish before serving. The fried herb lends texture and visual appearance to any dish. Some recipes call for jimbu to be added at the beginning stage of the cooking process, whereas other recipes require that it be added at the end.

People from the upper Mustang region of Nepal use jimbu for medicinal purposes, including stomach ailments, cough and cold, flu, and high altitude sickness.

Jimbu is available through online retailers or some local Nepali markets outside Nepal. As a substitute, some people use dried roots of garlic bulbs. But this alternative does not produce the same flavor as jimbu. If jimbu has been stored for a long period, it becomes crisp and crumbly and starts to lose its flavor. It gets stale quickly. For this reason, I recommend that you purchase jimbu in small quantities.

Timmur (Nepali Pepper)

Nepali *timmur, ban timmur,* or Nepali pepper is a relative of Szechwan peppercorn, Sichuan pepper, *Poivre chinois*, and Sancho pepper. Its scientific name is *Zanthoxylum armatum*.

Timmur is a highly pungent, sharp-tasting dried berry from the prickly ash shrub family. It is often mistaken for black pepper, but it has an entirely different flavor and is, in fact, not related to the black pepper family. Timmur grows in thorny bushes in high altitude areas of Nepal. The bushes are found wild throughout the hilly slopes of Nepal where the temperature is cold. When the berries ripen, they turn a deep red color around mid-September. The harvesting lasts for three to four weeks. Local farmers pick the berries by hand. The sharp thorns make the picking very difficult, and sometimes they have to use sticks to break the branches. The collected berries are dried in the sun until all the moisture has evaporated. They are then sorted by hand, cleaned of thorns, branches, and leaves. The dried berries are split into two halves and the shiny black seeds are removed because of their bitterness. The dried berries have a rough, wrinkled, and uneven surface and their aroma lies in the split covering of the pod, not in the seed.

The timmur berries are transported from the hilly area of Nepal in a *doko* (wicker basket) to Kathmandu markets for sale. If you visit the open-air markets around Indra Chowk or the historic Ason bazaar district, you will find many vendors setting up their *doko* or *nanglo* (wicker baskets or tray) full of timmur pepper for sale.

Nepalese describe the taste of timmur as *per-peraune*, which means "biting taste with an anesthetic feeling on the tongue." It is certainly an acquired taste for some people, but once you get used to it, you will appreciate its unique flavor. It should be used only in moderation; otherwise, it will overpower the dish.

Timmur is the most commonly used spice in Nepali fermented or preserved pickles and chutneys, especially in potato and tomato-based chutneys. Without timmur, the pickles taste flavorless and flat. It adds a unique pungency. Young green timmur gives a fresh twist to charcoal-roasted tomato achaar. Grinding or crushing the timmur pepper together with salt, dried chilies, and garlic in a mortar and pestle gives a delicious, tangy taste when used to season roasted corn and sliced cucumber or in many *sandheko* (salad-like) dishes. Whole timmur is also used to flavor some vegetable and lentil dishes, but it is removed before serving so that its unpleasant bite can be avoided. Timmur is also added to Nepali wild mushrooms to help remove any toxic elements. While trekking in the Muktinath, Mustang area, I observed locals using timmur extensively to flavor yak meat, and to make jerky, *momos* (stuffed dumplings), lentils, and vegetables.

During the rainy season, trekkers in the mountains use timmur to cure leech bites. It is also used as a home remedy to cure stomach ailments and toothaches.

The recipes in this book usually suggest grinding the timmur in a mortar and pestle to bring out the maximum flavor, but you can also use a spice grinder and then use a sieve to remove the husks. Timmur is best if ground fresh, because the flavor will be sharper. These days Nepali spice markets sell pre-ground timmur stored in sealed plastic bags, which may be convenient to use but will be less aromatic. I prefer to crush the pepper in small amounts as needed in a mortar and pestle.

To preserve the flavor and color of timmur, store the whole pepper in an airtight container in a cool, dry place, away from direct sunlight. Glass jars with tight-fitting lids are the best way to store them. Whole timmur will stay fresh up to two years while ground timmur may lose its aroma.

Substitute: Nepali timmur may not be available outside Nepal, but these days I have seen some online stores selling imported varieties. The closest substitute for timmur is Szechwan pepper or Chinese pepper, which has a similar if milder flavor.

The Unique Vegetables of Nepal

More than 60 percent of Nepal's population depends on agriculture for their livelihood and vegetables are important crops. The word "*tarkaari*" is used for cooked or uncooked vegetables. A typical Nepali meal consists of rice, lentils, and some kind of side vegetable dish. Vegetables are generally cooked with a minimum amount of spice and seasonings. They are simply fried, deep-fried, sautéed, mixed with other ingredients, made into gravy, made into patties, or stuffed. They are also made into pickles, salads, snacks, and even desserts. Most Nepali households do not store vegetables, so they are bought fresh every day.

While the Kathmandu valley is renowned for the seasonal vegetables grown in its fertile soil, the scarcity of arable land in many rural and hilly areas limits vegetable consumption to root vegetables and preserved vegetables. During peak harvest season, vendors bring a wide variety of dewy-fresh and organically grown vegetables to the market from different regions.

The most common vegetables in Kathmandu include green beans, cauliflower, cabbage, egg-plants, greens, okra, peas, potatoes, radish, squash, and tomatoes. Green leafy vegetables such as spinach and mustard greens are eaten daily in large quantities.

I get asked questions about Nepali vegetables on my blog on a near daily basis, so this chapter is intended to be a guide to unique vegetables of Nepal. I have listed the Nepali vegetables that you need to try at least once, if available, and recipes for these vegetables can be found in Chapter Seven. There are so many other vegetables, but I focus here on the more common ones:

Pumpkin Vine Shoots (Pharsi ko Muntaa)

Pumpkin vine shoots, considered a delicacy in Nepal, are the up-permost tender shoots, tendrils, leaves, and delicate stems from pumpkin plants. These shoots are harvested from the growing end of the vine (the top 3 to 4 inches) by pinching off the tender ends. The plants will put out a new shoot or growth after the vine has been harvested. Pumpkin vine shoots have a distinct light flavor that can be described as a cross between squash and spinach. They should be cooked within a day of picking for maximum freshness and flavor. Like any leafy green, its volume reduces by half after cooking. My husband grows a small patch of pumpkin vine in the corner of our home garden along with other vegetables. This summer the vine grew in abundance and we ate *muntaa* at least once a week. Once you taste these delicious vegetables, you will come back looking for more. Most parts of the pumpkin are edible: the flowers, the fleshy shell, the seeds (roasted), and the young shoots.

Chayote Squash (Ishkush)

Ishkush is a delicious mild flavored squash that grows on a climbing vine. It is a pear-shaped, lime-green squash with crispy white flesh and a single large, soft seed. In scientific journals, it is called *Sechium edules SW*. Chayote squash is one of the easiest vegetables to grow in warm tropical or subtropical climates. In Nepal, the chayote plant is treated as a summer annual or perennial and once it begins to grow, it can take over the whole garden. Its vine climbs wildly over and across

roofs, over fences, and up and around trees. The chayote plant does well where there is an abundance of full sun that helps yield fruits. It is a favorite and staple vegetable for those who live in the hilly parts of Nepal as one single plant can provide 75 to 90 squashes in a season.

The mild-flavored chayote squash is loved because it is versatile and can be blended with other ingredients and spices. It can be sautéed with other vegetables such as potatoes or fresh or dried beans. Sometimes, it is cooked with goat meat, lamb, or chicken. It also has an excellent storage life.

There are so many varieties of chayote squash with different shapes, sizes, and textures found in Nepal. While walking around the Kathmandu Ason vegetable market, I spotted chayote covered with thorny, prickly spines and asked the vegetable vendor if it tasted similar to the smooth-skinned variety. He told me that this variety is difficult to peel, but all varieties taste somewhat identical, except the over-matured, dry and tough ones will be "*ne mitho*" (bland in taste).

Other parts of the chayote plants are also used in Nepali cooking. The uppermost tender shoots and leaves of the chayote vine are called *ishkush ko muntaa*. They are harvested by pinching off the tender ends and are cooked similarly to pumpkin vine shoots. They are often served as a savory vegetable dish along with freshly boiled rice. The root of the chayote plant is called *ishkush ko jaraa* and is also cooked and eaten by some. They are a delicious addition to sautéed root vegetable dishes.

Balsam Apple (Barelaa / Chuche Karelaa)

Barelaa, or balsam apple, is a late summer vegetable that measures one to two inches long with a slightly curved end and soft and delicate texture. Its scientific name is *Momordica balsamina*. The pale green juicy fruit looks somewhat like a pointed gourd (*parvar* or *parvar*). It is picked and cooked when it is young and tender. The young fruit has a spongy flesh and multiple white seeds, while mature overripe ones have numerous black rough seeds which should be removed before cooking. Since this vegetable is quite delicate, it cooks quickly. To cook, cut into strips, remove seeds and stir-fry with potatoes or it can be made into a *saandheko* pickle dish, or simply cook like any common vegetable with spices. This seasonal vegetable can be found in abundance in Nepali vegetable markets during the summer season.

Mountain Ebony (Koiralaa ko Phool)

Koiralaa ko phool or Mountain Ebony (Botanical Name: *Bauhinia Variegata L.*) is the edible flower of the Bauhinia tree. The color of the flower varies from pink-white to light mauve-purple. The tree is a medium-size evergreen with orchid-like flowers with long buds. It is grown throughout the Himalayas in high altitude areas and packed with nutrients. The unopened buds and flowers are collected from trees and can be made into a vegetable curry, a salad-like dish, or pickled, but they must be boiled before preparing. It is a popular spring flower and has become an integral part of Nepali cuisine where it has been consumed for centuries as a seasonal delicacy with unique flavor. It is also used as an Ayurvedic herbal medicine as a cure for diarrhea and dysentery.

My memories of homemade *Koiralaa ko Achaar* (Mountain Ebony Potato Salad, page 256) is when our family cook, Thuli Bajai, used to make it when the flowers were in season in Spring. The flower blooming season only lasted for two to three weeks. Bajai told us that the raw and uncooked flowers are bitter, so should be cooked properly. Before cooking, she washed the flowers and buds, but did not soak the flowers in the water for an extended time as they quickly became waterlogged. The base of *Koiralaa ko achaar* is, of course, the freshly picked flowers. The first time I tried this recipe, I worried that the beautiful orchid-looking flower was too pretty to cook. Now I can't wait until spring to cook this delicious vegetable.

Mountain ebony is an extremely perishable flower and should be used within a day after it is purchased. It is in high demand during springtime in Nepal and sold in the local vegetable markets. Unfortunately it is not available in the US.

Nettle Greens (Sishnu ko Saag)

Sishnu, lekali sishnu, thulo sishnu, ghario sishnu, bhangre sishnu, or *patle sishnu* are Nepali names for edible nettle greens (*Uetica.sp.*). Nepal's best kept secret among wild green vegetables, the nettle is prized for its taste, nutrient value (iron, vitamin A and C), and healing properties. Nettle greens are traditional vegetables that grow like wild weeds along rivers, forests, walls, hedges, and many shaded trails. Nepalese have been eating nettle greens for centuries and they are popular in areas where there is a scarcity of other vegetables. Nettle greens are known for their sting, but cooking completely eliminates their stinging effect. The young tender leaves and shoots are cooked similar to any other leafy vegetables. Many people find nettle greens reminiscent of spinach. Some describe them as mild-flavored, earthy-tasting, and like a mixture of cucumber and spinach.

When nettle greens are picked or gathered, only the uppermost tender shoots and top green leaves are picked. The older, mature leaves from the lower part of the plants are tasteless. If you are trying to explore and collect nettle greens from the wild, be sure to use rubber gloves, tongs, or scissors. Make sure not to touch the shoots, leaves, or plants with your bare hands. Its sting is not pleasant!

I was lucky enough to find an elderly street vendor selling a bag full of freshly-picked nettle greens early in the morning at an open-air market near the Jana Baha area of Kathmandu. It is not common to see nettle greens sold like this since one has to go to the wild to collect them. The street vendor told me the nettle greens were picked by using Nepali metal tongs called *chimtaa*. She taught me how to collect, cook, and serve them. As she did she was singing the song, "*saag re sisnu khaaeko aanandi manle … haat kaa maila sun kaa thailaa, ke garnu dhanle?*" ("Sacks of gold are like collected dirt on your hands, what is one to do with all these wealth? It is better to eat nettles greens and cultivate happiness in your heart.")

Bamboo Shoots (Taamaa)

Bamboo shoots are the underdeveloped, young, edible shoots of the bamboo plant known as *taamaa* in Nepali. They have a unique flavor and texture, are considered a delicacy in traditional Nepali cuisine, and are a favorite wild vegetable for many. There are many varieties of bamboo plants growing throughout Nepal, but not all of them are edible. In the book *The Introduction of Nepalese Food Plants* under the section of "tender shoot vegetables" edible bamboo shoots are given the scientific name *Bambusa vulgaris Schrad*. The common name is feathery bamboo or *taamaa bans*.

The sprouting buds or shoots are dug out during springtime. They are cylindrical and covered with numerous layers of brown husks. Before the shoots are cooked, the outermost woody brown sheaths are removed one by one until the edible and tender layers are exposed. The edible portions are ivory to light-yellow/green in color. By the time the brown shoots are trimmed and cleaned, the original size of the shoot becomes much smaller.

Bamboo shoots are mild-flavored and mix well with most ingredients. They can be pickled, fermented, dried, or cooked with any combination of vegetables. Fermented bamboo shoots are made into a popular stew-like dish combined with black-eyed peas, potatoes, and several other herbs and spices called *taamaa-alu-bodi ko tarkaari*. The savory dish has a dominant bamboo flavor and is usually accompanied with freshly boiled rice as a part of the everyday Nepali traditional meal of *Daal-Bhaat-Tarkaari*. To make fermented bamboo, slice the fresh bamboo shoots into thin pieces, mix with salt, mustard seeds, turmeric, and mustard oil, and cure in the sun until they become slightly sour and flavorful.

Ash Gourd (Kubhindo)

Kubhindo, called ash gourd, wax gourd, white gourd, or winter melon (*Benincasa hispida*), is a pumpkin-like large gourd that grows on a vine. The gourd itself ranges from oblong to cylindrical and has a pale green skin with a chalky wax coating. It is cooked as a vegetable when young, and the ripe ones are made into crystallized candy or preserves. The mature gourd has a hard, tough shell with a firm, white flesh and can be stored for almost one year. It is a common vegetable grown in Nepal and in other parts of Southeast Asia. *Kubhindo* is offered to deities during Hindu rituals and other religious ceremonies. They are used during *Lakhee Naach* (masked demon dance ceremony) during the festival of Indra-Jatra in Nepal.

Taro (Karkalo-Gaava-Pidhaalu)

Karkalo (common names: *Colocasia*, Taro Leaf, *Dasheen*, *Arbi Patta*; botanical name: *Colocasia antiquorum*) is the Nepali name for the taro plant, which comes from a tuberous root. It is a tall-growing plant that has clusters of attractive, heart-shaped leaves resembling the beautiful ornamental variety of the elephant ear plant. The leaves are usually broad, bright green, and velvety to touch. In Nepal, we use all three parts of the plant including the leaves (*karkalo ko paat*), the young stalks (*gaabaa* or *gaavaa*), and the taro tubers or corms (*pidhaalu*).

The tender stalks and young leaves (*karkalo-gaava*) are cooked together just like spinach or mustard greens, and produce a delicate flavor akin to "spinach with silky texture." The uncurled part of the leaves are the most delicious part of the vegetable. When the young leaves and stalks are harvested, the stem will grow back and put out a small new leaf around the base of the root corm.

Taro tubers are a versatile vegetable; they can be prepared in a variety of ways including boiling, frying, and steaming, or they can be cooked with a combination of vegetables and lentils and used in soups and stews. They have a nut-like flavor and a smooth texture when cooked. Taro tubers are extremely nutritious and a good source of fiber.

A few words of warning: When the taro stalks and leaves are cleaned, the sap secreted by the stem can cause skin irritation and a temporary discoloration of the fingers to some sensitive skin, so it is good to wear rubber gloves when handling. To get rid of irritation, simply rub some salt on your fingers. Taro is also never eaten raw because it causes an itchy, stinging, and very irritating sensation to the throat, known as *kokyaoone* in Nepali. Once cooked, the irritating aspect is destroyed and adding lemon juice helps to further reduce its irritability.

Fiddlehead Ferns (Neuro)

Fiddlehead ferns are one of the most loved wild vegetables found in Nepal. Nepalese call this unique vegetable "*neuro*" which literally translates to "bent" or "curled" (*neehureko* or *jhukeko*). They are the young shoots of edible fern plants and they resemble the spiral end of a fiddle, for which they are named. In Nepal, they are collected by hand during springtime from woods, shady swamps, riverbanks, and damp fields. They can also be purchased from local markets.

The young shoots emerge from the ground around mid-April. The shoots in their coiled form remain for only a couple of days and they need to be picked before they open to beautiful lacy leaves, which cannot be cooked as they become stringy and bitter. They are extremely perishable and need to be cooked within a day or two after picking. Fiddleheads are covered with fuzz or paper-like covering and must be cleaned before cooking. Their taste is somewhat similar to asparagus-okra-spinach, but their texture is crunchier. Some say it has a flavor similar to an artichoke, maybe with a whiff of mushroom.

There are many ways to prepare fiddleheads. To preserve their beautiful green color, blanch the fiddleheads in salted water and then immediately rinse in cold water, then pan-sauté with butter, salt, garlic, and pepper. They are delicious in a salad-like dish with potatoes (*Saandheko Neuro*), with ground sesame seeds, salt, and chili pepper and tempered with fenugreek seeds and mustard oil. No matter how you cook them, *neuros* are a unique vegetable.

Banana Blossoms (Bungo)

Banana blossoms or buds are the tender hearts of unopened banana flowers called *keraa ko bungo* in Nepali. The rusty purple-colored blossoms have several sheaths and are roughly shaped like a heart. Banana blossoms are eaten as a cooked vegetable, made into spicy curries, or prepared as fresh pickles (*achaar* dish). Many people compare the taste of banana blossoms to fresh artichoke hearts, but I think they have their own distinct taste. Before cooking, you must strip off the non-edible outer tough sheath until the tender inner yellowish bud is revealed. *A word of warning:* before handling fresh banana blossoms, I recommend you rub your hands and knife with cooking oil to prevent the sap from discoloring your hands.

The first time I saw the banana flower was after I arrived at my cousin's farmhouse in the Tarai area of Nepal near Chitwan National Park. I admired a beautiful rusty-purple banana blossom that was hanging at the end of a stalk from a banana tree. I had no idea they were edible. Being born and raised in Kathmandu, the blossoms were not frequently seen in local vegetable markets there. The small bananas found in Nepal have small blossoms and the locals tell me that the fresh pickles made from small blossoms are much tastier with better flavor and texture. If you ever see banana blossoms in your fresh food or Asian produce markets, please try them. I am sure it will be a delicious treat!

Nepali Cucumber (Nepali Thulo Kankro)

This extremely rare variety of cucumber (*Bhadaure kankro*) is known in scientific journals as *Cucumis sativus L.Var. Sikkimensis Hook*, and is native to the Himalayan mountain areas of Nepal and Sikkim. Sir Joseph Hooker, a British botanist along with explorers in the 19th century, first discovered it in the eastern Himalayas in 1848. Here is part of what he wrote about it in his journals: "So abundant were the fruits, that for days together I saw gnawed fruits lying by the natives' paths by the thousands, and every man, woman and child seemed engaged throughout the day in devouring them."

Nepali cucumbers differ from the varieties available in the United States and other parts of the world. They are eaten fresh like the common green variety when they are young, but are also left on the vine to ripen further so that they can be made into pickles. These cucumbers look remarkably like small watermelons, large and oblong, but upon maturity the cucumber develops a thick rusty red-brown skin with a pure white crispy flesh. The ripe fruit can grow large—14 to 16 inches long and 6 to 8 inches wide.

Khalpi ko achaar, or pickled cucumbers, play a very important role in most Nepali households. They are commonly eaten with a traditional Nepali meal or paired with afternoon snacks. Nepalese have been making this pickle for centuries using a natural fermentation process. They believe that fermented pickles improve digestive issues especially after eating a spicy meal. Pickled cucumbers are a must during the festival of *Dashain* (see page 11), when a large amount of meat, along with other rich, fatty and spicy festive foods are consumed.

My husband and I and some of our friends have been successful growing our own Nepali variety of cucumber in our backyard gardens in the U.S. We let the healthy mature cucumber remain on the vine until the cold freeze comes to upstate New York and then make fermented pickles.

Tamarillo (Tyaamatar)

Tyaamatar is the Nepali name for a "tamarillo" or "tree tomato," an attractive plum-shaped fruit with meaty pulp and seeds. The botanical name of this fruit is *Cyphomamdra betacea*. It has a tough, bitter skin and is very tart but flavorful when ripe. Despite its appearance, it is not a true garden tomato although it resembles a medium-size pear tomato. There are many varieties of tamarillo, which come in different sizes, shapes, and colors. *Tyaamatar* is grown mostly in the central hilly regions of Nepal. It is not common in the Tarai regions. Ripe *tyaamatar* is used primarily to make chutney, similar to a tomato chutney (page 250).

A Day at a Nepali Vegetable Market

Vegetables (*tarkaari*) are one of the most important food groups in the Nepali diet. During peak growing season, you may see a local farmer heading to the market balancing a bamboo pole across his shoulders, holding two wicker woven baskets (*kharpan*) of freshly picked vegetables. At Nepali vegetable markets (*tarkaari bazar*), one can witness the proud harvest of vendors filling every tiny space with elaborate displays of vegetables and fruits. Greens such as spinach and mustard are neatly tied in small bundles and arranged in piles. Potatoes, onions, and shallots are skillfully arranged in wicker trays, baskets, or burlap sacks. Most Nepali households do not store vegetables, so they are bought fresh every day. On many street corners, vendors set up small stands of freshly picked fruits and vegetables such as green gooseberry, lapsi, guava, or tangerines. The vegetables are weighed on a hand-held scale, known as a *taraaju*.

Lapsi Fruit of Nepal
(Nepalese Hog Plum)

Lapsi fruit, also known as *labsi* or *lausi* (*Choerosos pondias*), are considered a native wild fruit of Nepal. In English, they are commonly referred to as Nepalese hog plums. The tall subtropical tree can be found growing in many hilly parts of the country. The fruit is greenish-yellow when ripe and roughly resembles a small oval-shaped plum. Harvesting season is from September to January. The fruits are allowed to remain on trees until they become fully ripe. Once they are completely yellowish-green and the thick pulp becomes soft and comes off easily from the branch, they are harvested by handpicking or shaking the tree. Some of the unripe green lapsi that have fallen from the trees are separated and left to ripen further.

Lapsi are an extremely sour fruit, even when fully ripe, and have a high vitamin C content. The fruit has a tough fibrous skin and pale yellow flesh, which is firmly attached to a large brown seed. The pulp is difficult to separate from the seeds, but once cooked it separates easily. Ripe lapsi have a pleasantly tart flavor and some people like to eat them fresh, but they are mainly used to make sweet and sour dried fruit nuggets or fruit leather (*titauraa, maadaa, paaun*) both sweet and salted. Lapsi are also pickled, cooked with vegetables, or used as a souring agent. It is believed to have health benefits in Newar culture, and a thin soup is prepared from the fruit pulp (*paun kwaa*) and served after a heavy meal to help digestion. The boiled tough skin (peel) of the lapsi fruit (*lapsi ko bokraa*) is also dried with or without adding seasonings. It becomes excessively brittle once dried, so it is not good for chewing, but is used as a souring agent for some pickles. Lapsi seeds (*lapsi ko gedaa*) are used as homemade spinning toys called *champati*. Children enjoy playing and comparing their record for the longest spin. The stony seeds are also used as a cooking fuel in some villages in Nepal.

Lapsi ko Maadaa, or *titauraa* are a great favorite fruit treat for many Nepalese, and if someone goes home to Nepal for a visit they always bring back several packages of store-bought lapsi chew. The commercially made, packaged, flavorful nuggets in multiple varieties with different shapes and sizes are sold in Nepali markets. They are named *lapsi peero maadaa, guleo lapsi ko titauraa*, regular *lapsi seto* candy, lapsi powder, sweet-sour candy, *jhol titaura*, and trekking fruits, etc. Making fruit leather is an ancient method of preserving fruits when there is an abundance of fruits in the season.

I have been making at least fifteen batches of fruit leather using different varieties of fruits every summer or fall for the past many years here in the United States to share with friends and family. I dry my fruit roll-ups in the food dehydrator because the sun is not very reliable in the area where I live. My children and grandchildren have always enjoyed the natural fruit snacks and while growing up, fruit leather was their regular "candy."

Making Fruit Leather

In Nepal, during the summer months at our house, making fruit leather, nuggets, chews, and pickles was a family affair. My mother and her kitchen helpers were busy making several batches of fruit leather when perfectly tree-ripened fruits with full flavor were in season. Some of the fruits came from our own fruit trees, such as persimmons, mangoes, pear and guavas, but the *doko* (basket) full of lapsi fruit were bought from the villagers who transported the fruit to Nepali markets from their nearby hilly farms.

As soon as the fruits were picked or bought, the kitchen helpers prepared the fruits by sorting, rinsing, boiling, and mixing them with spices or sweetener and mashing to make a smooth puree. It was then poured into a *naanglo* (wicker flat tray). The tray was covered with cheesecloth or nylon netting, and secured with a clothespin to protect the pureed fruits from insects and dirt. Several trays were placed in the sunny part of the house for them to sun-dry, usually in the *kausi* area (open space in the uppermost part of the house).

It would take several days for the fruit leather to dry, depending upon the intensity of sun. The fruit drying trays were always brought back inside when the sun set in the evening. They were ready when the fruit was fully dried and all the moisture had evaporated. The fruit leather had a leather-like appearance and chewy texture. They were removed from the tray, cut into bite-size pieces or simply rolled up into strips in sugar to protect them from air and moisture. The fruit leather was stored in an air-tight moisture-proof container or in plastic bags. (You had to make sure the nuggets or fruit leather was completely dry or else they may develop mold while being stored.) Sometimes, by the end of the drying process, my cousins and younger siblings slowly peeled and tore the fruit leather from the drying tray and enjoyed it so much that almost half of the fruit leather disappeared before it was ready to be cut and stored. We were addicted to this delicious special treat. The variations of hot and spicy ones were popular among younger crowds.

The Creative Art of Making Newari Mari

Savor the most traditional and festive sweets of Nepal in the narrow streets of downtown Kathmandu, Patan, and Bhaktapur area, where you will see many century-old local (Newari and Nepali) sweet shops filled with a variety of traditional sweets. The sweet shops are called "*Mari Pasal*" in Newari. "*Mari*" translates to "bread" and "*Pasal*" means "store." The sweets are neatly stacked up on back shelves or on the front shelves under glass. They are eaten throughout the day, at breakfast, lunch, or as teatime snacks. They are also offered to deities during prayers and puja ceremonies, and served as desserts for feasts.

The art of making *mari* is a centuries-old practice, passed down from generation to generation. When you walk around these sweet shops, you will observe the *haluwai pasale* (local professional sweet makers) and their busy staff members, stretching and designing dough into perfect sizes and shapes. Some are cut into diamond shapes, others are made into twisted ropes and fried in bubbling oil in a *kahari* (deep-frying pot). The wonderful aroma of freshly-made sweets permeates the air and entices you in. The *mari pasal* is always busy with customers who buy traditional sweets year around at any time of the day.

In Kathmandu, Shree Purna Ashok Mithai Bhandar is one of oldest sweet shops, located near Kasthamandap Temple near Maru Tole, established at least one hundred years ago by Purna Das Rajkarnikar. At present it is fully owned, operated, and managed by its fourth generation of family members. My family has always been a loyal customer and we have ordered sweets that are made in pure clarified butter (gheu) for every celebratory occasion. Back in 2008, when I was writing my first cookbook, *Taste of Nepal*, I asked the owner of the sweet shop to allow me to come to his store and observe his kitchen staff working in the kitchen. I promised not to distract his employees and told him my only purpose was to learn and understand the art of making classic sweets.

I was lucky enough to live within walking distance. I woke up early each day to arrive at the store just in time for the kitchen staff to begin their morning preparation routine. The back of the store leads to a small *chowk* (courtyard) where the kitchen is located. I sat in one corner and observed their ingredients, their step-by-step preparation, and cooking methods. I took notes and snapped pictures. The morning hour was busy preparing *jeri-swaari* (breakfast sweets) and small *sel-roti* (fried rice bread). There were no measurement guides. Everything was done with *andaj* (guesswork). The only measuring devices were the eyes and hands, and there were no hard and fast rules, yet every dish came out perfect. I was so grateful to observe them in their element. It fed my curiosity and I learned the basics of how to make traditional Nepali sweets.

There are the various types of sweet treats in Purna Bhandar. The most popular, *laakhaa-mari* bread, glazed or unglazed in various sizes is a Newari ceremonial bread. Other Newari *mari* are *roth* (triangle-shaped traditional cookies made with flour-butter-sugar), *khajuri* (flaky, buttery fried cookies shaped like curved bowl), *anarsaa* (rice flour patties topped with poppy seeds), *ain-themari* (flaky-crunchy cookies with icing), *gudhpaak* (fudge-like sweets made from edible gum & dry-fruits), *khaaja* (multi-layered pastries), *fini* or *phini* (sweet or plain puffed pastry), *pustakaari* (brown sweets made from edible gum, ground nuts, and *khuwaa*), *panjabimari* (variation of glazed savory pastry), *gulmari* (crunchy glazed sweets like thin noodles), *aitimari* (fried glazed pastry rings), *gosutamari* (twisted glazed donuts), and *chimtimari* (flaky decorative flower-shaped pastry). The visually appealing, more elaborate, uniquely flavored and textured *maris* are prepared during *Tihaar* Festival (see page 12) and Bhai-Tikaa Day (see page 13) in Nepal.

These are some of the photos I took of the bakers preparing the morning's pastries at Shree Purna Ashok Mithai Bhandar sweet shop in Kathmandu.

Laakhaamari
Newari Ceremonial Sweet Bread

Laakhaamari is a crunchy-flaky textured sweet bread, prepared for ceremonial occasions. This special bread comes from the Newar community, the indigenous people of Kathmandu. Although *laakhaamari* is a Newari sweet bread, it has gained popularity among many other Nepali ethnic groups over the years. It resembles a coiled, twisted rope and is prepared from ground rice, wheat flour, and black gram lentils.

The preparation of *laakhaamari* is an ancient culinary art that has been passed down orally for centuries. As a traditional festive dish, it is prepared during Newari wedding ceremonies. Before the formal marriage ceremony (*gwe*), the family members of the groom's party signal the approval of the forthcoming marriage by sending freshly prepared *laakhaamari*, with other sweets, fruits, and flowers to the bride's family. *Laakhaamari* is also given to relatives and friends to announce the wedding. The size and shape of the

bread varies, with larger ones sent to closer relatives to honor them and smaller ones sent to the invited guests.

Laakhaamari is prepared with pre-soaked, ground rice, ground black urad beans, wheat flour, butter, and water. All these ingredients are mixed together to form a pourable batter. It is then shaped into a round coiled design, deep-fried in a large Nepali frying pan until light golden brown. The finished product is allowed to rest before it is glazed with light icing to create a translucent satiny finish. The sweet bread is delicious by itself or served with other foods. The bread keeps well for at least a month at room temperature.

Making this bread at home is a glorious undertaking. It is time-consuming and requires extra effort, equipment, and skills. Even for a skilled cook, it may take more than a couple of hours to prepare just one *laakhaamari*. Because of this, these days it is not often prepared at home, but bought at specialty sweet shops (*Haluwai ko Pasal*). I have never tried to make this bread at home, but only watched how it is made in sweet shops. But I wanted to give a brief description about a centuries-old traditional art form.

The photos here are from Suresh Balami's sweet shop, The Yetkha Mithai Pasal, located south of the Nardevi temple in Kathmandu. I would like to thank Mr. Suresh and his brother Gyanu Balami for taking their valuable time to show me how to make this delicious bread.

Learning to Make
Dhindo the Nepali Way

Dhindo or *Dhido* (pronounced *dhee-dough*) sounds like some exotic dish from Nepal, but it is simply a thick porridge or mush made by cooking stone-ground cornmeal (*ghatta maa pidheko makai ko pitho*), millet flour (*kodo ko pitho*), or buckwheat flour (*phaapar ko pitho*) with salt and water.

Dhindo is a staple food in rural and middle mountain-area regions of Nepal, especially in dry areas where rice or wheat are difficult to grow. This hearty, filling dish is a nutrient powerhouse and is eaten with a dab of homemade *nauni*, *gheu* (clarified butter), *jhol tarkaari* (curried vegetables), or with various pickles and buttermilk or yogurt. *Gundruk-Dhindo* is the most common combination served in farming communities. *Gundruk* is a fermented and preserved leafy vegetable that is used to prepare a soup-like dish that is known as *gundruk ko jhol*. Nepalese who do hard physical labor consume enormous amounts of this nutritious meal.

Traditional *dhindo* meals are served on Nepali round plates called *thaal* made of stainless steel or brass. It is common to see large mounds of *dhindo* served in the middle of a *thaal* accompanied by side dishes in small portions. It is eaten with the right hand by first scooping up or tearing small bite-size pieces of *dhindo* with your fingers, then dipping or rolling them into the side dish. It is a Nepali tradition to always wash hands prior to eating and after the meal. *Dhindo* should be eaten steaming hot, right after cooking since it hardens once it cools.

Traditionally, *dhindo* is cooked in an iron pan with a long handle and rounded bottom called a *taapke*, which has excellent heat distribution qualities. It is typically stirred with a *panyu*, a large iron spoon with a long handle.

Due to its humble origins, *dhindo* meals were rarely found in the fancy Kathmandu restaurants, but these days, it is being introduced as an authentic, traditional Nepali meal. I enjoyed a

memorable *dhindo* meal from a local restaurant called Pate Dhido. The *dhindo* was made from millet flour (*kodo ko pitho*). Served with *dhindo* is a rich and flavorful chicken curry cooked with ginger-garlic, fresh green chilies, *saandheko gundruk* (salad-like gundruk dish), tiny bits of red chili sauce, and sautéed onions. The clarified butter is lightly browned with chopped garlic before pouring into the prepared *dhindo* to give it extra flavor.

When we ordered this dish, the kitchen staff started to prepare *dhindo* immediately after they received the order. I could smell the *dhindo* being cooked from my table only a few feet away. I got up and asked the chef if he would let me watch his cooking method. He cooked it in a copper pot. After vigorous stirring with a wooden spoon, the *fatfatee* chef (chatterbox) told me, "Look you can't avoid the messy splatters when you are stirring the mixture. Make sure there

Dhindo *served on a* thaal *with chicken curry.*

are no lumps. We call this process *beskari dhindo lai maskauda* in local terms. Buckwheat and millet *dhindo* is also pretty much cooked the same way except the color of the finished dish will be different. The taste of *dhindo* is usually bland, so it is always eaten with spicy liquids, and *dhindo* should be moist, neither runny, nor dry." He poured the steaming mush onto a brass plate. He added, "My basic cooking procedure for making our authentic *dhindo* is 1 cup millet flour, 4 cups of water plus some more, if needed, ½ teaspoon salt, or to taste, 1 cup cornmeal (coarse or medium-ground), 2 tablespoons clarified butter." He presented us with a traditional *dhindo thaal* and I did not know freshly-cooked steaming *dhindo* could be so good. I enjoyed every bite – served in its natural form with locally grown *raayo ko saag* (mustard greens) sautéed with dried red chilies, and the local chicken with spring onions. The pickle platter consisted of fiery tomato chutney and *khaadeko mula ko achaar* (pickled radish). For someone with simple tastes, nothing could be more satisfying than *kodo ko dhindo*. (*See* Dhindo *recipe, page 179.*)

Yogurt in Daily Life
Akshataa ko tikaa

Yogurt, called *dahi* in Nepal, is considered one of the country's most important dairy products and is consumed everywhere in different forms. Yogurt is not only used for culinary purposes, but it is also deeply rooted in Nepali cultural traditions, rituals, and religions. It is considered pure, auspicious, and sacred, and a must-have item for all festivals, feasts, and celebrations. Yogurt made in decorative clay pots (*kataaro*) are also presented to families to show gratitude and good will.

Many Nepalese eat yogurt during religious fasting days. It is also consumed as an auspicious blessed food before departing from home to travel. Many Nepalese believe that yogurt brings good luck and fortune so a fresh container of yogurt is placed in entrance ways for a special welcome and departure. Fresh plain yogurt is used in the preparation of *achetaa ko tikaa*, which is a red paste, prepared by mixing together rice grains, red vermillion powder, and plain yogurt. On auspicious occasions, the red *tikaa* is carefully applied on the forehead for family blessing (*see page II*).

Yogurt is considered one of the purest forms of food to be offered to the deities during religious festivals. One of the most essential divine liquids offered to deities, called "*Pancha Amrit*" (five nectars of immortality), consists of yogurt, milk, clarified butter, sugarcane juice, and honey. Plain yogurt is also offered to deities as a sacred offering, and later eaten as a blessed food. It is used in ritual bathing ceremonies, where the devotee pours plain liquid yogurt on the image of the god.

I was born in a family where yogurt was homemade almost every day. We called the yogurt "*ek raate dahi*" which translates to "yogurt made overnight" or "one-night yogurt." Most Nepali households make a small amount of yogurt on a daily basis with just two ingredients: fresh milk and live and active yogurt cultures (usually from a previous batch). A warm place to rest for the culture to incubate and a "do not disturb sign" are also important. The delicious yogurt will be ready in 6 to 8 hours. Yogurt made this way is typically consumed within a day or two before it starts to acidify and turn sour. Yogurt has been made basically the same way for centuries. Although most of the yogurt in Nepal is prepared from cow or water buffalo (*bhaisi*) milk, yak and goat-milk yogurt are also popular in certain mountain regions.

Nepalese like their yogurt fresh, plain, thick but not runny. Sour yogurt is called *amilo dahi*, and it is not liked by many. Due to lack of refrigeration in Nepali local life, after the homemade yogurt is set, it is kept at room temperature in the kitchen until used. Yogurt that is left in the natural stage starts to sour immediately. If the yogurt has become too tart, it is possible to mix in gram flour (*besan*) and several spices to make a creamy soup-like dish called *dahi kadi*, which is eaten with freshly steamed rice. Some Nepalese believe that when the yogurt starts getting sour, it actually preserves the yogurt.

Yogurt is also known as an ancient healing food. It is used in different forms to cure indigestion and intestinal infection and recognized as a cure for hangovers. It is also eaten to obtain a

soothing effect in the stomach after eating rich, spicy, and greasy foods. It has cooling properties to help tolerate warm days. Yogurt is also served at the end of feasts and celebrations because of its soothing quality and the benefits of probiotics to balance your digestive system.

The habit of making homemade yogurt stayed with me even after coming to the U.S. I usually make a large container of yogurt every week that lasts almost 8 to 10 days in the refrigerator. I usually make yogurt before going to bed and the next morning I am rewarded with a perfectly incubated overnight creamy yogurt. For festive occasions, I use my decorative clay pots called *kataaro* in Nepali. I have never used a thermometer to check the temperature of boiled milk, I just use my fingers to judge the temperature. If you like to eat yogurt often, you can try to make homemade yogurt today. Making yogurt at home is simple and easy, and does not require any special skills. Most of the equipment needed to prepare *"ek raate dahi"* is probably already in your kitchen. (*See recipe page 315.*)

A Day in Bhaktapur
Making Juju Dhau

All you need to know about "Juju Dhau – King of Yogurt" from Bhaktapur, Nepal

Bhaktapur, located in the eastern part of Kathmandu, is famous for its unique architecture, woodcarvings, pagoda-style temples, and narrow streets. Two sites within Bhaktapur, Bhaktapur Durbar Square and Changunarayan Temple, have been inscribed as UNESCO World Heritage sites.

Bhaktapur is also famous for its Juju Dhau, a delicious, creamy, sweetened custard-like yogurt. "Juju" means "king" and "dhau" mean "yogurt" in Newari, and "juju dhau" literally translates to "king of yogurt." It has been a delicacy since ancient times, from the Malla Dynasty to the Shah King's era. There are multiple competing stories about its origin. One popular version is that after the yogurt makers of Bhaktapur won a competition, the Malla kings dubbed it the "king of yogurt."

Juju Dhau is an important component of feasts and celebrations but can be enjoyed anytime as a daytime snack or as an after-dinner dessert. Sometimes, it is made in a small clay cup, sold, and consumed in the same container. Juju Dhau used to be available only in Bhaktapur, but these days, it is available all over Nepal, in supermarkets, Asan Chowk markets, and yogurt shops.

I wanted to find out more about this famous yogurt and asked my dear friend, Madhu, who took me to Bhaktapur to observe the juju dhau making process. I am also grateful to Mr. Shyam S. Dhaubhadel, founder of Siddi Memorial foundation, and the owner of Cafe Nayatapola in Taumadhi Square in Bhaktapur for arranging this tour. He introduced me to Mr. Nabin Pradhananga, a third generation juju dhau maker, who owns and operates a yogurt-making facility inherited from his great grandfather. He was happy to give us a tour. He told us he starts the process early every morning and buys milk from local buffalo or cow farmers or sometimes from out of town. He first showed us where he stores his collection of unglazed natural clay pots (maata ko kataaro or kala). He explained, "The clay pot is porous, so the excess liquid or moisture from the yogurt slowly evaporates and makes firm textured, creamy and thick yogurt. It also retains the proper temperature during the incubation period of yogurt making. The clay pots keep yogurt cool on hot summer days. All our yogurt is sold in the same clay pot that it was prepared in." He soaks the clay pots in water for several hours and drains them completely before adding milk and starter culture.

We then proceeded to the kitchen area, where several large, heavy-bottomed pots (karaahi) filled with buffalo milk (bhaisi ko doodh) were being heated over a wood-fired stove. His kitchen staff were stirring the milk constantly to prevent sticking until the milk had thickened. Mr. Pradhananga said this process could take about 1 to 1½ hours depending on the amount of milk used. Once the milk thickens, he adds sugar and lets the milk cool down a bit before he adds it to the kataaro. We went to a room filled with rice husks (bhus), which is the papery covering of rice grains. The husk helps to keep the temperature of the milk culture warm during its incubation period. Mr. Pradhananga showed us how each kataaro is placed on top of a rice husk neatly in a line. He made a little well and pushed the kataato half way to secure the pot. His staff members slowly poured the thickened milk into each container. After the milk cooled, they added starter culture (one spoonful at a time) to each individual container. He said an active yogurt culture (previously made yogurt) is needed for each new batch of yogurt. The starter culture is called "dahi ko beu" in Nepali and "dhau pusa" in Newari. He showed us the "starter," which was saved from the last batch of juju dhau. Then, his staff covered each kataaro with another empty kataaro. Finally, they placed a thick, heavy insulated cotton blanket (tagaeko oddane) on top of the yogurt containers. These containers are left undisturbed for several hours (average 3 to 4 hours on warm days, 5 to 6 hours on cold days) for the yogurt to set. The room must be warm for the culture growth. Mr. Pradhananga told us that the most important thing to keep in mind while making yogurt is that he prefers buffalo milk with high fat content, he prefers black clay pots, and uses a wood fire to heat the milk. He added smilingly, "A well-set yogurt will not drop off or fall even if you turn the kataaro upside down."

He said he would return when the yogurt sets and move the yogurt containers to shelves to rest, during which time, it thickens further and becomes more creamy and delicious. Some of the rice husks that are attached to the container have to be removed. Triangle wood stands called dhauka help to keep the containers stacked. He then loads the containers into a van, and transports them throughout the city for sale.

I thoroughly enjoyed my tour, and I encourage everyone to visit Bhaktapur and sample a bowl of juju dhau. Thank you so much Mr. Nabin Pradhananga for showing us how you make such delicious juju dhau.

The Leaf Plates of Nepal
Tapari, Dunaa, Botaa

A very attractive and large special occasion leaf plate that was stitched for my cousin's son's rice feeding ceremony in Kathmandu. The auspicious food items, floral offerings, and ritual objects are placed around the large quantity of cooked rice during the Paasne ceremony.

Tapari, dunaa, and botaa are disposable, multipurpose leaf plates and bowls made by stitching *saal ko paat* with small bamboo sticks. *Saal* trees (*shorea robusta*) are most commonly found in the Terai regions of Nepal and are used for timber and fuel. The leaves are used for plates and animal feed, while the seeds and fruits have Ayurvedic medicinal use. Nepalese use the fresh leaf plates and bowls for many occasions. Saal leaves are considered *chokho* (pure, sacred, and auspicious) in Nepal and are must-have items in many religious rituals. In many historical pictures, you will see Queen Mayadevi giving birth to Gautam Buddha under the saal tree (or Ashoka tree) in a garden in Lumbini in southern Nepal, so it is valued as a holy tree. In Kathmandu Valley, one can find typical Nepali pagoda temple architecture with very rich wooden carvings, and most of the temples are made of bricks and saal tree wood.

The shiny dark-green *saal ko paat* are collected by hand-picking from the lower branches of the tree. Some freshly fallen leaves are also collected from the ground. The leaves are then neatly stacked together, tied with a thin bamboo rope and made into bundles, then taken to the market for sale or supplied to a different vendor. In general, there are three different sizes and shapes of leaf plates made:

Tapari is a lightly curved plate made by stitching several saal leaves together with a fine bamboo stick (*sinka*). The shiny fresh green leaves are very flexible and have a lot of moisture, making it easy to twist, squeeze, and shape them into plates without breaking the leaves.

Dunaa is a medium-size bowl, either circular or rectangular and can be used to hold semi-liquid foods.

Botaa is usually made by using a single leaf, stitched together into a small bowl.

Machine-made dry leaf plates and bowls started to appear in Nepali markets only a few years ago. Now they are extensively used by street food sellers, fast-food vendors, restaurants, and hotels and even at picnics and outdoor parties as disposable plates. They are available in many local stores in Kathmandu. The demand for leaf plates is increasing rapidly because they are biodegradable and compostable making them environmentally friendly products.

Making leaf plates and bowls requires time and skills. My good friend, Krishna Maya Prajaapati, demonstrated how to create traditional leaf plates. She used twelve leaves to make a medium-size tapari. *Starting with the center part first, she placed two leaves in the middle, then arranges other leaves in a circular pattern (like a plate). The shiny side of the leaves are placed up. She stitched and attached all the pieces securely with ½-inch bamboo sticks creating a flat circular plate. Holding the flat leaf with one hand, she squeezed and folded with the other hand to make a slightly curved plate that is secured with a bamboo stick. Thank you, Krishna Maya, for showing me an excellent work of art!*

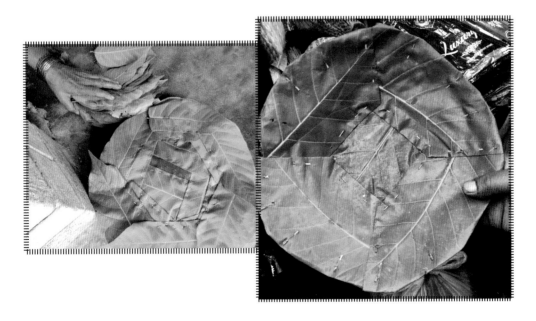

Chapter 2

THE NEPALI PANTRY & KITCHEN EQUIPMENT

A Guide to Nepali Ingredients
Nepali Pakaaune Saamaagri Haru

The following describes some of the special ingredients that are called for in this book. You will also find additional descriptions of unfamiliar ingredients in the recipes themselves. Please refer to both sections. Most of these ingredients are easily available through online retailers, some local Nepali markets outside Nepal, Asian and Middle Eastern grocery stores, or some health food stores and larger supermarkets.

Ajowan Seeds (*Jwaano*) Also known as *ajowain,* Bishop's weed, omum, or carom seeds, these are used extensively in Nepali cooking. These tiny gray-brown seeds have a striped surface and resemble celery seeds, but have a somewhat sharper and more pungent flavor. If the seeds are chewed plain, they are strong, bitter, and stinging, but their aftertaste is quite pleasant. They are usually lightly fried to release flavor and added at the beginning stages of the cooking process. Ajowan seeds are sometimes crushed in a mortar and pestle and added to batters. They are one of the most important spices in the much-loved Sprouted Bean Soup (*Kwanti*). The seeds are also chewed on their own to help with bloating, relieve flatulence, and aid digestion. It is believed that ajowan soup helps lactating mothers increase and maintain milk supplies. The seeds should be stored in an airtight container in a cool, dark place.

Asafetida (*Heeng*) Also called *hingu* (Sanskrit) or devil's dung, asafetida is used extensively in Nepali cooking to flavor and preserve food, as well as for its medicinal properties. Asafetida comes from an herbaceous fennel-like perennial plant. When mature, the stems are cut close to the roots releasing a milky substance that solidifies into a brownish, gummy mass. Asafetida is sometimes described as having an unpleasant and overpowering smell, due in part to the presence of sulfur. In Nepali, there is a saying, *"hing ne bhai pani hing ko taalo cha"* (translation: even if the asafetida is used up, its aroma lingers in the wrapping cloth). However, when used with discretion and in minute amounts, this spice mellows and adds a pleasant aroma to prepared food. Asafetida is commonly used in the preparation of daals, vegetable curries, and pickles. Almost all daal and bean dishes are cooked with asafetida, making them digestible since this spice offers relief from flatulence. It is readily available, labeled as *hing* at Indian grocery stores in powdered or solid forms. Most powdered forms are combined with rice, corn, or wheat flour to prevent lumping, or to reduce its overpowering smell, and sometimes to increase its weight. The powdered form is convenient, but of a less intense flavor. Solid pieces of asafetida are brown in color and come in irregular shapes. Some people prefer to buy the solid form because its flavor is more concentrated. In my recipes, I use the powdered form, but if you decide to purchase solid asafetida, you can grind it as needed. The flavor of asafetida is definitely an acquired taste, and for some people who are not familiar with the spice, it may take some time. Asafetida should be stored in an airtight container because of its strong smell.

Atta Flour (*Gahu ko Pitho*) Also known as chapatti or durum whole wheat flour, this fine-textured flour is processed from low-gluten wheat and used in making most unleavened breads. Since this flour is low in gluten, it is easier to knead and roll.

Black-Eyed Peas (*Bodi*) Also known as cow peas, these kidney-shaped beans are tan or cream colored with small black markings or "eyes," which they maintain even after cooking. The outer skin of the bean is somewhat thick and not easily digestible, so they should be soaked for at least six hours or until soft before cooking and then cooked thoroughly. They can be mixed with vegetables and cooked as a curried dish.

Black Salt (*Bire Noon, Kaaloo Noon*) Black salt, *kaalaa namak* in Hindi, is a special type of Indian mineral salt. Although it is known as black salt, it is not black. The powdered version of black salt is brownish-grey, while the solid form is violet to purple-brown. This salt has a sharp, distinct, tangy taste, and may contain small quantities of mineral and iron. It is used in small quantities, as it has a tendency to overpower the dish. It is mainly used in the preparation of fried snacks, appetizers, and fresh chutneys, sprinkled on raw vegetables and fruits, and added to spicy yogurt dishes. It is one of the ingredients used in Nepali seasonal salt mixture. Black salt is very salty and certainly an acquired taste, and cannot be used interchangeably with table salt or sea salt. It is available in solid or powdered form. The solid form can be easily pounded in a mortar and pestle or in a blender before using. It should be stored in a well-sealed container in a cool dry place.

Buckwheat Flour (*Phaapar ko Pitho*) Buckwheat belongs to the sorrel and rhubarb family and has triangular seeds. It is not related to wheat, is not a true grain, and has no gluten. It has a nutty flavor and is a high source of protein. Buckwheat roti is eaten during fasting days when other grains are avoided. It is available at Indian and health food stores, and at some regular supermarkets. It should be stored in an airtight container.

Cardamom, Black (*Alainchi*) Native to the sub-Himalayan region, black cardamom is the dried fruit of a perennial herbaceous plant of the ginger family. Apart from its usage in India, Nepal, and other Asian countries, black cardamom is not common. The pod is oval shaped and dark brown, and its size ranges from ¾ to 1 inch. The pod is tough and leathery with deep wrinkles. Each pod contains several moist brown seeds that are sticky, flavorful, and once crushed, emit a pleasant smoky aroma with a hint of camphor. When cooked, the spice enhances and intensifies the taste of food without overpowering a dish. Some people describe black cardamom as an inferior substitute to green cardamom, but it is considered a valuable spice in Nepal. It is an entirely different flavor compared to green cardamom and should not be used as a substitute. It is one of the ingredients used to make Nepali *garam masalaa* spice blends and is also used in meat curries, rice

dishes, and pickles. Many Nepalese chew black cardamom after dinner or any time of the day to freshen the breath and palate. It is also used as a home remedy for digestive disorders and considered beneficial to teeth and gums. Black cardamom is available in Indian food stores. Look for pods with moist, sweet seeds, and a smoky fragrance. Old pods with splits and cracks will have poor quality seeds with no flavor. The seeds quickly lose their flavor once the pods are opened, so store the pods whole and grind the seeds as needed.

Cardamom, Green (*Sukumel*) The dried unripe fruit of a perennial bushy plant of the ginger family, green cardamom pods are three-sided, smooth-skinned, and contain reddish-brown seeds. The seeds are sticky and have a highly aromatic flavor with a hint of eucalyptus. Because of its high price, it is used sparingly. When a recipe calls for whole cardamom, the pods are cracked leaving the seeds intact, adding a subtle flavor to a dish. Sometimes the pods are removed before the food is served. For recipes that call for ground cardamom, I prefer to crush the seeds in a mortar and pestle rather than use pre-ground cardamom because the seeds begin to lose their flavor once the pods are opened. Cardamom is one of the most important ingredients in Nepali sweets, and is also popular in meat and vegetable curries, sweet preserved pickles, and beverages. It is also one of the ingredients used to make Nepali *garam masalaa*. Cardamom seeds are also chewed after dinner or any time of the day to freshen the breath. Many people carry a small bag of cardamom pods to chew as needed. Cardamom is also used in Ayurvedic medicine to treat various maladies such as digestive disorders and headaches, and is known to cure nausea and vomiting. Cardamom pods, both green and bleached

white, are available whole, seeded, or ground in Indian food stores and most supermarkets. Look for high-quality whole pods that are plump and have brownish-black seeds with a strong scent. If the pod is wrinkled and dried up, the seeds will have no flavor. Pre-ground cardamom powder is convenient, but it will be less aromatic.

Cassia Leaves (*Tejpaat*) From an aromatic evergreen tree, this herb is also known as Indian cassia, cinnamon leaves, and *tej patta*. The leaves are oblong shaped and usually have three prominent veins. The dried leaves have a warm, sweet, and distinct cinnamon aroma. They are usually lightly sautéed for all kinds of spiced meat and fish curries, savory rice dishes, lentils, and some vegetables and are usually removed from the dish before it is served. Cassia leaves are one of the important spice ingredients in the preparation of Nepali *garam masalaa*. The leaves are also known to have some medicinal properties for the treatment of colic and diarrhea. They are available in Indian food markets often under the name "Indian Bay Leaves." They should be stored in an airtight container in a cool dark place.

Chickpea Flour (*Besan*) Also known as Bengal gram flour or *chana* flour, this flour is pale, yellow-colored, and finely milled from brown chickpeas. It has a nutty flavor and is used often as a batter for fritters, sweet dishes, and as a thickener. Look for this flour in Indian grocery stores or larger well-stocked supermarkets.

Chickpeas, Brown (*Kaalo Chanaa*) Brown chickpeas are similar to white chickpeas in shape, but are smaller and more wrinkled, with a thick seed coating. Despite their physical similarity to white chickpeas, they have a different flavor and texture with an earthy aroma and nutty taste. Chickpeas should be soaked in water before cooking. They can be cooked in bean dishes, toasted, fried to make crunchy snacks, or sprouted.

Chickpeas, White (*Sukeko Chanaa*) Also known as Bengal gram or garbanzo beans, white chickpeas are irregular-shaped, cream-colored beans somewhat larger than peas. They have a thick wrinkled skin and are normally soaked in water before using, which cuts down the cooking time. After soaking, the beans double in size and the wrinkles smooth out. They are cooked as regular bean dishes, mixed with salads, or sprouted.

Chickpeas, Yellow Split (*Chana ko Daal***)** These are also known as split Bengal gram and come from the brown variety of chickpeas. They resemble yellow split peas or pigeon peas, but are slightly larger and have a bright yellow color with stronger flavor and nutty aroma. This daal takes a long time to cook and will not disintegrate, but holds its shape. It is usually pre-soaked before cooking. Yellow split chickpeas are difficult to digest, so are always cooked with a generous amount of ginger and asafetida.

Cilantro (*Hariyo Dhania ko Paat***)** The fresh green leaves and tender stems of the coriander plants are a favorite herb in the Nepali kitchen. In Nepal it is known as *hariyo dhania* and most refer to this aromatic herb as fresh coriander, rather than cilantro. The seeds and leaves have completely different flavors and aromas and cannot be substituted for one another. Fresh cilantro has a distinct and sharp flavor, whereas the seeds are much milder. A small amount of chopped fresh cilantro is sprinkled on nearly every dish as a garnish and to add extra flavor. Cilantro is also combined with highly seasoned meat or vegetables to tone down spiciness. Some families freeze the fresh leaves for future use. Frozen leaves may offer colors and flavors in the dish but wouldn't work well for garnishing. Cilantro is sold year-round in most supermarkets and in Indian, Latin American, and Asian food markets. Make sure it is bright green and avoid wilted leaves. It can be stored in the refrigerator for up to one week in a plastic bag lined with a paper towel. The rooted variety can be kept longer in a glass of water, root-end down, covered with a plastic bag in the refrigerator. Change the water every other day and use as needed.

Cinnamon and Cassia Bark (*Daalchini***)** One of the oldest known and most aromatic spices, cinnamon is the dried inner bark of a tropical evergreen tree. The bark is reddish-brown in color, pungent, sharp tasting, and easily breakable. It is used either whole or ground to flavor sauces, rice, desserts, and syrups, and is brewed with milky tea. Cinnamon is also one of the components of Nepali spice blends, such as *garam masalaa*. It is available whole or ground in any supermarket or Indian food store. Cinnamon sticks keep indefinitely, but ground cinnamon loses its flavor more quickly. Both should be stored in an airtight container. In Nepal, a small stick of cinnamon is sometimes chewed with cardamom and cloves after a heavily spiced meal to freshen the breath and palate.

Clarified Butter (*Gheu***)** Clarified butter (*gheu* in Nepal) is made by heating unsalted butter until all the milk solids separate and can be removed. This butter imparts a wonderful flavor and is extensively used in Nepali cooking. It is easy to make at home and is sold as "ghee" in jars of various sizes in Indian groceries and some supermarkets. (*See recipe, page 314.*)

Cloves (*Lwang***)** The dried buds of a tropical evergreen tree, cloves are reddish-brown in color with a rounded flower head. They are one of the most important Nepali spices, used both for culinary and medicinal purposes. In Sanskrit, cloves are called *deva kusuma*, meaning "the flower of the gods" or "auspicious bud." Cloves are either used whole or ground to flavor many savory Nepali dishes but rarely in sweet dishes. When gently sautéed, the spice swells and releases a pleasant aroma. Cloves are also used in pickles and are an important component in Nepali *garam masalaa* mixtures. Cloves can overpower a dish, particularly when ground, so they should be used sparingly. Buy them whole, not ground, as ground cloves lose their potency quickly.

Aside from its culinary use, cloves are also used to freshen one's mouth. Nepalese chew cloves throughout the day, alone or with green or black cardamom or cinnamon sticks and betel nuts. Chewing cloves is certainly a cultivated taste, and at first they can be bitingly sharp, hot, and leave a lasting numb sensation in the mouth, but once you get used to it you enjoy the taste. Cloves act as a quick home remedy for relieving toothaches by simply tucking them in the affected corner of the mouth and chewing slowly to release the oil. This also helps to minimize tooth decay and eliminate halitosis. Cloves are used to cure nausea and flatulence and promote digestion, especially after eating fatty and spicy food.

Coriander Seeds (*Dhaniya ko Geda*) The dried, ripe fruit of a hardy annual plant from the parsley family, coriander seeds are beige or yellowish-brown in color, slightly smaller than peppercorns, with longitudinal ridges, that can be easily split into halves. They have a very pleasant and sweet aroma, with a hint of citrus. It is a valued spice in Nepali cooking and extensively used as a flavoring agent in nearly all dishes. Coriander is an important ingredient in Nepali garam masalaa mixtures. The combination of cumin and coriander is one of the most common seasonings in Nepali cuisine. In many recipes, both coriander leaves (cilantro) and seeds are used in the same dish to create a wonderful flavor. Coriander seeds are available both whole and ground at Indian grocery stores. I usually purchase whole seeds and grind them in small quantities as needed because ground seeds lose their potency quickly. To bring out their flavor, you can also toast the seeds carefully before grinding and store them in an airtight container.

Cumin Seeds (*Jeera*) In Sanskrit, cumin seeds are called *sugandhan jeeraka*, meaning "good smelling with digestive properties," indicating that the spice has been in use since ancient times for digestive disorders. Cumin seeds are gray-green, oblong, ridged, and thicker in the middle with pointed ends, somewhat resembling caraway or fennel seeds in appearance, but their flavor and aroma is entirely different. They have a sharp, pungent, and slightly bitter taste. The seeds are used extensively in Nepali cooking— whole, ground, or lightly crushed. Cumin seeds are an essential ingredient in Nepali spice blends. Ground cumin has a distinct, strong, and powerful flavor and should be used carefully in measured quantities; otherwise, it may dominate a dish. Cumin seeds are available either whole or ground at most supermarkets. Ground cumin seeds lose potency once it ages, so grind them fresh or purchase in small quantities.

Cumin Seeds, Black (*Kaalo Jeera*) The black variety of cumin seeds comes from a small, slender, annual herb. It is similar to regular cumin seeds except for their dark brown color and length. These seeds are warm, pungent, and mildly bitter, with a sweet scent. They are called *shahi jeera* in Hindi, meaning "king cumin" because of their distinct features. This spice is used more widely in Indian-Kashmiri cuisine than Nepali. Because it is relatively rare, black cumin is used only in small amounts to flavor rice dishes, meat curries, and fried snacks.

Fennel Seeds (*Saunp* or *Saunf*) The strong-smelling fennel plant has bright green stalks, lacy, dark green leaves, and mustard yellow flowers, which turn into seed-heads when ripe. Seeds are collected before they mature and are dried. These slightly curved seeds are oval-shaped with ridges, greenish-yellow, and look somewhat like plump cumin seeds. They are an aromatic spice with a mild licorice flavor. All parts of the fennel plant are edible, including the young tender shoots, leaves, and stalks, as well as the seeds. Fennel seeds are often offered at the end of a meal as a digestive or to freshen the mouth. The seeds are sometimes toasted to bring out their flavor and mixed with coconut, melon seeds, and sugar crystals before chewing. They are available in most supermarkets and the higher quality seeds will be bright green, which indicates freshness. The seeds can be ground in a spice grinder or with a mortar and pestle as the recipe indicates.

Fenugreek Seeds (*Methi ko Geda*) An indispensable spice in Nepali cooking, these brownish-yellow rectangular seeds are very hard and highly aromatic. They come from an annual herb of the legume family that grows about two feet high with white flowers that form long, slender pods. When the pods mature, they are dried, and the seeds are removed. The seeds have a very strong, unpleasantly bitter taste in the raw stage, but when cooked, they emit a wonderful aroma. They are used in small quantities, and in many recipes the whole seeds are first fried in oil to bring out the maximum flavor. But be forewarned, frying fenugreek seeds gives off an unpleasant smell that may linger for days without proper ventilation. Fenugreek seeds can also be soaked, sprouted, and used in salads or pickles. The young and fresh green leaves (*methi ko saag*) of the fenugreek plant are also used; they have a pleasant bitter flavor that is an acquired taste. Fenugreek seeds, as well as fresh and dried leaves, are available in Indian grocery stores.

Garlic (*Lasoon ko Poti*) Fresh garlic is one of the most liberally used ingredients in Nepali cooking. Raw garlic has a strong flavor, but its pungency reduces once it is cooked. Peeled, sliced garlic does not keep very well, so peel only the amount required for each recipe. Leave the bulb intact with the skin on when storing. Crushed garlic is much stronger than chopped or whole garlic. Nepalese use stone mortar and pestles to crush garlic until it is completely smooth. Sometimes the garlic is crushed with a little salt to bring out even more flavor. Crushed garlic starts losing its intensity after a few hours, so should be used right away. Garlic powder is more convenient to use, and you can substitute it, but the flavor is not the same as fresh garlic. Some orthodox Brahmins in Nepal do not eat garlic due to religious reasons, but garlic's healing qualities are gaining popularity. Purchase garlic with firm, plump bulbs and dry skins. Avoid soft, sprouting bulbs and store garlic in an open container at room temperature in a well-ventilated area. If the bulbs are broken, individual cloves will not store well.

Garam Masalaa A dry spice blend. See Chapter 15, Spice Blends & Basic Recipes, pages 310 and 311, for recipes for two homemade garam masalaa.

Ginger (*Aduwa* or *Aduwaa*) Although fresh ginger is sometimes called gingerroot, it is actually an underground creeping rhizome. The attractive plant has long leaves, and grows up to three feet tall, forming rhizomes that are dug up from the ground as they mature. Fresh ginger has cream to light brown skin with a pale yellow flesh, and provides the freshest flavor and spicy biting taste. Fresh, dried whole (*sutho*), and powdered ginger are available at Indian and Asian food stores and most supermarkets. For best results, always choose ginger that is firm and unwrinkled. It can be kept for several weeks in the refrigerator, wrapped in a paper towel to absorb moisture. Peeled and sliced ginger does not keep very well, so it should be peeled as needed. Fresh ginger paste is also available at some Asian and Indian grocery stores and should be refrigerated after opening. Powdered ginger is convenient, but has a different flavor and should not be substituted for fresh ginger. Aside from its culinary use, both fresh and dried ginger are valued for their medicinal properties, particularly to soothe indigestion, loss of appetite, and especially flatulence. They are also used to relieve coughs and sore throats.

Goddess Basil (*Tulasi*) Considered sacred in the Hindu tradition, this annual herb is traditionally grown in the courtyard of many Nepali homes or in a pot and worshiped in the morning and evening. Goddess Basil has small aromatic leaves, which are either green or purplish. In addition to their religious uses, fresh or dried basil is used to make a soothing herbal tea, and is believed to help treat common colds, headaches, and stomach disorders.

Green Gooseberry (*Amalaa*) Also called Indian gooseberry, *emblica* or *amalaki*, green gooseberries come from trees grown at the foot of the Himalayan Mountains. The tree has feathery leaves, and the fruit is light yellow to green, round, firm, and tart. Gooseberries are picked by hand or by shaking them from the tree. They are then gathered from the ground and transported to markets in a conical wicker basket (*doko*). Nepalese regard whole gooseberries as sacred and offer the fruit to deities during worship. They may be eaten raw, but are usually formed into nuggets and dried, made into preserves, or pickled with spices. Gooseberries possess high nutritive value and are known for their medicinal properties. They are believed to help prevent aging and to treat diarrhea and hemorrhages. Gooseberries are available in Indian markets, frozen and dried, but occasionally you may find fresh ones.

Jimbu Also known as Himalayan aromatic leaf garlic, jimbu is a dried aromatic herb that is virtually unknown outside the Himalayan region. The herb looks like dry brownish-green grass and has a distinct flavor somewhat similar to garlic and shallots. It is found wild throughout many regions of Nepal. The leaves and tender stems are carefully picked and dried, which weakens the flavor, but this is reversed by browning them in hot oil until fully fragrant. Nepalese have a remarkable fondness for this herb and they use it as a tempering spice to flavor daals, vegetables, salads, and pickles. Generally, a small pinch of jimbu is sufficient to flavor a dish and it should be used with discretion. The fried herb lends texture and visual appeal to any dish. As the herb ages, it loses its flavor, so purchase it in small quantities. Jimbu is available through online retailers or some local Nepali markets outside Nepal. Some people substitute the dried roots of the garlic bulb, although this does not produce the same flavor as jimbu. (*For more detailed information, see page 30.*)

Kidney Beans (*Raajma ko Daal*) These kidney-shaped beans have a red firm skin with cream-colored flesh, and are cooked similar to other beans. They are first soaked in water to improve the texture and to quicken the cooking time, and then they are slowly simmered with fresh herbs and spices until tender.

Lapsi Fruit (*Nepalese Hog Plum*) Also known as *lausi*, these are a native fruit of Nepal. The tall subtropical tree can be found growing in many parts of the country. The fruit is greenish-yellow when ripe and roughly resembles a small oval-shaped plum. It is extremely sour, even when fully ripe, and has a high vitamin C content. The fruit has a tough fibrous skin and pale yellow flesh that is firmly attached to a large brown seed. The pulp is difficult to separate from the seeds, but once cooked it separates easily. A ripe lapsi has a pleasantly tart flavor and some people like to eat it fresh, but it is mainly used to make dried fruit nuggets or fruit leather, both sweet and salted. It is also pickled, cooked with vegetables, or used as a souring agent. The stony seeds (*champati*) are used as a cooking fuel and some children play with the seeds like round marbles. Lapsi is not available outside Nepal. (*For more detailed information, see page 40.*)

Lentils, Red or Pink (*Musuro ko Daal*) Also known as *masoor daal*, these round lentils have brown seed coatings and are very popular in Nepal. They are available whole (*singo musuro ko daal*) or split (*musuro ko daal*). When cooked, whole lentils retain their shape and do not disintegrate into mush. The split, skinless variety is quick cooking with a delicate nutty flavor and turns golden yellow when cooked. The whole lentils with skins can be sprouted or stir-fried and made into crunchy snacks. Generally, neither variety needs soaking before cooking.

Mango Powder (*Amchoor*) Made from tart, unripe, green mangoes (which are peeled, sliced, dried, and finely ground), mango powder is very tart with a pleasant, mild, citrus flavor. It is used to add tartness to various dishes, more commonly vegetable dishes than meat dishes, and is frequently used to flavor snacks. The light brown-colored powder is available in Indian grocery stores in sealed plastic bags.

Mung Beans (*Moong Daal*) Also known as green grams or *mugi ko daal*, these legumes are extensively used in Nepali cooking. They are known for their lightness and for being easily digestible. These tiny oval-shaped beans come in three forms. Split yellow mung beans without skins (*pahelo moong ko daal*) are the most common daal in Nepal and are considered the most delicious and easiest to digest. They can be soaked, drained, and fried into crunchy snacks. This daal is also frequently prescribed for sick people with digestive disorders. Split green mung beans with skins (*khoste moong ko daal*) are used to prepare basic daal or combined with rice to make a soft rice porridge. Whole green mung beans with skins (*singo moong ko daal*) are cooked by themselves or combined with other legumes. They can be soaked and used in salads, stir-fried, deep-fried, or sprouted, and are used to make the traditional Nepali mixed sprouted bean dish *Kwanti* (Sprouted Bean Soup, *page 123*).

Mustard Oil (*Tori ko Tel*) Mustard oil is an extremely pungent, yellow-colored oil that comes from pressed mustard seeds. In the raw state, the oil has a bitter, sharp flavor, but once it is heated to the smoking point, the pungency mellows and the oil imparts its delicious flavor to food. It is used extensively in making pickles and chutney as it acts as a preservative. Nepalese apply mustard oil to hair to promote healthy growth and use it in massage for relief from aches and pains. Mustard oil is available in Indian and Asian stores, and some well-stocked supermarkets.

Mustard Seeds (*Rayo or Sarsyun*) These small round seeds come from the mustard plant, a common annual field crop in Nepal. They range from reddish-brown to a dark brown color, but when crushed they are yellow on the inside. They have a pungent, sharp flavor, but when fried in oil, they impart a mellow nutty flavor. Nepalese use ground or coarsely ground mustard seeds to make pickles because of their wonderful preservative properties that discourage mold and bacteria. They are also used to perk up vegetable dishes. Yellow mustard seeds (*sarsyun*) are used to cook fish and are believed to eliminate fishy odors. The tender leaves of the mustard plant, called mustard greens (*raayo ko saag*), are also cooked into a delicious vegetable dish. The seeds are pressed to extract fragrant mustard oil. Mustard is used as a home remedy to cure flatulence and to promote digestion. Mustard seeds are available whole, split, or powdered at Indian grocery stores, Asian markets, and regular grocery stores.

Nutmeg and Mace (*Jaiphal & Jaipatri*) Nutmeg and mace are known for their strongly aromatic, warm, fresh, and nutty flavor. Both nutmeg and mace come from the fruit of the nutmeg tree. Mace is the lacy, light orange colored, fibrous membrane that covers the nut of nutmeg fruit. The mace is removed from the nutmeg, dried and ground, and used as a spice. It has a mild flavor compared to nutmeg and is used in a spice mixture. Some Nepali *garam masalaa* contains mace and nutmeg with a combination of other spices. Ground nutmeg and mace are frequently used to season strong-flavored meats like game, venison, and organ meats. They are also used with cardamom to prepare milk-based sweet dishes and yogurt desserts. Nutmeg should be used in moderation, a small pinch is generally sufficient to flavor a moderate-sized dish. Purchase whole nutmeg and grind or grate it as needed, because its flavor deteriorates and it loses its potency soon after grinding. Whole nutmegs keep indefinitely if they are stored in an airtight container, away from sunlight. In addition to its culinary uses, nutmeg is also used as a home remedy to aid digestion, treat diarrhea, cure nausea, and improve appetite. Nutmeg oil is also used in soap, perfume, and ointments.

Peas, Dried (*Sukeko Thulo Kerau*) Available in green and yellow varieties, these peas are used whole or split, with or without the skins. When split and skinless, they are consumed as daal, while the whole peas are eaten as a form of vegetable curry. They can also be soaked, sprouted, made into salads, or mixed with other vegetables. They are sometimes toasted and puffed for snack foods. Dried peas do not require soaking before cooking, but soaking shortens the cooking time.

Peas, Field (*Sukeko Hariyo Saano Kerau*) These tiny peas resemble garden peas, with smaller and narrower pods, each containing tightly packed almost round, smooth peas. Once dried, they become green-gray in color and resemble mung beans, but are much harder. Field peas are usually grown for drying, but are also eaten fresh. The podded bushy plants are sold bundled in Nepali markets during the spring. The dried peas require soaking for more than twelve hours before using them. They are most commonly pickled, used in salads, or cooked with vegetables.

Peppercorns (*Marich*) One of the most widely used spices in the world, black pepper is also known as *pippali* in Sanskrit, which means "berry." Black pepper has a very pungent, hot, and biting taste, and thus should be used in moderation. It is available whole, finely ground, or crushed. Although pre-ground pepper is convenient, the essential oils released by grinding peppercorns fade quickly, so it is best if purchased whole and ground as needed. It should be stored in an airtight container away from sunlight. Peppercorns are recognized as having medicinal qualities such as promoting digestion, reducing bloating and flatulence, and relieving nausea.

Pigeon Peas (*Rahar ko Daal*) Also known as red gram, yellow lentils, *arhar*, or *toor*, pigeon peas are usually sold split without skins. This daal has a slightly nutty taste, is easy to digest, and resembles yellow split chickpeas. In Nepal, *rahar ko daal* is considered the king of daal, because of its delicious flavor, and it is always cooked for feasts. These lentils are available dry and oiled. The oily kind look glossy because they are coated with castor oil to prevent spoilage. Oiled pigeon peas should be rinsed in hot water before cooking.

Poppy Seeds (*Khus Khus*) These small, dried, pale yellow, black, or beige seeds come from the capsules of the opium poppy. They add a crunchy texture and nutty flavor to any dish, and are especially popular as a topping for breads. They can be purchased at Indian grocery stores and most supermarkets. These seeds contain oil that turns rancid quickly, so it is best if they are stored in the refrigerator.

Nigella Seeds (*Mungrelo*) Also known as black cumin, black onion seeds, and *kalonji*, these are small, triangular, black seeds with a rough surface and white interior. They have a lingering flavor described as peppery, nutty, and bitter. The whole seed is not very strong, but when crushed they have a distinct pungent flavor. Nigella seeds are often confused with onion seeds, but they are quite different and should not be substituted. The seeds are usually fried or toasted to enhance their flavor, and cooked with meat and fish curries, with mild vegetables such as pumpkin, and used extensively in preserved pickles. They are available whole in small packets in Indian grocery stores.

Radish Seeds (*Mula ko Beu*) The dried edible seeds of the radish plant, radish seeds are reddish-brown in color with a pungent, sharp, and peppery taste, and a hint of radish flavor. When the radish plant reaches its full height, its yellow flowers become seedpods. The seeds are harvested, separated, and collected by threshing. They are used in small quantities because of their overpowering taste and mainly as a pickling spice. These seeds are used in the ground form and they can be easily crushed with a mortar and pestle.

Rice Flakes, Pressed (*Cheuraa or Chewraa*) Also known as *ba-jee*, pressed rice flakes are prepared from soaked or parboiled rice that has been flattened by large heavy rollers into flat flakes. They are dehydrated and the finished product is a ready-to-eat rice flake. In Nepal, the old-fashioned method of pounding the grains in a heavy wooden mortar with a pole still exists in many villages, and is preferred by many, although it is slowly being replaced by machines. The dried rice flakes have uneven edges and a rough texture, and resemble rolled oats. They are extremely light, with no particular aroma, a bland taste, and vary in thickness, texture, and color according to the types of rice used to prepare the flakes. *Cheuraa* is very popular throughout Nepal because it can be consumed without further cooking, stores well, is easy to carry, and is light and healthy. Plain, toasted, or fried rice flakes are eaten with vegetables or meat, eggs, yogurt, pickles, and as a mid-day snack between meals. It is also served as a breakfast food. *Cheuraa* is sold in plastic bags in Indian grocery stores under the name *poha*, *chidwa*, or *chura*. Before use, the flakes need to be picked over to remove any foreign matter. Store them in a cool dry place in a covered container to keep out moisture.

Rice Flour (*Chaamal ko Pitho*) This white flour is made by grinding rice grains into powder. It is available in Indian or East Asian grocery stores and some health food stores, as well as well stocked supermarkets. Store in a dry, tightly closed container.

Saffron (*Kesar*) The dried stigmas of the saffron crocus flower are known as saffron. Each flower contains three bright red stigmas that are handpicked, an extremely labor-intensive process, making it one of the world's most expensive spices. The stigmas are dried until they shrink into slender, delicate thread-like strands with a bright orange-red color and delicate aroma. Saffron is used in small amounts to flavor various Nepali dishes. The threads are usually crushed and infused in warm liquids to extract their full aroma and flavor and to give an even color to the dish. Some cookbooks suggest toasting saffron strands before crushing them to extract more flavor. I do not recommend this method, and it is also not necessary to bring out the intense aroma by toasting. Saffron is also available in the ground form in an airtight container, dated and labeled with the source in Indian, Middle Eastern, and regular supermarkets. Good-quality saffron has a strong pleasant flavor, and is light, glossy, and soft to touch. It should be stored in a cool dry place away from sunlight, for its flavor diminishes and it becomes dry and brittle as it ages. Ground saffron loses its potency more quickly and can be easily adulterated with fillers unless you get it from a reputable spice vendor.

Sesame Seeds (*Til*) Sesame seeds are flat, small, oval seeds that come from the annual tropical sesame plant. They can be white, black, or various shades of brown. White sesame seeds are shiny, slippery, and easy to crush and remain white even after cooking. They are used mainly in desserts and bread preparations. The black varieties have a strong bitter taste and are not used much in Nepali cooking, but they are considered sacred and are used in various religious ceremonies and rituals. Light brown sesame seeds are much preferred and are usually toasted to bring out their nutty flavor. They are available at most supermarkets and in Indian, South Asian, and Middle Eastern grocery stores. Due to their high oil content, sesame seeds turn rancid quickly. It is best if they are purchased in small amounts and used as needed. They should be kept in an airtight container in a cool and dry place.

Soybeans, Fresh and Dried (*Bhatmaas*) Also known as *bhatmaas ko kosa* and edamame, soybeans grow on an annual bushy plant that produces green shell beans covered with fuzz. The shelled beans are similar in size and color to green peas and slightly smooth to the touch, with a firm and crisp texture. Soybeans have received universal recognition because of their nutritional value, especially their high protein content. Both fresh and presoaked beans are an excellent source of fiber and are used to make vegetable curries, stews, and soups. They are also sometimes sprouted before using in soups. Toasted soybeans make an ideal snack. Fresh green soybeans are occasionally available at Asian and Indian grocery stores, and frozen and dried soybeans are available at many well-stocked supermarkets.

Tamarind (*Imili or Imilee*) Thick reddish-brown pods of a large tropical evergreen tree with ferny leaves native to Asia, tamarinds are three to six inches long, irregularly curved at the ends, and shaped somewhat like a large peapod. As the pod matures, they develop shiny, black seeds surrounded by pulp and coarse fiber. When dried, the brittle shells crack open and the pulp dehydrates into a sticky, sweet-and-sour paste. Tamarind is used as a souring agent in many Nepali dishes. It is available at Indian or Asian grocery stores in different forms: compressed (with or without seeds) into fibrous blocks, concentrated, powdered, and sometimes whole dried pods. If you are using compressed pulp, you need to soak it in water before using.

Timmur (*Nepali Pepper*) Also known as *ban timmur*, this is a highly pungent, sharp-tasting dried berry from the prickly ash shrub family. It is often mistaken for black pepper, but it has an entirely different flavor and is, in fact, not related to the black pepper family. When the berry matures, it splits into two halves with a shiny black seed. It has a rough, wrinkled, and uneven surface and the aroma lies in the split covering of the pod, not in the seed. Nepalese describe its taste as *per-peraune*, which means "biting taste with an anesthetic feeling on the tongue." It should be used only in moderation, otherwise it will overpower the dish. Timmur is the most commonly used spice in Nepali pickles and chutneys. The pickles will taste flavorless and flat without timmur and this kind of pungency is important in Nepali pickles. Whole timmur
is also used to flavor some vegetable and lentil dishes, but it is removed before serving so that the unpleasant bite can be avoided. It is also used to cook Nepali wild mushrooms to remove any toxic elements. While trekking in the Muktinath area, in the Mustang district of Nepal, I observed locals using timmur extensively to flavor yak meat, and to make jerky, *momos* (stuffed dumplings), lentils, and vegetables. Timmur is found wild throughout the hilly slopes of Nepal where the temperature is cold. During the rainy season, some use timmur to cure leech bites. It is also used as a home remedy to cure stomach ailments and toothaches. The recipes in this book usually suggest grinding the berries in a mortar and pestle to bring out maximum flavor, but you can also use a spice grinder. Use a sieve to remove the husks. **Substitute:** Nepali timmur is not easily available outside Nepal, but you may substitute Szechwan pepper or Chinese pepper, which has a similar, if milder flavor. (*For additional information, see page 31.*)

Turmeric (*Besaar Haledo*) Used in nearly all Nepali dishes to add color and flavor, ground (*besaar*) and fresh turmeric (*haledo*) are the most important spices in Nepali cuisine. The plant is native to southeastern Asia (probably India) and is cultivated throughout the warmer areas of the world. The plant belongs to the ginger family and has a rhizome that looks similar to fresh ginger but has short, round, finger-like stems and an orange color. To produce ground turmeric, fresh turmeric is boiled or steamed, peeled, dried, and ground to a powder. Making your own ground turmeric is a lengthy process, and requires a lot of time and effort, but some people prefer this authentic version. Preground turmeric is yellow-orange in color, lightly aromatic, slightly bitter, and pungent. A small amount (¼ to 1 teaspoon) of turmeric is sufficient to color and flavor a dish. Excessive turmeric can overwhelm the other flavors of the food. Turmeric is added to nearly all Nepali dishes, including breads and pickles. It also has antiseptic properties and therefore is rubbed onto slaughtered animals to help preserve the meat. Fish is rubbed with salt and turmeric to eliminate any fishy smell. Because of its color, turmeric is sometimes confused with saffron, but the flavors are in no way similar. Turmeric has a religious significance in many Hindu ceremonies and rituals. Turmeric is available either fresh, dried, or powdered at Indian grocery stores and well-stocked supermarkets. The color of ground turmeric tends to fade and becomes unpleasant if the spice has aged. One has to be very careful when using turmeric powder, as it tends to stain clothes, cooking utensils, cutting boards, and work surfaces and is difficult to clean.

Urad Beans (*Maas ko Daal*) Also known as black gram, urad beans resemble whole mung beans, but are smaller and have a dull black seed coat. It takes a long time to soften this daal while cooking, and it is known to be the slowest cooking bean and difficult to digest. When cooked, each bean doubles in size and becomes slippery. Since the beans are heavy and hard to digest, many people cook them with a generous amount of ginger, garlic, and ground asafetida. They are available in three forms. Split white urad beans without skins (*maas ko chhata ko daal*) are creamy-white or ivory-colored skinned split beans resembling yellow split mung beans in texture but have a blander taste. Split black urad beans with skins (*kaalo maas ko daal*) are used for a popular Nepali daal preparation called *Jhaaneko kaalo maas ko daal*. They are also combined with rice to make soft rice porridge and are soaked, ground, and used to make many snacks. The soaked and ground batters are mixed with chopped vegetables and made into sun-dried nuggets. Whole black urad beans with skins (*singo maas ko daal*) are small, oval, shiny or dusky black beans. They are cooked the same way as any basic daal dish, or soaked and sprouted.

Urad Flour (*Maas ko Pitho*) This is an off-white colored flour made from dried, split, and skinless urad beans. It is used by itself, or combined with other flours and made into breads or savory fried snacks. Look for urad flour in Indian grocery stores.

Yogurt We use regular plain whole-milk or non-fat yogurt in our Nepali recipes (see page 315 for making yogurt at home). We do not use the thicker Greek yogurt.

Commonly used Equipment in the Nepali Kitchen

Bhaadaa Kuda Haru

The Nepali *bhancha kotha* (kitchen) is beautiful in its simplicity. Preparing food does not require any fancy gadgets and most basic utensils found in the average Western kitchen will suffice. Most food is cooked on the stovetop and villagers in rural parts of Nepal still use homemade clay stoves (*chulo*) and cook on wood or charcoal fires. Gas, kerosene, and electric stoves, however, have replaced these clay stoves in Kathmandu and many other parts of Nepal. Traditionally, kitchens occupied the top floor of the house and wood was the main source of cooking, so pots and pans were designed to fit wood-burning stoves. Some traditional cooking utensils made of iron, brass, copper, and bronze, with elaborate engraving, are still used in Nepali households, but they have slowly been replaced by modern and more functional utensils. To prepare the recipes in this book, you do not need to purchase special kitchen equipment. However, listed below are some of the more commonly used items that can be useful in making authentic Nepali dishes. Most of these are available through online retailers or at Indian or Asian supermarkets.

Rolling Pins (*Chaukaa and Belnaa*) *Chaukaa*, small round platforms usually made of wood, stone, or marble are used for rolling out dough. *Belnaa* are rolling pins usually made of wood. They are wide in the middle and have tapered ends. Their grip and weight is suited for rolling thin, round breads.

Wok-Shaped Pan (*Karaahi*) A wide, round-bottomed pan, with two side handles, resembling the Chinese wok. It can be used for almost any method of cooking, including deep-frying, stir-frying, steaming, or braising. A *karaahi* is made of heavy cast-iron and can withstand high cooking temperatures. It also absorbs heat quickly, distributes it evenly, and retains it for maximum efficiency, even at low temperatures. This pan comes in a variety of sizes and materials, such as brass, iron, and stainless steel, and the two handles on the sides make it easy to rotate or move while cooking. It is the choice of many cooks, and is one of the most indispensable cooking utensils in Nepali kitchens.

Pressure Cooker (*Presar Kooker*) A pressure cooker is a pot in which steam pressure builds up so that food cooks quickly at high temperatures. It is available in stainless steel or heavy-duty aluminum, which are both good conductors of heat. Pressure cookers are popular in modern Nepali kitchens as they cook food in a short time. Nowadays pressure cookers are used to cook everything including rice, meats, daals, and some vegetables.

Spice Box (*Sanduke or Masalaa Dani*) A *sanduke*, a round stainless steel spice box that stores dry spices, is found in most Nepali homes and generally kept by the side of the stove. It contains seven round bowls, along with a small teaspoon measure that fits inside the box. It has a tight-fitting lid to ensure that the spices are not exposed to air and do not mix together. These are one of the most convenient utensils in Nepali kitchens as you can pick up all seasonings and spices you require from one single container. The bowls are filled with commonly used spices, such as ground cumin, ground coriander, fenugreek seeds, ground chili, garam masalaa, ground turmeric, and salt.

Dumpling Steamer (*Momo pakaune bhaadaa*) Stacked steamers are mainly used for steaming stuffed dumplings (*momos*). They are made of aluminum or stainless steel and comprised of two to three racks with holes allowing steam to pass through. The bottom pot holds water and has a domed lid that prevents water from dripping onto the steamed food. The top rack accommodates a large quantity of food. They are generally available in Asian supermarkets.

Griddle (*Taabaa or Taawaa*) A *taabaa* is a heavy iron griddle or skillet used to cook Nepali breads. It is slightly concave and comes in various sizes, but the most common ones are nine inches in diameter. A *taabaa* does not usually have a handle, but some varieties do have a circular loop handle, and modern ones have wooden handles. After much use, *taabaas* become well-seasoned.

Frying Pan (*Tai Taapke*) A *tai taapke* is a classic Nepali pan used especially for deep-frying. It is made of heavy cast-iron, has a flat bottom, and a long handle that does not get hot during cooking. There are many sizes and varieties, and some smaller *taapkes* are designed for frying eggs so that they cook without breaking the yolk. A *tai taapke* is great for cooking Nepali *se-roti*, as it distributes heat evenly.

Cast-Iron Pan (*Falaam ko Taapke*) This traditional cast-iron pan with a long handle and rounded bottom is mainly used to prepare black urad beans (*maas ko daal*). When the *daal* is simmered in this pot, it transforms into a deep black color with rich flavor. Almost all Nepalese households possess this pan. It is known for its excellent heat distribution during cooking. The pan is heavy, durable, and ideal for cooking vegetables or preparing entire meals.

Round Tray and Bowls (*Thaal-Kachauraa*) Traditionally Nepali meals are served on a *thaal-kachauraa*, which is a round metal tray (*thaal*) with small bowls (*kachauraa*). When serving Nepali meals, rice and bread are placed directly on the *thaal*, while other preparations, such as meat, vegetables, and lentil puree, are placed in the individual bowls that surround the tray. This way the rice does not get mixed up with other dishes and it lets you sample each individual dish separately.

Divided Plates with Compartments (*Khande Thaal*) A *khande thaal* is a metal tray that is divided into compartments or sections. It can be round or square, and the most common ones are made of stainless steel. When using a *khande thaal*, rice is placed in the largest compartment and the vegetables, meats, lentils, pickles, and curry dishes are placed in the surrounding compartments. This allows you to taste each dish individually and to mix the tastes and textures to see what combination and sequence you prefer. *Khande haals* are one of the most important and indispensable items in the Nepali kitchen.

Mortar and Pestle (*Khal*) This multi-purpose grinding tool is used to grind herbs, spices, nuts, and seeds into powders and pastes. A mortar and pestle is one of the most practical kitchen tools. They are made of a variety of materials, such as stone, brass, iron, marble, or hardwood. They are especially effective when grinding small quantities of ingredients.

Round Wicker Tray (*Naanglo*) Made from sturdy bamboo strips and reeds, this tray is mainly used to separate hulls, stones, and foreign material from grains. It is one of the most important and practical kitchen items used for sorting and sun-drying spices and vegetables, or just storing objects.

Kitchen Knife (*Chulesi*) A *chulesi* is a special Nepalese knife designed to be used while the user is sitting on the ground. A heavy wide-blade that is slightly curved is molded and attached to a wooden block. To use the *chulesi* one needs to sit on the ground and hold the wooden block with one foot and then the vegetable or meat is cut by using both hands feeding it through the blade, pushing it against it. One certainly needs special skill to use it.

Gagro (water container) A *gagro* is a pot shaped like an expanded vase with a rounded bottom and a narrow neck. It comes in different sizes, hand-carved with intricate designs, in brass, copper, or clay. Almost every Nepali household uses this water container.

Theki (yogurt container) A *theki* is a wooden container that comes with a long churning stick. They are used for churning yogurt and to prepare butter or buttermilk.

Chapter 3

SNACKS, APPETIZERS & SAVORIES

KHAAJAA RA CHAMENAA

Life in a Nepali household is always busy. Visitors, friends, and relatives often drop in casually. These unplanned comings and goings are a part of everyday social life. The people of Nepal are warm and hospitable, and they take pride when family and friends visit. If you go to someone's house, the host will automatically offer you a beverage accompanied by some kind of snack as a welcoming gesture.

The word *khaajaa* is derived from the Nepali word for snacks that literally translates as "*khaa eat*" and "*jaa go*." The host usually ask the guests, "*khaajaa khayer matrai janus*" ("please have some snacks before leaving"). A typical Nepali snack will be salty, spicy, sweet, and sour. Some snacks are served by themselves and others are combined with other dishes. Sometimes deep-fried salty or sweet crackers like *nimki*, or *furindanaa* (savory snack mixes) are prepared ahead of time and stored in an air-tight container. They are served along with a cup of hot milky tea when guests drop in at unexpected hours and are convenient when there's no time to prepare a warm snack.

Nepalese eat two full meals a day, one around mid-morning and another after sunset. But it seems that they are always snacking in between, perhaps because the gap between the two meals is so long. Nepali *khaajaa* provides a much needed energy boost between the two main meals.

There are so many varieties of snacks that it is difficult to name them all here. One of the most popular snacks are *cheuraa* (pressed rice flakes) served with a combination of fried or curried vegetables, meat, egg, yogurt, or preserved or fermented pickles. Other favorite snacks include *pakaudas* (fritters made from seasonal vegetables and potatoes), stuffed samosas, *tarkaari ko chop* (vegetable patties), *furindaana* (mixed fried snacks), and a variety of sweet dishes. *Poori-tarkaari*, which is a puffed fried bread served with vegetables, is extremely popular as a mid-afternoon snack. *Momos* (dumplings), accompanied by various dipping sauces, are also very popular. During the sunny afternoons of the winter season, Nepalese may snack on a fruit salad made from pomelo *(bhogate saandheko)* and spices.

Snacks are most often served mid-afternoon along with hot or cold beverages. Although traditional Nepali meals do not usually start with appetizers, many of the dishes from the "Snack" and "Meat" chapters of this book can serve as an appetizer.

SPICED PEANUTS

Badaam Saandheko

Makes 4 to 6 servings

Even when guests arrive unexpectedly, snacks and beverages must be served in Nepalese homes and the following recipe is super quick to make. This is one of the most delicious, crunchy, spicy snacks to munch on with drinks. In the Nepali language, "*badaam*" is "peanut," and "*saandheko*" is "marinated," so this is a marinated peanut dish. If you are making this dish way ahead of time, assemble all ingredients except peanuts beforehand and then mix the peanuts in just before serving so that they don't get soggy textured.

3 cups dry-roasted peanuts, unsalted
1 medium red onion, finely chopped
1 tablespoon finely julienned fresh ginger
2 medium cloves garlic, finely chopped
6 to 7 green onions (white and pale green parts), finely chopped
½ cup finely chopped cilantro
3 to 5 hot green chilies, finely chopped (adjust to taste)

1 teaspoon ground cumin
½ teaspoon ground turmeric
Salt to taste
3 tablespoons freshly squeezed lemon or lime juice
2 tablespoons mustard oil

In a large bowl, combine all the ingredients. Taste and adjust salt and seasonings. Cover and set the mixture aside to allow seasonings to blend well for 10 minutes. Transfer the mixture to a platter and serve at room temperature.

SPICY POTATO SALAD

Makes 4 to 6 servings

Aalu Saandheko

Aalu saandheko is a much loved and popular dish in Nepal. This delicious, freshly made, salad-like dish can be a snack or appetizer or a side dish with a Nepali main meal. Any variety of small yellow or red thin-skinned potatoes are perfect for this dish. The potatoes should not be overcooked or undercooked. Try to use fresh lemon or lime juice instead of bottled lemon juice as the preservatives take away the flavor of natural lemon. Over the years I have learned countless ways of making this dish, and here I share my favorite.

8 to 10 small potatoes (about 3 pounds)	1 teaspoon ground cumin
2 tablespoons fresh ginger, peeled and finely julienned	1 teaspoon cayenne pepper powder
4 medium cloves garlic, finely chopped	¼ teaspoon timmur, finely ground with a mortar and pestle (Nepali pepper; *see page 31*)
4 fresh (hot or mild) green chilies, finely chopped	¼ cup fresh lemon or lime juice
1 cup finely chopped cilantro	Salt to taste
4 to 5 green onions, white and pale green parts, cut into ¼-inch slices	3 tablespoons mustard oil
1 large red onion, finely chopped (about 1½ cups)	1 teaspoon fenugreek seeds
2 medium ripe tomatoes, chopped (about 2 cups)	2 dried red chilies, halved and seeded
	½ teaspoon ground turmeric

Place the potatoes and enough water to cover in a medium-size saucepan and bring to boil over high heat. Reduce the heat to medium-low, cover the pan, and continue cooking until the potatoes are fork-tender, 20 to 25 minutes.

Drain the potatoes and when cool enough to handle (do not pour cold water over them to cool the potatoes, as this will water down their flavor), peel and cut the potatoes into 1-inch cubes. Place the potatoes in a large bowl and combine them with the ginger, garlic, green chilies, cilantro, green onions, red onions, and tomatoes and mix well. Add cumin, cayenne pepper powder, timmur, lemon juice, and salt and mix well. Set aside.

Heat the mustard oil in a small skillet over medium-high heat until faintly smoking. Add the fenugreek seeds and red chilies and fry until seeds are dark brown and fragrant, about 5 to 7 seconds. Add turmeric and remove the pan from heat and pour the entire contents over the potatoes and mix thoroughly. Taste and adjust salt and lemon juice. Cover the bowl and let the *aalu saadheko* stand for 15 minutes at room temperature to absorb seasonings. Transfer to a serving dish and serve.

BATTER-FRIED VEGETABLES

Makes 4 to 6 servings

Pakaudaas

Pakaudaas, batter-based savory fritters, are very popular in Nepal. This recipe is versatile, so feel free to choose your favorite ingredients and spices. The key to making the perfect *pakaudaa* lies in the quality of ingredients and heating the oil to proper temperature. If the oil is not hot enough, the fritters will absorb too much oil. Also, a thick batter will overwhelm the vegetables and make doughy fritters, but if the vegetables are too wet, the batter will be runny. Serve with chutney or dipping sauce.

2 cups chickpea flour (*besan*)	½ teaspoon cayenne pepper powder
½ cup finely chopped cilantro	¼ teaspoon freshly ground black pepper
2 fresh mild green chilies, minced	Small pinch ground asafetida
1 teaspoon salt, adjust to taste	2 cups vegetable oil
1 teaspoon ajowan seeds	1 medium onion, sliced ¼-inch thick and
1 teaspoon minced fresh ginger	separated into rings
1 teaspoon ground cumin	1 small eggplant, sliced ⅛-inch thick
1 teaspoon ground coriander	¼ head cauliflower, cut into 1-inch florets
½ teaspoon ground turmeric	(about 2 cups)

In a medium-size bowl, combine the chickpea flour, cilantro, green chilies, salt, ajowan seeds, ginger, cumin, coriander, turmeric, cayenne pepper powder, black pepper, and asafetida. Gradually add 1 to 1½ cups of water to make a smooth batter with the consistency of thick cream. Cover and set aside for 20 minutes. When the batter is well rested it will thicken slightly. If the batter seems too thick, add some water; if it feels too thin, add more chickpea flour

Heat the oil in a heavy deep skillet over medium-high heat until it reaches 350-375 degrees F. Test the readiness of the oil by placing a drop of batter into the hot oil. If it bubbles and rises to the surface immediately, it is ready. Dip a vegetable slice into the batter, making sure it's completely coated. Shake off any excess and gently place it in the hot oil. Fry, turning a few times, until golden brown and crispy, 2 to 3 minutes (fry a few pieces at a time, but do not crowd the pan). With a slotted spoon, remove the *pakaudaa* draining as much oil as possible, and transfer it to a paper towel-lined platter. Repeat with the remaining vegetables. Transfer the *pakaudaas* to a platter and serve immediately while still crispy.

Variations: The following work well made into *pakaudaas*: ⅛-inch-thick-slices of Asian eggplant; ⅛-inch-thick slices of zucchini; stemmed spinach; stemmed, seeded, and thinly sliced bell peppers; shredded cabbage; whole green chilies, with a small slit cut in the middle; thin slices of crustless bread, cut into triangles; peeled and deveined shrimp, patted dry; bite-size pieces of fish fillet; ½-inch thick slices of paneer cheese; or sliced hard-boiled eggs.

Batter-Fried Chicken Fritters / *Kukhuraa ko Pakaudaa*

BATTER-FRIED CHICKEN FRITTERS

Makes 6 to 8 servings

Kukhuraa ko Pakaudaa

This batter-based flavorful snack is crunchy on the outside but juicy and tender on the inside. Care should be taken with the temperature of the oil while frying the chicken as frying in extremely hot or smoking oil will brown the chicken quickly on the outside and leave it raw inside, but frying on low heat will make them chewy and rubbery. These can be served as an appetizer or snack with tomato chutney and a beverage.

2 pounds of skinless, boneless chicken breast or thighs, cut into 1-inch pieces (make them as uniform as possible)	¼ teaspoon ground black pepper
	½ teaspoon ground turmeric
	1 teaspoon salt (adjust to taste)
1 cup besan (chickpea flour) plus 2 tablespoons as needed	1 tablespoon minced fresh ginger
	2 medium cloves garlic, finely minced
3 tablespoons rice flour	2 fresh mild green chilies, cut into cubes
1 medium red onion, thinly sliced	¼ cup finely chopped fresh cilantro
1 teaspoon ajowan seeds	2 tablespoons fresh lemon juice
1 teaspoon ground cumin	2 cups vegetable oil
1 teaspoon cayenne pepper powder, or to taste	

In a large bowl, combine the chicken, chickpea flour, rice flour, onion, ajowan seeds, cumin, cayenne pepper powder, black pepper, turmeric, salt, ginger, garlic, green chilies, cilantro, and lemon juice. Gradually add 3 tablespoons of water and mix well using your hands until all the ingredients are fully coated. Cover and set aside to marinate for 30 minutes. When the mixture is well rested, it should be just thick enough to form into fritters. If the batter is too runny, add some chickpea flour; if too thick, sprinkle in some water.

Heat the oil in a deep heavy skillet over medium-high heat until it reaches 350 degrees F. Test the readiness of the oil by adding a small piece of the batter. If it bubbles and immediately rises to the surface, it is ready. Scoop up about 2 tablespoons of the chicken mixture and gently drop it into the oil. Fry, turning a few times, until golden brown and crispy, 4 to 5 minutes. With a slotted spoon, remove the chicken *pakaudaa*, draining as much oil as possible, and transfer to a paper towel-lined platter. Repeat with the remaining batter frying four or five pieces at a time, but do not crowd the pan. Transfer to a platter and serve immediately, while still crisp.

FISH FINGERS/PATTIES

Maachaa ko Bari

**Makes 4 to 6 servings
(15 to 20 small fish fingers/patties)**

Fish fingers (British English) or fish sticks (American English) or *Maachaa ko Bari* (Nepalese) are delicious fried snacks or appetizers that can be made from a variety of fish. In this recipe, fish is cooked with fresh herbs and spices, shaped into sticks (resembling store-bought fish sticks) or patties, and deep fried. These are generally served warm with chutney and dipping sauce or just a squeeze of lemon juice.

---

1 pound potatoes, any variety

2 cups vegetable oil, divided

1 medium onion, finely chopped (about 1 cup)

3 to 4 mild fresh green chilies, finely chopped

2 teaspoons minced fresh ginger

2 medium cloves garlic, minced

1 teaspoon cayenne pepper powder or adjust to taste

1 teaspoon ground cumin

1 teaspoon ground coriander

½ teaspoon ground turmeric

2 to 2½ pounds firm white fish fillet, picked over for bones and cut into 2-inch pieces

1 teaspoon salt, adjust to taste

1 cup finely chopped cilantro

4 to 5 green onions (white and pale green parts), finely chopped

2 tablespoons fresh lemon or lime juice

2 eggs, lightly beaten

1 cup dry bread crumbs, plus more if needed

1 lemon, cut into wedges

Place the potatoes and enough water to cover in a small saucepan and bring to a boil over high heat. Reduce the heat to low, cover, and cook until the potatoes are tender, 20 to 25 minutes. Drain, and when cool enough to handle, peel, mash coarsely, and set them aside.

Heat 2 tablespoons of the oil in a medium-size skillet over medium-high heat. When the oil is hot, add the onions and fry until lightly browned, about 5 minutes. Stir in the green chilies, ginger, garlic, cayenne pepper powder, cumin, coriander, and turmeric and mix well. Reduce the heat to medium, add the fish and salt, and cook, stirring frequently, until the fish is cooked through and all the moisture has evaporated, about 8 minutes. Add the mashed potatoes, cilantro, green onions, and lemon juice and continue cooking until the mixture is dry. Transfer to a bowl and cool to room temperature before using.

With a lightly oiled hand, scoop out 2½ tablespoons of the fish mixture and roll into a 2-inch-long cylinder or round pattie, your preference. Place on a platter and repeat with the remaining mixture. Dip each stick in the beaten eggs, let the excess drip off, then roll it in the bread crumbs, and shake off the excess. Repeat until all the fish sticks/patties are coated with bread crumbs.

Heat the remaining oil in a large nonstick or cast-iron skillet over medium-high heat until it reaches 350 to 375 degrees F. Test the readiness of the oil by sprinkling a pinch of bread crumbs into the hot oil. If it bubbles and they rise to the surface immediately, it is ready. Place six or seven fish sticks/patties in the oil and fry, turning carefully once or twice, until browned and crispy, 2 to 3 minutes. Remove them with a slotted spoon, draining as much oil as possible, and transfer to a paper towel-lined plate to drain. Repeat with the remaining fish sticks/patties, skimming the surface of the oil occasionally and removing any burnt bread crumbs before adding the next batch.

Transfer the fish sticks/patties to a platter and serve with the lemon wedges and your favorite chutney or dipping sauce.

URAD BEAN FRITTERS

Makes 6 to 8 servings

Maas Baaraa

Baaraas are light and spongy urad bean fritters that resemble small doughnuts. Traditionally, the soaked urad daal is ground using a *silouto* and *bachhaa* (stone slab and roller), giving it a smooth and fluffy consistency, but this recipe uses a food processor or blender to produce an equally good result. They are best served fresh but can be stored overnight. *Baaraas* are not an everyday foodstuff, but are associated with special religious and ceremonial occasions. During the ten days of the Dashain festival (page 11), they are prepared fresh each morning and offered to the deities for sacred offerings (*naivedya*). They are also distributed among friends and families and consumed as a blessed food that Nepalese call *prashad*.

2 cups split black urad beans with skins (*kaalo maas ko daal*)	1 tablespoon minced fresh ginger
	Small pinch ground asafetida
Salt, adjust to taste	2 cups vegetable oil

In a large bowl, soak the beans for at least 6 hours or overnight. When soaked, the beans swell and double in size and weight. Rub the beans between your hands vigorously to loosen the outer black covering. The coating will come off easily and float in the water. Skim them off, drain the beans, add fresh water, and repeat the process until most of the coatings are removed. Drain the beans in a colander.

Place the drained beans in a food processor or blender and process, adding just enough water to make a semi-thick smooth puree with no grainy bits of beans remaining. You may have to do this in two batches. Place the bean puree in a bowl and add salt, ginger, and asafetida and whisk the batter by hand (*phaune*) until it is light and spongy. Cover the bowl and allow the mixture to rest at room temperature for at least 10 minutes.

Heat the oil in a large heavy skillet over medium-high heat until it reaches 350 to 375 degree F. Test the readiness of the oil by dropping a little batter into the hot oil. If it bubbles and rises to the surface immediately, it is ready. With moistened fingertips, scoop up 2 tablespoon of the batter, place in your palm, and shape into a round and flat patty. Make a hole in the center of the patty. Immediately gently slide the patty into the hot oil. The *baaraa* will sink to the bottom first, but will rise up and double in size. Flip it over a few times, until both sides are light brown and it is cooked through, about 2 to 3 minutes. Remove with a slotted spoon, draining the excess oil, and place the fritter on a paper towel-lined plate. Repeat with the remaining batter. Serve the fritters warm or at room temperature.

Urad Bean Fritters / *Maas Baaraa*

Snacks, Appetizers & Savories

CHICKEN AND URAD BEAN PATTIES

Makes 6 to 8 servings

Woh

Woh (also called *Wo* or *Newari Baaraa*) are griddle-cooked patties made from urad or mung beans or a combination of both. They are light and spongy daal patties that resemble small flat pancakes. The following savory and classic recipe is from Deepa Pradhan's kitchen, who shared her Newari culinary passion by showing me how to create *woh*. This version is cooked with soaked and ground split black urad beans (*kaalo Maas ko daal*) and ground chicken, along with other spices. Ground chicken adds a unique flavor to these daal patties. *Woh* is similar to *baaraa* (see page 82), the difference is *baaraa* is deep-fried, whereas *woh* is griddle-cooked with only small amounts of oil, making it a relatively healthier version. These daal patties are delicious on their own, but serving them with other dishes rounds out a wonderful lunch or snack. Deepa prefers to make her *woh* with split green moong beans (*khoste mung ko daal*) and ground chicken breast for a lighter version.

2 cups split black urad beans	1 teaspoon ground cumin
¾ pound ground chicken or turkey	Small pinch ground asafetida
½ teaspoon salt, adjust to taste	2 finely chopped fresh mild green chilies
1 tablespoon minced fresh ginger	½ cup finely chopped cilantro
1 teaspoon minced garlic	1 cup oil

In a large bowl, wash and soak the urad beans for at least 6 hours or overnight, until doubled in volume.

Rub the beans between your hands vigorously to loosen the outer black skins. The coating will come off easily and float in the water. Skim off coating, drain the beans and add fresh water, and rub again until most of the coatings are removed. Place the drained beans in a blender or food processor and process adding just enough water to make a semi-thick smooth puree.

Place the bean puree in a bowl and add ground chicken, salt, ginger, garlic, cumin, asafetida, green chilies, and cilantro and whisk until it is light and spongy. The batter should be easily spreadable. If the batter is too thick, add 1 to 2 tablespoons of water and beat with a fork or hand until fluffy. Cover the bowl and allow the mixture to rest at room temperature for at least 10 minutes.

When ready, heat a non-stick skillet or griddle over medium-high heat. To ensure that the griddle is at the right temperature, test by splashing a few droplets of water on the griddle. If the droplets bounce and splutter, then it is ready; if the water evaporates immediately, it is too hot. Adjust the heat accordingly. Add 1 tablespoon of oil to coat the griddle. Add about

½ to ¾ cup of the bean mixture onto the center of the griddle. Using the back of a spoon or your hand spread the batter gently in a circular motion to create a 4-inch circle. You can place 2 or 3 patties on the griddle at a time, without crowding. Cook until the edges start to crisp and the underside starts to brown, about 2 minutes. Turn the patties over and drizzle 1 teaspoon of oil around the edges and top. Cook until browned on both sides.

Transfer to a serving dish and keep warm until served.

PEA AND POTATO SAMOSAS

Makes 25 to 30 samosaa

Tarkaari ko Samosaa

These fried turnovers filled with vegetables, meat, or a combination, are one of Nepal's most popular snacks. Traditionally served with chutney or dipping sauce, I like to serve them as a light lunch with yogurt or salad.

Dough:
2½ cups all-purpose flour plus extra for rolling
¼ cup fine-grain semolina
½ teaspoon ajowan seeds, crushed
½ teaspoon salt
¼ cup vegetable oil

Vegetable filling:
2 pounds potatoes, any variety
2 to 3 cups vegetable oil, divided
1 teaspoon cumin seeds
1 medium onion, finely chopped (about 1 cup)

2 fresh mild green chilies, chopped
1 tablespoon minced fresh ginger
3 medium cloves garlic, minced
2 teaspoons ground coriander
1 teaspoon ground cumin
1 teaspoon cayenne pepper powder
1 teaspoon salt, adjust to taste
½ teaspoon ground turmeric
2 cups frozen peas, thawed and thoroughly drained
1 cup finely chopped cilantro
4 to 5 green onions (white and pale green parts), finely chopped
2 tablespoons fresh lemon or lime juice

To make dough: combine the flour, semolina, ajowan seeds, and salt in a bowl. Rub in the oil until the mixture resembles a coarse meal. Gradually add ¾ to 1 cup of water until the dough holds together. Knead the dough until semi-firm, adding a little flour if it feels too sticky or a little water if it is too firm. Cover with a damp towel and set aside for 1 hour.

Prepare filling: Place the potatoes and water to cover in a large saucepan and bring to a boil. Reduce the heat to low, cover, and cook until the potatoes are tender, 20 to 25 minutes. Drain, and when cool enough to handle, peel and cut the potatoes into ¼-inch cubes and set aside.

Heat 3 tablespoons of the oil in a medium-size saucepan over medium-high heat until hot, but not smoking. Add the cumin seeds and fry until lightly browned and fragrant, about 5 seconds. Add the onions, green chilies, ginger, and garlic. Stir frequently until the onions are soft but not brown, about 5 minutes. Stir in the coriander, cumin, cayenne pepper powder, salt, and turmeric. Add the peas and potatoes and cook, stirring for 5 minutes. Remove from the heat and stir in cilantro, green onions, and lemon juice. Transfer to a bowl and cool to room temperature.

Assemble samosas: Place the dough on a lightly floured work surface. Knead it again until it is soft and pliable. Divide into fifteen balls and coat them with flour. Flatten one ball with a rolling pin and roll into a 7-inch circle. Cut the circle in half. Moisten the straight edge with water and fold the semicircle in half again, squeezing along the moistened edge to seal it. Now you have a triangle-shaped cone. Pick it up with your thumb and forefinger. With your other hand, fill the cone with 3 to 3½ tablespoons of filling. Moisten the top edges and press together. Do not over stuff or the samosa may open while frying. Repeat with the remaining dough and filling. While working, make sure to keep the dough covered so it does not dry out. Place the filled samosas in a single layer on a tray, cover, and set aside until you are ready to cook.

Heat the remaining oil in a deep, wide skillet over medium-high heat until it reaches 350 to 375 degrees F. Gently drop some samosas in the oil, cooking 4 to 5 at a time. Fry turning frequently, until they are crisp and golden brown. Remove with a slotted spoon and drain on a paper-towel-lined platter. Repeat until all samosas are fried. Serve immediately.

CHICKEN CHOWELAA
Kukhuraa ko Chowelaa

Makes 4 to 6 servings

Chowelaa is a well-known dish in Nepal and comes from the Newar community of Kathmandu. The chicken is boiled or roasted, cut into bite-size pieces, and combined with fresh herbs and spices. The intense flavor of this dish is achieved through the addition of tempered spices—spices fried in oil. This is an extremely versatile dish, and can be served hot, chilled, or at room temperature as a snack, appetizer, or part of a Nepali meal.

2 pounds skinless, boneless chicken breasts or thighs, poached until fork tender, cut into bite-size pieces
1 medium red onion, finely chopped (about 1 cup)
¼ cup finely chopped cilantro
4 or 5 green onions (white and pale green parts), finely chopped
4 fresh mild or hot green chilies, finely chopped
3 tablespoons fresh lemon or lime juice
1 tablespoon minced fresh ginger

1 teaspoon ground cumin
1 teaspoon cayenne pepper powder
½ teaspoon ground turmeric
¼ teaspoon timmur (Nepali pepper; *see page 31*), finely ground with a mortar and pestle
⅛ teaspoon freshly ground black pepper
Salt to taste
2 tablespoons mustard oil
¼ teaspoon fenugreek seeds
2 dried red chilies, halved and seeded
3 to 4 medium cloves garlic, slivered

In a medium bowl, combine cooked chicken, onions, cilantro, green onions, green chilies, lemon juice, ginger, cumin, cayenne pepper powder, turmeric, timmur, black pepper and salt to taste.

Heat the mustard oil in a small skillet over medium-high heat. When the oil is hot, but not smoking, add the fenugreek seeds and dried red chilies and fry until the fenugreek seeds turns dark brown and the chilies become reddish-brown and fragrant, about 5 to 7 seconds. Add the garlic and fry until crisp but not brown, about 7 seconds. Immediately pour the entire contents of the pan into the chciken mixture and toss well. Cover the bowl and allow the seasonings to develop for at least 10 minutes. Transfer the mixture to a serving dish and serve.

POTATOES AND PRESSED RICE FLAKES

Makes 4 to 6 servings

Aalu Cheuraa

This is my favorite mid-afternoon snack and I make it frequently for a quick lunch served with yogurt and pickle. The ingredient list may look long, but the dish is simple to prepare. It is a convenient snack to pack for a picnic or short outing as it can be eaten at room temperature.

3 cups pressed rice flakes (*cheuraa; page 65*)	1 tablespoon brown sesame seeds
2 tablespoons clarified butter (*gheu*; page 314) or vegetable oil	1 teaspoon minced fresh ginger
	1 teaspoon salt, adjust to taste
1 dried red chili, halved and seeded	½ teaspoon ground turmeric
1 teaspoon brown mustard seeds	½ teaspoon ground cumin
½ teaspoon cumin seeds	½ teaspoon ground coriander
Small pinch ground asafetida	½ teaspoon cayenne pepper powder
2 medium potatoes, peeled and cut into ½-inch cubes (about 2 cups)	½ cup chopped cilantro
	4 to 5 green onions (pale green parts), chopped
¼ cup raisins	
2 tablespoons halved raw cashews	1 tablespoon lemon juice

Spread the rice flakes on a large platter and pick out any foreign matter such as unhusked rice, stems, or powdery flakes and discard. Wash, rinse, and drain the rice flakes until water runs clear. Put the rice flakes in a medium-size bowl, cover with cold water, and soak for 1 minute. The softened rice flakes should be firm, not mushy or lumpy. Drain completely.

Heat the clarified butter in a heavy-bottomed pot over medium-high heat. When it is hot, add the dried chili, mustard seeds, and cumin seeds and fry until they are lightly browned and the mustard seeds pop and are fully fragrant, about 5 seconds. Sprinkle in the asafetida first, then add the potatoes and fry, stirring from time to time, until they are lightly browned and tender, about 5 minutes. Add the raisins, cashews, and sesame seeds and stir well. Add the ginger, salt, turmeric, cumin, coriander, and cayenne pepper powder and continue cooking for 1 more minute. Add the drained rice flakes and stir gently to mix. Reduce the heat to medium-low, cover, and cook until the potatoes are well mixed with rice flakes. Mix in the cilantro, green onions, and lemon juice and serve.

Variation: Use any combination of vegetables or soaked and cooked brown chickpeas to make a colorful *cheuraa* dish. Make sure the vegetables are cut into ½-inch pieces and cooked thoroughly before adding them in and follow the recipe above.

YOGURT WITH PRESSED RICE FLAKES

Makes 2 servings

Dahi-Cheuraa

Dahi-Cheuraa is a mixture of yogurt and pressed rice flakes and is one of the most popular foods in Nepal. This soothing comfort food is eaten any time of the day, as a mid-afternoon snack or as a light lunch, but I usually serve it for breakfast. In Nepal, one very common demeaning insult is to call someone "*dahi-cheur-manche*," which translates to "a person who is untrusting, shady, tricky, undependable, and untrustworthy." It derives from the fact that *dahi cheuraa* blends well, just like a smooth talker can blend in with whoever they are talking to.

---

1 cup pressed rice flakes (*cheuraa; page 65*)   1 to 2 tablespoons sugar, or to taste
2 cups plain yogurt (preferably whole-milk)   Chopped nuts and/or fruit (optional)

Spread the rice flakes on a large platter and pick out any foreign matter such as unhusked rice, stems, or powdery flakes and discard.

In a small bowl, combine the rice flakes, yogurt, and sugar. Let the mixture stand, covered at room temperature, until the yogurt is absorbed and the flakes soften, about 10 minutes. Add the chopped nuts and/or fruits, if using.

PRESSED RICE FLAKES WITH GREEN PEAS
Cheuraa-Matar

Makes 4 to 6 servings

Cheuraa-matar is my father's favorite mid-afternoon snack. I like to make this dish at the height of the season from spring to early summer when fresh peas are tender and can be easily bought at the local farmer's market. Although shelling fresh peas is tedious, it is worth the delicate taste they add to this snack.

3 cups pressed rice flakes (*cheuraa; see page 65*), thick variety	Small pinch ground asafetida
2 tablespoons clarified butter (*gheu; page 314*)	2 cups shelled fresh peas
1 dried red chili, halved and seeded	2 fresh mild green chilies, split lengthwise
½ teaspoon cumin seeds	½ teaspoon ground turmeric
2 small cassia leaves	½ teaspoon ground cumin
1 medium onion, finely chopped (about 1 cup)	½ teaspoon ground coriander
4 small cloves garlic, chopped	Salt to taste
1½ teaspoons minced fresh ginger	½ cup finely chopped cilantro
	4 to 5 green onions (white and pale green parts), finely chopped

Spread the rice flakes on a large platter, pick out any foreign matter such as unhusked rice, stems, or powdery dusty flakes and discard. Wash, rinse, and drain the rice flakes until the water runs clear. Put the rice flakes in a medium-size bowl, cover with plenty of cold water, and soak for 1 minute. The softened rice flakes should be firm, not mushy. Drain.

Heat the clarified butter in a heavy saucepan over medium-high heat. When it is hot, add the dried chili, cumin seeds, and cassia leaves, and fry until lightly browned and fragrant, about 5 seconds. Add the onions, garlic, ginger, and asafetida and cook until soft. Mix in the peas, green chilies, turmeric, cumin, coriander, and salt to taste and cook, covered, stirring occasionally, until the peas are cooked, 8 to 10 minutes.

Gently stir in rice flakes. Reduce the heat to medium-low, cover, and cook until the spices have soaked into the rice flakes, about 5 minutes. The finished dish should be moist, tender, and fluffy. If the mixture is too dry, stir in ¼ cup of warm water and cook for 5 minutes more. Mix in the cilantro and green onions, and serve the mixture hot or at room temperature.

SWEET FRIED PRESSED RICE FLAKES

Guleo Taareko Cheuraa

Makes 6 to 8 servings

This is a delicious and quick method of converting pressed rice flakes into a crunchy snack. When fried, rice flakes double in size and become snow white in color. Fried *cheuraa* is versatile and can be served sprinkled with sugar or salt as a mid-afternoon snack with beverages or with meat, vegetables, or pickles. The fried flakes can also be combined with nuts, fried potato shreds, fried lentils, and spices to make a crunchy snack mix.

---

2 cups pressed rice flakes (*cheuraa; page 65*), thick variety

2 to 3 cups vegetable oil
2 to 3 tablespoons sugar, or to taste

Spread the rice flakes on a large platter and pick out any foreign matter such as unhusked rice, stems, or powdery flakes and discard.

Heat the oil in a deep skillet over medium-high heat until it reaches 350 to 375 degrees F. If the oil is too hot, the rice flakes will brown too quickly, but if the temperature is not hot enough, they will absorb too much oil and be soggy. Test the readiness of the oil by placing a few rice flakes in the hot oil. If the flakes expand and rise to the surface immediately, the oil is ready.

If you have a fine-mesh metal strainer, place ½ cup of rice flakes at a time in the strainer and lower them into the hot oil. The flakes will sink first, then bubble and foam, and within a minute, they will expand to fluffy white flakes. Stir constantly and fry until the flakes float to the surface, which occurs very quickly. Immediately remove the flakes from the oil and drain on paper towels. (Either lift the strainer or you can use a slotted spoon.) Repeat with the remaining rice flakes.

Mix the fried rice flakes with the sugar and serve. You can also cool to room temperature and store in an airtight container for 2 to 3 weeks.

AJOWAN CRACKERS

Makes 4 to 6 servings

Jwaano Haale ko Namkeen

Namkeen or *nimki* are deep-fried flour crackers flavored with ajowan seeds, which provide a distinct flavor and can be used whole or crushed. They are a popular light snack food, usually served with hot tea or cold beverages. *Namkeen* can be made ahead of time, but should be stored in an airtight container.

2½ cups all-purpose flour plus extra for rolling	3 tablespoons clarified butter (*gheu; page 314*) or unsalted butter, melted
1 teaspoon ajowan seeds, lightly crushed in a mortar and pestle	2 tablespoons plain yogurt, mixed with 2 tablespoons water
1 teaspoon salt	2 to 3 cups vegetable oil
Small pinch baking soda	

In a medium-size bowl, mix the flour, crushed ajowan seeds, salt, and baking soda. Add the butter and rub it into the flour mixture with your fingers until the mixture resembles a coarse meal. Stir in the yogurt mixture and then gradually add ¼ to ½ cup of water to form a dough that comes together. Knead until the dough is semi-firm. If it is too sticky, add 1 to 2 tablespoons more flour; if it feels too firm, add a little water and knead some more. Cover the dough with a damp kitchen towel and set aside at room temperature for 10 minutes.

When the dough is well rested, place it on a lightly floured flat surface and knead for 1 minute. Divide the dough into four balls. Dust one of the balls generously with flour, and roll it out ⅛-inch thick. Cut the rolled dough into 1-inch diamond shapes. Repeat the process with the remaining dough. Set aside.

Heat the oil in a heavy deep skillet over medium-high heat until it reaches 350 to 375 degrees F. Test the readiness of the oil by placing a small piece of dough into the hot oil. If it bubbles and rises to the surface slowly, it is ready. Add several pieces of dough at a time and fry, stirring as needed, until they are golden brown and crisp, 3 to 4 minutes. With a slotted spoon, remove them, draining as much oil as possible, and transfer to a paper towel-lined platter. Fry the remaining pieces the same way. When they have cooled, store them in an air-tight container. These crackers keep well for 1 month.

GREEN SOYBEANS IN PODS

Makes 4 to 6 servings

Useneko Hariyo Bhatmaas Kosaa

This is a popular, delicious, and healthy snack cooked and served in a natural way. Nepalese eat these boiled soybeans by squeezing the savory pods with their lips and pushing beans directly into their mouths. The boiled beans have great nutritional value and are practically addictive. Take care to select pods that are bright green, fresh, tender, and sweet. Fresh, unshelled soybeans are occasionally available in Asian food markets, health food stores, or well-stocked larger supermarkets, but frozen ones are widely available, both shelled or unshelled. This recipe uses fresh soybeans, but if you use frozen soybeans, then reduce the cooking time.

1 pound green soybeans in pods Seasoned Salt Mixture; or Nepali Seasoned 　Salt (page 312)	**Seasoned Salt Mixture:** ¼ cup salt 2 teaspoons ground black pepper 1 teaspoon ground timmur (Nepali pepper; 　*see page 31*) 1 teaspoon ground red pepper

Mix all the ingredients for the Seasoned Salt Mixture and store in a dispenser with large holes for sprinkling.

In a large bowl, combine soybeans with some of the seasoned salt mixture and mix thoroughly by rubbing the mixture into each bean pod. Set them aside for 20 to 25 minutes. This will bring out the bright green color of the soybeans.

Bring a large pot of water to a rolling boil over high heat. Add the soybeans and boil until they are tender, 10 to 15 minutes. Remove one pod and test for doneness by squeezing it and pressing the beans out. The beans are cooked if they come out easily. Drain the pods in a colander. Transfer them to a serving bowl or basket. Serve warm or at room temperature.

NEPALI-STYLE CORN ON THE COB
Poleko Makai

Makes 6 to 8 servings

Fresh sweet corn is so good all by itself that it does not need much spicing up, but this recipe adds a new dimension to ordinary corn. Each row of kernels is scored and marinated with spices. Then the corn is roasted on a grill, bringing out the intense flavor of the spices.

6 to 8 ears corn	½ teaspoon cayenne pepper powder
¼ cup butter, softened	⅛ teaspoon timmur (Nepali pepper; *see page*
2 fresh mild green chilies, minced	*31*), freshly ground with a mortar and pestle
1 tablespoon fresh lemon or lime juice	⅛ teaspoon freshly ground black pepper
1 teaspoon minced fresh ginger	Salt, adjust to taste
1 medium clove garlic, minced	1 lemon, cut into wedges

Remove and discard the husks and silks from the corn. Hold each ear firmly and score each row of kernels with a sharp knife. When the kernels are pierced, a milky liquid may be released.

In a small bowl, combine the butter, green chilies, lemon juice, ginger, garlic, cayenne pepper powder, timmur, and black pepper and mix well. Add salt to taste. Spread the spice mixture evenly over each ear of corn and rub the entire surface, making sure each kernel is covered. Set them aside about 10 minutes to allow the flavors to be absorbed.

Preheat a charcoal or gas grill to medium-high heat for 10 minutes.

Place the ears of corn directly on the grill and roast, turning occasionally, until they are dotted with black and brown marks. Transfer the corn to a platter, garnish them with the fresh lemon wedges, and serve warm.

SAMAY BAJI

Samay Baji is a traditional Newari food platter consisting of multiple dishes and flavors combined together and served in a single plate, and represents celebration and festivities in the Newar community. The authentic dish is made regularly in many Newari households during family celebrations, birthdays, and weddings, when someone is going away for a long journey, and as sagun food. Sagun is a ceremony that involves the presentation of auspicious food items, flowers, fruits, and sweets to gods for good luck, happiness, longevity, and best wishes. *Samay Baji* is also eaten during major Nepali festivals, such as Indra Jatra, Bijaya Dashami, Laxmi Puja and Bhai Tika, Bisket Jatra and Yomari Punhi. These days, a *Samay Baji* platter is served as a starter food in many Nepali restaurants, or as a light lunch. In a typical *Samay Baji* platter, you may find a combination of the following dishes: *cheuraa* (pressed rice flakes), grilled and marinated meat, fried boiled eggs, fried soybeans, julienned ginger, lentil patties, potato salad, bean dishes, small fried fish, and homemade wine. This is an extremely versatile dish, and can be served at room temperature as a snack or appetizer. There are many variations of this dish—some cooks add radish pickle, bamboo shoots curry, *pau-kwaa* (lapsi pickle), and yogurt—but this is my simplified version.

2 cups *cheuraa* (pressed rice flakes), dry roasted
1 cup *swaya baji* or *samay* (puffed rice)
1 cup roasted or fried soybeans, split or whole
1 cup dried black-eyed peas (bodi), soaked overnight, boiled and fried
10 to 12 medium cloves garlic, peeled whole, fried in oil until light brown
½ cup peeled and julienned fresh ginger, fried in oil until light brown
1 cup dried fish (*sidra maachaa*), fried in oil until crunchy
8 to 10 hard-boiled eggs, peeled and fried until light brown
1 recipe *Woh* (Chicken and Urad Bean Patties; page 84)
1 recipe *Chamsoor-Paalungo Saag* (Spinach with Garden Cress; page 155)
1 recipe *Alu ko Achaar* (Spicy Potato Salad with Sesame Seeds; page 254)
1 recipe *Khukuraa ko Sekuwaa* (Grilled Chicken; page 201)

Samay baji **presentation Nepali way:** once you are ready to serve, select the right size plates and add pressed rice flakes in the middle of the plate, top with lentil patties and some fried fish, and add all side dishes neatly arranged around the plate. Add a small amount of garlic and ginger around the plate. Serve smaller portion sizes in the beginning, there is always room for second helpings.

Chapter 4

RICE DISHES

BHAAT / BHUJAA

Rice is cultivated in many regions of Nepal, and is one of its most important crops. The rice seedling transplanting and harvesting seasons are times of great anticipation and happiness in the community. Nepali farmers celebrate the occasion with a feast accompanied by music and dance. In the hilly part of the country, however, land conditions and lack of rain make rice difficult to grow and thus an expensive luxury. In these higher elevations, locals eat corn, millet, wheat, barley, and buckwheat.

Rice is a versatile food that can be simply boiled, steamed with butter, or cooked with a variety of ingredients such as spices, herbs, nuts, vegetables, meat, lentils, and beans. Plain boiled rice acts as a neutral food to eat with highly spiced curries, chutneys, pickles, and gravies. Nepalese like their rice tender, light, and fluffy with each grain separate and not mushy.

Uncooked rice is called *chaamal*, and cooked rice is referred to as *bhaat* or *bhujaa*. Rice is grown under a wide range of conditions and a number of varieties are produced in Nepal, varying in size, shape, color, flavor, and fragrance. The most expensive variety is *masino chaamal* or *basmati chaamal* (long-grain white rice), which is prized for its delicate, distinct flavor and texture. Medium- to short-grain white rice, called *saano-thulo maarsi chaamal*, is usually flatter and oval in shape. *Usineko chaamal* (parboiled rice) is slightly yellowish in color, less flavorful, less expensive, and takes longer to cook. Pressed or flattened rice flakes known as *cheuraa* are one of the most common rice products consumed in Nepal. Rice is also ground to make flour that is then made into fried or steamed snacks, breads, and sweet dishes.

Preparing Rice

Rice is very easy to cook and does not require any special skills. If you follow a few basic guidelines, you will not have any trouble making perfectly cooked rice. Most of the recipes in this chapter use long-grain white rice or basmati rice, both of which are readily available in most supermarkets or Indian grocery stores. I usually cook rice after preparing the accompanying dishes that go with it, as they can be easily reheated, so then the rice is steaming hot when served.

Cleaning and Washing

Most commercially bagged rice, such as the supermarket varieties (in plastic, cloth, or burlap bags) has been cleaned and sorted, so there is rarely any need to pick through it. Be sure, however, to pick over imported rice or rice from open bulk containers for unhulled grains, stems, pebbles, or any tiny broken rice. To clean it, spread the rice on a large platter or a wide round wicker tray (or a *naanglo*, if available). Pick through a small portion at a time, and discard any foreign particles.

I always rinse rice thoroughly under cold running water before cooking to remove any floating husks or impurities that may have collected during milling and processing. To wash the rice, place it in a large bowl and cover with cold water. Gently rub the grains between your hands and remove anything that floats. Slowly pour the milky water out, holding back the grains with one hand. Repeat this process several times until the water runs clear.

Soaking and Draining

I recommend soaking rice (especially basmati) before cooking it as it shortens the cooking time and keeps each grain separate and fluffy. Soaking also makes the rice grains less likely to stick together. I recommend soaking for at least 20 minutes, but recipes vary, and some dishes only need washing and rinsing. To soak the rice, place it in a large bowl and cover with cold water, set aside. For cooking everyday rice (long-grain rice) by the absorption method, soak the rice for 20 to 25 minutes before cooking, but if you are in a hurry, omit the soaking. You will still get good results. I also prefer to cook the rice in the same water in which it has been soaking.

Cooking

Rice can be cooked in any pot that has good heat distribution and a tight-fitting lid. In Nepal, rice is traditionally cooked in a heavy, round-bottomed, brass pot called a *kasaudi*. The pot has a narrow neck to retain moisture, and the heavy bottom distributes the heat evenly so that the rice cooks in an energy-saving fashion and can be kept warm for a long time. Today, the more convenient and popular electric rice cooker has replaced the *kasaudi* in many Nepali households.

Cooking Methods

There are several methods of cooking rice and each cook has their own techniques, formula, and preference. Some prefer to boil rice in plenty of water on the stovetop. When the rice is almost cooked, the starchy water is poured off, and the rice is cooked over low heat until each grain is light and fluffy. In the absorption method, an exact amount of water is added to the rice and brought to a boil, then covered and simmered on the stovetop until the water has been absorbed and the rice becomes tender and fluffy. Rice can also be cooked by first sautéing it in oil, adding a measured amount of water, and then simmering it, covered, until the water has been absorbed. Finally, if you own an electric rice cooker, and follow the directions correctly, you should be able to make perfect, fluffy rice that stays warm for hours without losing quality every time. If you enjoy rice and cook it often, it may be worth purchasing a rice cooker.

Whichever method of cooking you use, be sure to leave the rice undisturbed for five to ten minutes, covered in the same pot so that the trapped steam finishes off the cooking process, known as *tharak marne* in Nepali. Sometimes while cooking rice, the grains stick together on the bottom of the pan and form a thin, golden brown crust cake, which is called *maamuri*, and is considered the most delicious part of cooked rice.

Most Nepali cooks do not measure water for rice, but make an educated guess based on a finger measurement. Typically, rice is washed, drained, and placed in a pot. The water is poured into the pot, and the cook inserts a finger into the water. The level of water above the rice should be just above the first joint of the middle finger. The rice is then cooked by the absorption method. When cooking a large quantity of rice I add about 1¼ inches of water above the rice. However, the measurement and cooking time depend on many factors, such as the age of the grain, type of rice, type of pot, whether the rice has been presoaked or not, and the heat source. With each type of rice, it is necessary to cook it once in order to find out the best way to cook it. A little experimentation will help to achieve the best results. I have found that I need to adjust the amount of water and cooking time with each variety of rice, but the basic guideline is for 1 cup of long-grain white rice, use 1½ to 2 cups of water, and for 2 cups of rice, use 3½ to 4 cups of water. Rice expands to two or three times its original size after cooking, so that generally 1 cup of uncooked rice yields 2½ to 3 cups of cooked rice.

PLAIN STEAMED RICE

Makes 4 to 6 servings

This is my basic everyday recipe for cooking rice. In this absorption method, the rice is cleaned and rinsed in a few changes of cold water, and soaked in a measured amount of water. It is then simmered while covered until all the water has been absorbed into the rice. This recipe works for any variety of long-grain or medium-grain white rice. I prefer to make moist and tender rice with each grain separated, so that it is not sticky or dry. Plain rice is a versatile dish that can be served with mild or highly seasoned curries, vegetables, or lentils.

> 2 cups long-grain white rice

Put the rice in a medium-size bowl, pour 3¾ cups water over it and soak for 20 minutes. Transfer the soaked rice and water to a heavy saucepan over medium-high heat. Bring to a rapid boil, uncovered, stirring gently from time to time. Once it comes to a full boil, reduce the heat as much as possible, cover, and simmer until the liquid has been absorbed by the rice and each grain is separate and tender, 15 to 20 minutes. Do not stir or uncover while the rice is simmering. Remove the pot from the heat and let the rice rest, undisturbed, for 5 to 10 minutes before serving. Uncover, fluff the rice gently, and serve. If you are not planning to serve it immediately, leave the rice covered in the pan to prevent it from drying out.

PLAIN BOILED RICE

Makes 4 to 6 servings

This is another basic method of cooking rice, using a larger quantity of water than the absorption method. When the rice is almost cooked, the starchy water is drained off, and the rice is cooked until it is fluffy. Although with this method much of the nutrients are drained away from the rice, the milky water (*bhaat ko maad*) is always reserved and used as a thickening agent for soups and curries or as animal feed.

> 2 cups long-grain white rice

Put the rice in a large heavy saucepan with 8 cups of cold water and bring to a boil over medium-high heat, uncovered. Cook for 8 to 10 minutes. Pinch a grain of rice between your thumb and finger. If it is cooked but still a little hard in the center, the rice is three-quarters cooked, indicating that it is ready to be drained. Drain the milky water through a fine-mesh strainer or sieve. Adjust the heat to the lowest possible setting and cook the rice, covered, until it is tender with each grain separated, 10 to 15 more minutes. Remove from the heat and let the rice rest undisturbed for 5 to 10 minutes before serving. Uncover, fluff the rice gently, and serve.

BUTTERED RICE
Makhani Bhujaa

Makes 4 to 6 servings

This is another basic way of making rice by the absorption method but using clarified butter. This recipe is prepared with aromatic basmati rice, which is a high-status grain cultivated in the foothills of the Himalayas. When cooked with clarified butter, it increases to twice its length and has a distinct delicate flavor and fluffy texture. This variety of rice is expensive and reserved for special occasions. Basmati rice can be found in large supermarkets or Indian markets, where it is less expensive. Imported basmati rice needs to be picked over, rinsed in several changes of water, and soaked before cooking. Each type of basmati rice absorbs water differently, so you may need to adjust the water slightly depending on the dryness and age of the grain.

> 2 cups basmati rice
> 2 tablespoons clarified butter (*gheu;
> page 314*) or regular unsalted butter,
> at room temperature
>
> ½ teaspoon salt
> 2 cassia leaves
> 4 whole cloves

Put the rice in a medium-size bowl, cover it with plenty of water, and leave to soak for 20 minutes.

Drain and place the rice in a heavy saucepan with the butter, salt, cassia leaves, cloves, and 3¾ cups of cold water. Bring to a rapid boil over medium-high heat, uncovered, stirring gently from time to time. Once it comes to a full boil, adjust the heat to the lowest possible setting, cover, and simmer until the liquid has been absorbed and the rice is tender with each grain separated, 15 to 20 minutes. Do not stir or lift the lid during simmering.

Remove the pan from the heat and let the rice rest, covered and undisturbed, for 5 to 10 minutes before serving. Uncover, fluff the rice gently, and serve. If you are not planning to serve it immediately, leave the rice covered in the pan to prevent it from drying out.

Note: This recipe can be prepared with any variety of good-quality long-grain white rice and can also be cooked in an electric rice cooker as well.

FRIED RICE
Bhuteko Bhaat

Makes 4 to 6 servings

This recipe is so versatile that any combination of vegetables, meats, eggs, nuts, and spices can be used. If you do not have leftover rice, you can cook fresh rice, but make sure to cool it completely before frying, or else it will be mushy. Rice usually hardens when cooled, but cooking over low heat and occasionally sprinkling in a little water will soften it. Fried rice is considered a complete one-dish meal and can be served by itself or with salad, yogurt, and pickles.

1 tablespoon vegetable oil
2 eggs, lightly beaten
¼ cup clarified butter (*gheu; page 314*)
½ teaspoon cumin seeds
1 medium onion, halved lengthwise and
  thinly sliced
3 or 4 cloves garlic, finely chopped
8 ounces fresh mushrooms, sliced (about
  2 cups)
1 small red or green bell pepper, cored and
  chopped (about 1 cup)

2 medium carrots, peeled and cut into
  ½-inch slices (about 1 cup)
1 cup frozen peas, thawed and drained
1 cup finely diced cooked meat (chicken,
  turkey, pork, or lamb)
4 to 6 cups cold cooked rice
Salt, adjust to taste
½ teaspoon freshly ground black pepper
4 to 5 green onions (white and pale green
  parts), finely chopped

Heat the oil in a small skillet over medium-high heat. Add the eggs and cook, without stirring, until set. Transfer the eggs to a platter. When cool enough to handle, julienne and set aside.

Heat the clarified butter in a heavy skillet over medium-high heat. When hot, add the cumin seeds and fry until lightly browned and aromatic, 5 to 7 seconds. Add the onion and garlic and cook until they are soft. Stir in the mushrooms, bell pepper, carrots, peas, and meat and sauté until the vegetables are half cooked, 5 to 7 minutes.

Stir in the rice, salt, and pepper, breaking up any clumps of rice and stirring until the rice is heated through and lightly browned. If the rice becomes dry and starts to stick to the skillet, add 1 to 2 tablespoons of water at a time, keep stirring and let the rice absorb the water before adding more. Stir in the green onions and julienned egg. Transfer the rice to a serving dish and serve hot.

AJOWAN RICE
Jwaano-Bhaat

Makes 4 to 6 servings

This recipe is one of the quickest and most flavorful ways of using leftover rice (*baasi bhaat*) to create a delicious dish. In addition, ajowan seeds are known to aid and stimulate digestion. Rice usually hardens as it cools, so sprinkle in 2 to 3 tablespoons of water while cooking to moisten it—in Nepali, we call this "*pani chamkhera bhutne tarika.*" This dish can be served as a light lunch with vegetables, pickles, and yogurt.

¼ cup clarified butter (*gheu; page 314*)
1½ teaspoons ajowan seeds
2 dried red chilies, halved and seeded
1 medium onion, halved lengthwise and
   thinly sliced

3 medium cloves garlic, finely chopped
4 to 6 cups cold cooked rice
Salt, adjust to taste
4 to 5 green onions (white and green parts),
   thinly sliced

Heat the clarified butter in a heavy skillet over medium-high heat. When hot, add the ajowan seeds and chilies and fry until lightly browned and aromatic, 5 to 7 seconds. Add the onion and garlic and cook, stirring until soft.

Adjust the heat to medium-low and mix in the rice, a little at a time, separating any clumps. Add some salt to taste and continue stirring until the rice is heated through and begins to brown slightly. If the rice becomes dry and sticks to the skillet, add 1 to 2 tablespoons of water at a time and keep stirring. Let the rice absorb the water before adding more.

The finished rice should be soft. Mix in the green onions, transfer to a serving dish, and serve hot.

Urad Bean and Rice Khichari / *Maas ko Khichari*

URAD BEAN AND RICE KHICHARI

Makes 4 to 6 servings

Maas ko Khichari

Khichari is a delicious and nutritious Nepali comfort food of rice and daal cooked into a creamy porridge. Warm spiced *gheu* is added just before serving for extra flavor. It is accompanied by vegetables, pickles, or yogurt. The rice and daal are usually soaked to shorten the cooking time, but you can omit this step if you wish.

1½ cups long- or short-grain white rice	½ teaspoon ground turmeric
1½ cups split black urad beans, with skin (*kaalo maas ko daal*)	Small pinch ground asafetida
	3 tablespoons clarified butter (*gheu; page 314*), divided
1 tablespoon minced fresh ginger	
1 teaspoon salt, adjust to taste	1 teaspoon cumin seeds

Combine the rice, urad beans, ginger, salt, turmeric, asafetida, 1 tablespoon of the clarified butter, and 7 to 8 cups of cold water in a heavy saucepan and bring to a boil over medium-high heat. Reduce the heat to low, cover, and simmer, stirring frequently, until the rice and daal soften, 25 to 30 minutes. If the *khichari* is too thick, add a few tablespoons of boiling water a little at a time. Remove from the heat and keep it covered until ready to serve.

Before serving, heat the remaining 2 tablespoons clarified butter in a small skillet over medium-high heat. When hot, add the cumin seeds and fry until lightly browned and aromatic, 5 to 7 seconds. Pour the entire contents over the *khichari*, mix well, transfer to a serving dish, and serve hot.

MAGHE SANKRANTI

Traditionally, *khichari* made with split black urad beans is prepared and served during the celebration of *Maghe Sankranti*, which is observed during the month of January. During this festive occasion, people take holy baths in the rivers, go to the temples, and visit their most respected elderly relative, friends, and family and receive and give blessings.

In addition to *khichari*, they feast on certain food items during the festival: *chaaku* (sweet made from retreated molasses), *tilauri* and *til ko laddu* (a chewy candy made out of sesame seeds and sugar), *gheu* (freshly made clarified butter), *sakhar-khand* (sweet potatoes), *pidaalu* (taro roots), *tarul* (yams), and *paalungo ko saag* (green leafy vegetables like spinach). All food consumed during the festival focuses on healthy eating, and is geared towards warming up the body during cold days, good nourishment, a lifetime free of disease, and purification of one's body.

PEAS PULAAU
Keraau ko Pulaau

Makes 4 to 6 servings

This is an easy recipe and makes a perfect light lunch with any gravy-based meat dish or with plain yogurt. To make it more festive, use basmati rice, which will give it a special touch. If fresh peas are not available, frozen peas are a good substitute. A typical festive Nepali meal always includes *pulaau*, most common ones are made from meat or mixed vegetables.

---

2 tablespoons clarified butter (*gheu; page 314*)

1 teaspoon cumin seeds

3 small cassia leaves

4 green cardamom pods, crushed

2 black cardamom pods, crushed

4 whole cloves

1 (1-inch) stick cinnamon, halved

1 medium onion, finely chopped (about 1 cup)

1 teaspoon minced fresh ginger

2 small cloves garlic, finely chopped

2 cups long-grain white rice (any variety), rinsed and soaked in cold water for 20 minutes, drained

2 cups shelled fresh or frozen peas, thawed and drained

1 teaspoon Nepali garam masalaa (*page 310*)

1 teaspoon salt, adjust to taste

½ teaspoon ground turmeric

Heat the clarified butter in a heavy saucepan over medium-high heat. When hot, add the cumin seeds, cassia leaves, green and black cardamom pods, cloves, and cinnamon and fry until they begin to puff up, darken, and give off a pleasant aroma, 5 to 7 seconds. Add the onion, ginger, and garlic and cook until they are soft, about 5 minutes. Add the rice and continue frying, stirring constantly, until the onion is translucent, about 2 minutes.

If fresh peas are used, add them with 3¾ cups of cold water, the *garam masalaa*, salt, and turmeric and bring the mixture to a rapid boil, uncovered, stirring gently occasionally. Once it comes to a full boil, adjust the heat to the lowest setting, cover with a tight-fitting lid, and simmer until the liquid has been absorbed and the rice is tender, with each grain separated, 15 to 20 minutes. Taste and add additional salt if needed.

If frozen peas are used, add them now, and cover. There is no need to stir. Remove the pan from the heat and let the rice rest covered, undisturbed, for 5 to 10 minutes so that the trapped steam cooks the peas. Uncover, fluff the rice, gently mix in the peas, and transfer the rice to a platter. If you are not planning to serve it immediately, leave the rice covered in the pan to prevent it from drying out.

MUNG BEAN JAAULO RICE

Makes 4 to 6 servings

Moong ko Daal ko Jaaulo

Jaaulo is a soft cooked rice and daal dish. It is served as a one-meal dish, and considered a soothing comfort food in Nepal. When cooked with the skinless variety of mung beans, rice becomes very light and nutritious. The traditional version of this recipe does not usually contain garlic, but I have added a whole head of garlic for extra flavor. A mild and simpler version of *jaaulo* is given to infants as baby food. It is also served to people who suffer from stomach pain or other digestive disorders. I grew up in a household where *jaaulo* was served in the morning as a nourishing breakfast food.

1½ cups long or short-grain rice
½ cup split yellow mung beans, without skins
  (*pahelo moong ko daal*)
6 to 8 small cloves garlic, peeled
½-inch piece fresh ginger, peeled and
  cut into 2 slices

3 tablespoons clarified butter (*gheu*), divided
1 teaspoon salt, adjust to taste
½ teaspoon ground turmeric
2 small cassia leaves
¼ teaspoon fenugreek seeds
Small pinch ground asafetida

Combine 7 cups of water, the rice, beans, garlic, ginger, 1 tablespoon of the clarified butter, salt, turmeric and cassia leaves in a heavy-bottomed pot. Bring the mixture to a boil over medium-high heat. Reduce the heat to simmer, cover, and cook, stirring frequently, until the rice and beans are soft and have become the texture of creamy porridge, 25 to 30 minutes.

Heat the remaining 2 tablespoons clarified butter in a small skillet over medium-high heat. When hot, add the fenugreek seeds and fry until the seeds turn dark brown and fragrant, 5 to 7 seconds. Remove the skillet from the heat and immediately sprinkle in the asafetida. Pour the entire contents over the prepared rice. Cover and allow the rice to absorb the seasoning for 5 minutes. Uncover and mix well. Remove the cassia leaves and ginger pieces before serving. Serve hot.

Note: *Jaaulo* can be made ahead of time and reheated. Once cooled, it tends to thicken, so add a small amount of boiling water and reheat to the desired consistency.

VEGETABLE JAAULO

Makes 4 to 6 servings

Tarkaari ko Jaaulo

Jaaulo is a one-dish meal of rice and two different variety of daals, considered a soothing comfort food in Nepal. This version is spicier and is enhanced with herbs and a variety of vegetables to round out the flavor. A mild version, given to infants and people suffering from stomach pain or other digestive disorders, was served for breakfast in my home growing up.

¼ cup clarified butter (*gheu; page 314*)
¼ teaspoon fenugreek seeds
2 small cassia leaves
½ teaspoon ground turmeric
Generous pinch ground asafetida
1 medium onion, finely chopped (about 1 cup)
1 tablespoon minced fresh ginger
4 small cloves garlic, finely chopped
2 medium potatoes, peeled and cubed (about 2 cups)

¼ head cauliflower, separated into 1-inch florets (about 2 cups)
1 cup long- or short-grain white rice
¼ cup split pink or red lentils, without skins (*musuro ko daal*)
½ cup split yellow mung beans, without skins (*pahelo moong ko daal*)
1 teaspoon ground cumin
1 teaspoon ground coriander
1 teaspoon salt, adjust to taste
1 cup frozen peas, thawed and drained

Heat the clarified butter in a heavy pot over medium-high heat. When hot, add the fenugreek seeds and fry until they darken and become fragrant, 5 to 7 seconds. Add the cassia leaves, turmeric, and asafetida, then immediately add the onion, ginger, and garlic. Fry, stirring constantly until they are lightly browned, 5 to 7 minutes.

Stir in the potatoes, cauliflower, rice, lentils, mung beans, cumin, and coriander. Add 7 cups cold water and the salt and bring the mixture to a boil. Then reduce the heat to low and simmer, partially covered, until the beans are soft, stirring frequently, 25 to 30 minutes. The mixture should disintegrate into a creamy porridge.

Stir in the peas and cook for 5 minutes more. If the porridge seems too thick, add a few tablespoons of boiling water. Transfer to a serving dish and serve.

TEMPERED RICE
Jhanne ko Saada Bhaat

Makes 4 to 6 servings

This is a family recipe, our favorite way of adding flavor to cooked rice by pouring spice-infused butter (*jhanne*) over the rice just before serving it. Traditionally, homemade clarified butter (*gheu*) is melted and added to the rice directly on the individual plates before serving. The spices listed below are the most commonly used. However, each family has their own spice blend. Sometimes a fried egg is served on top of the rice.

3 tablespoons clarified butter (*gheu; page 314*)	2 cloves garlic, thinly sliced
½ teaspoon ajowan seeds	1 teaspoon salt, adjust to taste
2 dried red chilies, halved and seeded	4 to 6 cups hot freshly cooked white rice

In a small skillet, heat the clarified butter over medium heat. Add the ajowan seeds and chilies and sauté until lightly browned and fragrant, 5 to 7 seconds. Immediately add the garlic and salt and sauté until the garlic is crisp. Pour the entire contents directly over the prepared rice. Cover and let the rice rest for 5 minutes so the flavor develops. When you are ready to serve, uncover and fluff the rice.

TEMPERING / *JHANEKO*
Tempering (*Jhaneko*) simply means adding more flavor to cooked dishes. In this process, oil or clarified butter (*gheu*) is heated separately in a pan with several spices and herbs. It is cooked until the spices release distinct aroma and turn a few shades darker, then the entire contents is poured in the prepared dish.

Chapter 5 LEGUMES— DRIED BEANS, LENTILS, PEAS

DAAL

There are a few basic things to be aware of before cooking daal. All imported daal must be picked over for tiny stones, dirt, or any foreign matter. To clean the daal, spread it on a large platter, pick through it carefully, and discard any foreign matter. Wash the daal by placing it in a large bowl and adding cold water to cover. Remove anything that floats. Gently rub the daal between your hands and slowly pour off the water, holding the daal back with one hand. Rinse and drain the cloudy water several times until it runs clear. Personally, I discard the soaking water and rinse the daal with fresh cold water before cooking it. Some kinds of daal may need to be soaked before cooking to soften the lentils, and other varieties can be cooked without soaking. Most varieties of daals are available in the US through online retailers or some local Nepali markets, in Indian grocery stores, and at some larger supermarkets. In Nepal, the word "daal" is a generic word used for both the uncooked legumes and the recipe they are made into.

TEMPERED YELLOW MUNG BEANS

Makes 4 to 6 servings

Moong ko Daal

This is one of the most common types of daal, made from skinless split yellow mung beans, which cook quickly and do not require soaking. There are just two basic steps in cooking this recipe: first simmer the beans, and then add tempered spices and butter. Be careful not to overcook the beans or they will become pasty and gooey. This daal is considered a comfort food in Nepal and soothes an ailing stomach when served with plain boiled rice. It is nutrient-packed and is often served to toddlers in the form of *jaaulo* (one-pot rice-lentil dish; page 109).

1 cup split yellow mung beans, without skins
  (*pahelo moong ko daal*)
1½ teaspoons minced fresh ginger
1 cassia leaf
1 teaspoon salt, adjust to taste
½ teaspoon ground turmeric
1 tablespoon clarified butter (*gheu; page 314*)
1 tablespoon fresh lemon or lime juice
¼ cup finely chopped cilantro
1 small tomato, chopped (about ½ cup)

Tempering spices
2 tablespoons clarified butter (*gheu*)
1 teaspoon cumin seeds
Small pinch ground asafetida
1 tablespoon fresh ginger, finely julienned
2 large cloves garlic, thinly sliced

Combine the mung beans, minced ginger, cassia leaf, salt, turmeric, 1 tablespoon clarified butter, and 3½ cups of water in a large, heavy saucepan. Bring the mixture to a quick boil over medium-high heat, uncovered, stirring occasionally to make sure the beans do not boil over or stick together. There is no need to skim off the foam that rises to the surface, as it contains flavor. When it comes to a full boil, reduce the heat to low, cover, and simmer gently until the beans are tender and have doubled in volume, 20 to 25 minutes. If necessary add more water to attain a soupy consistency and simmer for 5 more minutes. Remove from the heat and set aside, covered.

Prepare tempering spices: In a separate small skillet, heat 2 tablespoons clarified butter over medium-high heat. Add the cumin seeds and fry until lightly browned and fragrant, about 5 seconds. Add the asafetida and then immediately add the julienned ginger and garlic and fry until crisp. Remove the skillet from the heat, immediately pour the entire mixture into the daal and stir well. Cover and allow the seasonings to develop for 5 minutes.

Mix in the lemon juice. Transfer to a serving dish, sprinkle the cilantro and tomatoes on top and serve.

SPLIT WHITE URAD BEANS
Chiplo Daal

The pale ivory-colored split urad beans are called *chhataa ko daal* in Nepalese. These beans do not require soaking and can be cooked in a pressure cooker to speed up the cooking process. As the beans swell and thicken, they become creamy with a slippery texture and are called *chiplo daal*.

¼ cup clarified butter (*gheu; page 314*)
2 dried red chilies, stemmed (optional)
1 teaspoon cumin seeds
½ teaspoon jimbu (Nepali aromatic herb; *see page 30*)
1 teaspoon ground turmeric
2 small cassia leaves
Generous pinch ground asafetida

1 medium onion, halved and thinly sliced
4 to 5 medium cloves garlic, finely chopped
1½ tablespoons minced fresh ginger
1 medium tomato, chopped (about 1 cup)
1 cup split white urad beans, without skins (*maas ko chhataa ko daal*)
1 teaspoon salt, adjust to taste

Heat the clarified butter in a large, heavy pot over medium-high heat. When hot, add the chilies, cumin seeds, and *jimbu* and fry until fragrant and dark, about 5 seconds. Add the turmeric, cassia leaves, and asafetida, then immediately add the onions, garlic, and ginger. Cook until the onion is soft, about 5 minutes, stirring frequently. Add the tomatoes and cook until slightly soft.

Add the urad beans, salt, and 4 cups of water and bring the mixture to a boil, stirring occasionally to make sure it does not boil over or stick together. After it comes to a full boil, reduce the heat to low, cover, and simmer gently, stirring from time to time, until the beans are tender and fully cooked, 30 to 40 minutes. If needed, add ¼ cup water or more to attain a soupy consistency and simmer an additional 5 minutes. Transfer the daal to a serving dish and serve hot.

TEMPERED BLACK URAD BEANS

Makes 4 to 6 servings

Maas ko Daal

Maas ko daal, or split black urad/gram beans, need little introduction in Nepali cuisine. They are among the most loved type of daal, considered flavorful, satisfying, and extremely nutritious. *Maas ko daal* differ from other daals in that they are cooked in an iron pot (*falaam ko tapke*). When simmered in this pot, the daal transforms to a deep black color with rich flavor. To create an authentic Nepali taste the preferred combination of spices for *Maas ko daal* is jimbu (Himalayan herb), whole dried red chilies, asafetida, and fresh garlic.

1 cup split black urad beans, with skins
(*kaalo maas ko daal*)
1½ teaspoons minced fresh ginger
1 teaspoon salt, adjust to taste
½ teaspoon ground turmeric
⅛ teaspoon timmur (Nepali pepper; *see page 31*)
1 tablespoons clarified butter (*gheu*)

Tempering Spices
2 tablespoons clarified butter (*gheu*)
2 or 3 dried red chilies, halved and seeded
½ teaspoon jimbu (Nepali aromatic herb; *see page 30*)
Generous pinch ground asafetida
1 tablespoon finely julienned fresh ginger
2 large cloves garlic, thinly sliced

Combine the urad beans, minced ginger, salt, turmeric, timmur, 1 tablespoon clarified butter, and 3½ cups of water in a deep, heavy pot. Bring the mixture to a quick boil over medium-high heat, uncovered, stirring occasionally to make sure the beans do not boil over or stick together. Cook for about 20 minutes.

Reduce the heat to low, cover, and simmer gently until the beans are tender and have doubled in volume, about 55 minutes. If necessary, add more water to attain a soupy consistency and simmer 5 more minutes. Remove the pot from heat and set aside.

Prepare tempering spices: In a small skillet, heat 2 tablespoons clarified butter over medium-high heat. Add the chilies and jimbu, and fry until light brown and fragrant, about 5 seconds. Add the asafetida, then immediately add the julienned ginger and garlic and fry until crisp, about 10 seconds.

Immediately pour the entire tempering mixture into the daal and stir well. Cover and allow the seasoning to develop for 5 minutes. Transfer the daal to a serving dish and serve hot. The daal will thicken if not served at once. You can reheat it with 3 or 4 tablespoons of water if needed.

Variation: Add 1½ cups of diced taro vegetable, combine and cook together for a delicious dish.

BLACK URAD BEANS / MAAS KO DAAL

Black urad beans are grown in the warm and sub-tropical temperatures of Nepal. The small beans looks similar to green mung beans in size and shape. The seed color of *maas ko daal* varies according to types. The type with shiny black-green and dusky colors is regarded as the best type. They are used in three forms: whole urad beans with skin, split white urad beans without skin, and split black urad beans with skin. For my culinary research, I visited the village of Geetanagar-Amarbasti in the Chitwan District in the Narayani zone of Southern Nepal. The villagers were busy harvesting *maas ko daal* by their traditional methods—pulling the plants, cutting, thrashing, and gathering the seed pods. While I was taking pictures, the village women were whispering to each other, "*here ne kuirini le tashbir khicheko*" ("look a *kuirini* is taking picture of maas ko daal'). I replied to them smilingly in Nepali, "*ma kuirini hoina, baahir dherai baseko matrai*" ("I am not *kuirini*, but lived outside Nepal for a long time"). The word *kuirini* is a Nepali slang word for tourist. I can understand why they thought I was a tourist, because of the way I was dressed and how I was taking photos, but I wanted them to know that Nepal was also my home.

MAHAARAANI DAAL

Daal Mahaaraani

Makes 4 to 6 servings

"Mahaaraani" means "fit to serve a queen" and indeed this dish is. This is my family's favorite daal. A succulent and delicious slow-cooked dish, it is easy to prepare and extremely nutritious. This recipe combines three varieties of daals, each with a distinct flavor and texture. It is the traditional combination of daals, but any varieties can be used.

½ cup split yellow mung beans, without skins (*pahelo moong ko daal*)
½ cup split pink or red lentils, without skins (*musuro ko daal*)
½ cup split yellow pigeon peas, without skins (*rahar ko daal*)
1 tablespoon minced fresh ginger
2 medium cloves garlic, finely chopped
1 teaspoon salt, adjust to taste
½ teaspoon ground turmeric
2 cassia leaves
1 tablespoon clarified butter (*gheu; page 314*)

Tempering spices:
4 tablespoons clarified butter (*gheu*)
2 dried red chilies, halved and seeded
1 teaspoon cumin seeds
⅛ teaspoon jimbu (Nepal aromatic herb; see page 30)
Small pinch ground asafetida
1 medium onion, finely chopped (about 1 cup)
1 tablespoon finely julienned fresh ginger
2 medium cloves garlic, thinly sliced
2 medium tomatoes, finely chopped (about 2 cups)
½ cup finely chopped cilantro
3 to 4 green onions (white and green parts), finely chopped

In a large, heavy pot, combine all the mung beans, lentils, and pigeon peas with the minced ginger, chopped garlic, salt, turmeric, cassia leaves, 1 tablespoon clarified butter, and 4 cups of water. Bring the mixture to a boil over medium-high heat, uncovered, stirring occasionally to make sure the beans do not boil over. There is no need to skim away the foam that rises to the surface, because it contains flavorful ingredients. When it comes to a full boil, reduce the heat to low, cover, and simmer gently until the mixture is soft and fully cooked, 20 to 25 minutes. If needed, add more water to attain a soupy consistency and simmer for 5 more minutes. Remove the pot from the heat and set aside, covered.

Prepare tempering spices: In a separate small skillet, heat 4 tablespoons clarified butter over medium-high heat. When hot, add the chilies, cumin seeds, and jimbu, and fry until lightly browned and fragrant, about 5 seconds. Add the asafetida first, then immediately add the onion, julienned ginger, and sliced garlic and cook until soft. Add the tomatoes, cilantro, and green onions and cook, stirring constantly, about 2 minutes. Remove from the heat and immediately pour the entire mixture into the cooked daal and stir well. Lower the heat to medium-low, bring the daal back to a simmer, and cook for 10 minutes to develop the flavors. Transfer the daal to a serving dish and serve hot.

RED LENTIL DAAL
Musuro ko Daal

Makes 4 to 6 servings

Brightly colored split lentils are known as *musuro ko daal* in Nepal and are nutritious, quick to cook, light, and easily digestible. These shiny round lentils are coral colored, swell double their volume, and turn golden yellow after cooking.

---

1 cup split pink or red lentils, without skins (*musuro ko daal*)

2 small cassia leaves

2 large cloves garlic, finely chopped

1½ teaspoons minced fresh ginger

1 teaspoon salt, adjust to taste

½ teaspoon ground turmeric

1 tablespoons clarified butter (*gheu, page 314*)

1 tablespoon fresh lemon or lime juice

¼ cup finely chopped cilantro

2 to 3 green onions (white and pale green parts), finely chopped

1 small tomato, chopped (about ½ cup)

Tempering spices:

2 tablespoons clarified butter (*gheu*)

½ teaspoon cumin seeds

Small pinch ground asafetida

In a large, deep, heavy pot, combine the lentils, cassia leaves, garlic, ginger, salt, turmeric, 1 tablespoon clarified butter, and 3½ cups of water. Bring the mixture to a quick boil over medium-high heat, uncovered, stirring occasionally to make sure the lentils do not boil over or stick together. (Do not skim away the foam that rises to the surface, as it contains flavor.) Reduce the heat to low, cover, and simmer gently until the lentils are tender and fully cooked, 20 to 25 minutes. If necessary, add more water to attain a soupy consistency and simmer for 5 more minutes. Remove the pot from the heat and set aside.

Prepare tempering spices: In a separate small skillet, heat 2 tablespoons clarified butter over medium-high heat. Add the cumin seeds and fry until they darken and become fragrant, about 5 seconds. Sprinkle in the asafetida and immediately pour the entire mixture into the cooked daal and stir well. Cover and allow the seasonings to develop for 5 minutes.

Mix in the lemon juice, transfer the daal to a serving dish, sprinkle with the cilantro, green onions, and tomato, and serve.

MIXED FIVE DAAL
Panchamukhi Daal

Makes 4 to 6 servings

This recipe combines five different varieties of daal in equal amounts. Each has a distinct taste and texture, giving this dish a lot of flavor and making it a delicious accompaniment to any rice dish, roti bread, stir-fried vegetables, and pickles.

3 tablespoons clarified butter (*gheu*)
1 teaspoon cumin seeds
1 (1-inch) cinnamon stick
2 small cassia leaves
½ teaspoon ground turmeric
Large pinch ground asafetida
1 large onion, finely chopped (about 1½ cups)
3 to 4 medium cloves garlic, chopped
1 tablespoon minced fresh ginger
2 medium tomatoes, chopped (about 2 cups)
¼ cup split yellow mung beans, without skins (*pahelo moong ko daal*)
¼ cup split pink or red lentils, without skins (*musuro ko daal*)
¼ cup split white urad beans, without skins (*maas ko chhataa ko daal*)
¼ cup split yellow pigeon peas, without skins (*rahar ko daal*)
¼ cup split yellow chickpeas, without skins (*chana ko daal*)
1 teaspoon salt, adjust to taste
½ cup finely chopped cilantro

Heat the clarified butter in a large heavy-bottomed pot over medium-high heat. Add the cumin seeds and fry until lightly browned and fragrant, about 5 seconds. Add the cinnamon stick, cassia leaves, turmeric, and asafetida, then immediately add the onions, garlic, and ginger. Cook until the onions are soft, about 5 minutes, stirring frequently, then add the tomatoes and cook until slightly soft.

Add the mung beans, lentils, urad beans, pigeon peas, chickpeas, salt, and 4½ cups of water and bring the mixture to a quick boil, stirring from time to time to make sure it does not boil over. Reduce the heat to medium-low, cover, and cook until the daal are tender, 40 to 45 minutes. If necessary, add ½ cup of water or more to maintain a moderately thick consistency. Transfer the daal to a serving dish, sprinkle the cilantro on top, and serve hot.

Mixed Five Daal / *Panchamukhi Daal*

SPLIT PIGEON PEA DAAL

Makes 4 to 6 servings

Rahar ko Daal

In Nepal, *Rahar daal* is considered the king of daals. They have a slightly nutty taste, are easy to digest, and resemble yellow split peas. This is a mild daal made with yellow split pigeon peas which are available dry or lightly coated with oil. The oil preserves freshness and protects the pigeon peas from insects. If you are using this type, make sure to wash them several times in hot running water to remove the oil completely. My mother's kitchen helper, Laxmi Bajai, suggests, "not to add salt while simmering the daal, because it slows down the cooking time." She always emphasizes her method, but in my experiment with several batches with or without salt, I did not see much difference and I am back to my regular method of simmering with salt.

---

1 cup split yellow pigeon peas, without skins (*rahar ko daal*)
1 tablespoons clarified butter (*gheu*)
1 (1-inch) cinnamon stick
1½ teaspoons minced fresh ginger
1 teaspoon salt, adjust to taste
½ teaspoon ground turmeric
2 small cassia leaves

1 tablespoon fresh lemon or lime juice
¼ cup finely chopped cilantro

Tempering spices:
1 tablespoon clarified butter (*gheu*)
1 teaspoon cumin seeds
2 whole cloves
Small pinch ground asafetida

In a deep, heavy pot, combine the pigeon peas, 1 tablespoon clarified butter, cinnamon stick, ginger, salt, turmeric, cassia leaves, and 3½ cups of water. Bring the mixture to a boil over medium-high heat, uncovered, stirring occasionally to make sure the mixture does not boil over or stick together. When it comes to a full boil, reduce the heat to low, cover, and simmer, stirring from time to time, until the pigeon peas are tender and have doubled in volume, 25 to 30 minutes. If necessary, add more water to attain a soupy consistency and simmer for 5 more minutes. Remove the pot from the heat and set aside.

Prepare tempering spices: In a separate small skillet, heat 2 tablespoons clarified butter over medium-high heat. When hot, add the cumin seeds and fry until lightly browned and fragrant, about 5 seconds. Add the cloves and asafetida, remove the skillet from the heat, immediately pour the entire mixture into the daal, and stir well. Cover, and allow the seasoning to develop for 5 minutes.

Mix in the lemon juice. Transfer the daal to a serving dish, sprinkle the cilantro on top, and serve.

I captured this image of freshly harvested pigeon pea pods and shelled ones on a visit to Nepal. The farmer, Tek Bahadur Thapa, who showed me the plant explained, "we leave the pods on the plant until they have completely dried up and become leathery before harvesting them." The name "pigeon peas" has nothing to do with pigeons, but they are a well-known protein powerhouse and are one of the most delicious daal with a wonderful flavor.

SPROUTED BEAN SOUP

Makes 4 to 6 servings

Kwaanti ko Ras

According to a time-honored tradition, this delicious soup is prepared from a colorful array of mixed sprouted beans and served in July and August, during the Nepali Sacred Thread Festival (*Janai Purnima* or *Kwaanti Purnima; see page 10*). Traditionally, the sprouts are prepared from a combination of nine different kinds of colorful beans. This wholesome soup is highly nutritious and aids digestion and soothes an upset stomach. Today, *kwaanti* soup is cooked regularly in many Nepali households, and one does not have to wait for festival time to enjoy it. Although this dish can be prepared quickly in a pressure cooker, some cooks believe that the sprouts do not absorb the seasoning in the shorter cooking time. While cooking *kwaanti* there is no need to mash the beans to thicken the soup. Some sprouts, like mung beans, cook faster than others and by the time the whole dish is cooked, they will become mushy, making the dish just the right texture.

2 cups mixed sprouted beans (*see How to sprout beans, page 124*)
2 tablespoons clarified butter (*gheu; page 314*)
4 to 6 large cloves garlic, sliced
2 fresh mild green chilies, split lengthwise
½ teaspoon ground turmeric
Generous pinch ground asafetida
1 medium onion, halved lengthwise and thinly sliced
1 teaspoon ajowan seeds
1 teaspoon salt, adjust to taste
2 medium tomatoes, chopped (about 2 cups)
4 teaspoons minced fresh ginger

1½ teaspoons ground coriander
1 teaspoon garam masalaa (*page 310*)
1 teaspoon ground cumin
½ teaspoon cayenne pepper powder
2 cassia leaves
¼ cup finely chopped cilantro

Tempering spices:
1 tablespoon mustard oil
2 dried red chilies, halved and seeded
⅛ teaspoon jimbu (Nepali aromatic herb; *see page 30*)
½ teaspoon ajowan seeds

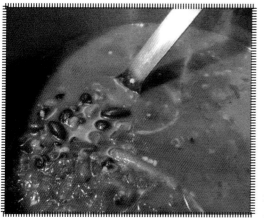

Rinse the sprouted beans in several changes of running water. Discard any seed coatings that come loose and float to the top of the water. Drain and set aside.

Heat the clarified butter in a heavy saucepan over medium-high heat. Add the garlic, green chilies, turmeric, and asafetida and fry for 10 seconds. Add the onion slices and cook, stirring constantly, until lightly browned, about 7 minutes. Mix in the sprouted beans, 1 teaspoon ajowan seeds, and salt and cook, stirring from time to time, until lightly fried and the moisture from the sprouts has evaporated, about 5 minutes. Add the tomatoes, ginger, coriander, garam masalaa, cumin, cayenne pepper powder, and cassia leaves and cook until the tomatoes have softened, about 3 minutes.

(continued next page)

Stir in 4 cups of water and bring the mixture to a boil. Reduce the heat to medium-low, cover the pan, and simmer. Check occasionally to see if the water has evaporated or the beans are soft. If not, add more water and continue cooking, covered. The beans are ready when they are soft when pressed between your fingers, 45 minutes to 1 hour. Remove the beans from the heat and keep covered.

Prepare tempering spices: In a small skillet, heat the mustard oil over medium-high heat until it faintly smokes. Add the dried chilies, jimbu, and ½ teaspoon ajowan seeds and fry until dark brown and highly fragrant, about 5 seconds. Remove the skillet from the heat, immediately pour the entire mixture onto the soup and stir well. Cover and let stand 10 minutes before serving. Transfer the soup to a serving dish, sprinkle the cilantro on top, and serve.

HOW TO SPROUT BEANS AND LENTILS

Mixed sprouted beans are known as *kwanti*, *quaanti*, or *biraula* in Nepal and are cooked a number of ways: in soups, vegetable stir-fries, salads, or with meats. Sprouted beans have been used since ancient times and are an excellent source of protein, vitamins, minerals, and fiber. Making your own sprouts is not as complicated as it might seem; in fact, it is quite easy and straightforward. In choosing the dried beans to sprout, I usually pick organically grown beans, which are available in the US at Indian markets, health food stores, and some specialty shops, but you can use any good quality beans. Keep away from insect-damaged ones, which are marked by holes.

Listed below is the traditional combination of beans, but any other combination may be substituted. Just use a total of 2½ cups of any variety of legumes. I usually prefer smaller beans, as they yield a better flavor.

½ cup whole green mung beans, with skins (*singo moong ko daal*)
½ cup whole black urad beans, with skins (*singo maas ko daal*)
¼ cup dried black-eyed peas (*bodi*)
¼ cup dried whole green or yellow peas (*sukeko thulo kerau — hariyo, pahelo*)
¼ cup dried soybeans, brown or white (*bhatmaas*)
¼ cup dried whole brown chickpeas (*kaalo chana*)

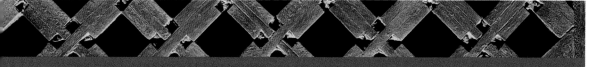

2 tablespoons dried whole yellow chickpeas (*thulo chana*)

2 tablespoons dried kidney beans (*raato bodi*)

2 tablespoons dried fava beans (*bakulla*)

2 tablespoons dried small field peas (*sukeko hariyo saano kerau*)

Cleaning: Inspect the beans carefully before soaking and remove any foreign materials such as small stones, weeds, seeds, soil, or leaves—once sprouted, it is very difficult to pick out and remove these foreign materials. Certain beans, such as whole black urad beans or Nepali field peas need to be cleaned particularly thoroughly, as they often contain tiny black stones. Wash, rinse, and drain the legumes several times until the water runs clear. Discard anything that floats.

Soaking: As a rule, for each cup of beans, use 4 cups of room temperature water. I do not recommend hot water, because it may cause the beans to sour or the outer skins to break. Very cold water will slow the rehydration process. Once the beans are soaked, they will swell and double in size. The soaking water should always be discarded. In a large bowl, mix all the beans together, add enough room temperature water to cover, and leave them to soak for 10 to 12 hours at room temperature.

Sprouting: Drain and rinse the beans thoroughly. Wrap the drained beans in a cheesecloth or muslin cloth and secure it. Place them in a colander or any porous container, as growing sprouts need ventilation. Place the colander in a cupboard, pantry, or any dark, warm, humid place to encourage sprouting. Check them occasionally, and sprinkle with a few drops of water if needed to keep the beans moist, but not wet. Twice each day (morning and evening), remove the beans from the cloth and rinse under running water, drain the beans, tie them back in the cheesecloth, and return to the warm place. Repeat the process until the beans sprout, which may take 2 to 3 days. The size of the sprouts will vary according to the combination of beans. They are ready when the sprouts are about ¼-inch long. Do not allow the sprouts to grow too long, as they will become tasteless. To stop further sprouting, drain completely and store in a plastic bag in the refrigerator.

How to use: When preparing the sprouted beans for cooking, it is not necessary to remove the outer covering of the beans or pluck off the sprouts. Some sprouted beans cook faster than others (mung beans cook faster than other large legumes, for instance). When you are cooking the mixed sprouted beans, the soft textured beans may become mushy by the time the cooking process is finished, which is normal.

Storing Sprouts: Properly stored fresh sprouted beans will keep for up to 1 week in the refrigerator. They should be completely drained because the wet sprouts spoil quickly. Put them in a container or plastic bags lined with an absorbent paper towel before placing them in the refrigerator. Try to use the sprouted beans within a week, when they are most flavorful.

Makes 6 to 7 cups

MUNG BEAN NUGGET STEW

Makes 4 to 6 servings

Moong Titauraa ko Ras

This delicately flavored dish is a traditional favorite of many Nepalese and is cooked regularly in my home. This delicious stew, actually a cross between soup and stew, is prepared with mung bean nuggets (*titauraa*). It is served with plain boiled rice and considered a soothing dish. Commercially prepared ready-made mung bean nuggets are available at Nepali or Indian grocery stores, by the names *mung dal titaura*, *mung dal badi* or *badian*. These nuggets may be substituted, but homemade nuggets are fresher and more flavorful and have an authentic Nepali taste.

3½ tablespoons clarified butter (*gheu, page 314*) or unsalted butter, melted
1½ cups mung bean nuggets, homemade (*opposite page*) or store-bought
2 medium potatoes, peeled and cubed the same size as the nuggets (about 2 cups)
1 tablespoon minced fresh ginger
2 small cloves garlic, chopped

1 teaspoon ground cumin
1 teaspoon ground coriander
½ teaspoon ground turmeric
1 teaspoon salt, adjust to taste
1 medium tomato, chopped (about 1 cup)
2 fresh mild green chilies, split lengthwise
½ cup finely chopped cilantro

Heat 2 tablespoons clarified butter in a heavy saucepan over medium-low heat. When hot, add the nuggets and fry them until golden brown on all sides, stirring constantly. (Watch carefully and do not burn them, as this process only takes a few minutes.) With a slotted spoon, remove the nuggets, drain them on paper towels, and set aside.

Increase the heat to medium, and add the remaining 1½ tablespoons butter and the potatoes to the same pan. Fry until the potatoes are lightly browned, about 5 minutes. Add the ginger, garlic, cumin, coriander, turmeric and salt and mix well. Stir in the tomatoes, green chilies, and half of the cilantro and continue cooking until the tomatoes are soft and all the juices have evaporated, about 5 minutes.

Add 3 cups of cold water and bring to a boil. Add the browned mung bean nuggets, lower the heat to medium-low, and cook, covered, stirring from time to time, until the potatoes are tender, the nuggets soften, and the sauce thickens, about 15 minutes. Transfer the stew to a serving dish, garnish it with the remaining cilantro, and serve.

HOMEMADE MUNG BEAN NUGGETS

Makes 75 to 80 nuggets

Moong ko Titauraa

Mung bean nuggets are common throughout Nepal and usually made at home. These sun-dried nuggets are made from split yellow mung beans. They are easy to prepare and dry quickly because they are small in size. The nuggets can be stored in an airtight container for up to six months. They are delicious in the stew on opposite page.

4 cups split yellow mung beans, without skins (*pahelo moong ko daal*)	1 to 2 tablespoons chickpea flour, or as needed (*besan*)
Generous pinch ground asafetida	Vegetable oil, as needed
½ teaspoon salt	

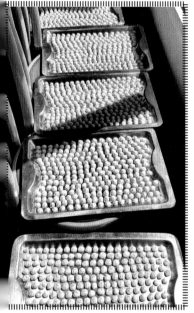

In a large bowl, soak the beans with enough water to cover for at least 6 hours, then drain.

Place the drained beans in a food processor or blender and process, adding a little water at a time as needed, to make a thick, smooth batter that can be shaped. You may have to do this in two batches. Use just enough water to facilitate blending. Transfer the batter to a bowl and mix with your fingers or a fork until the batter is light and spongy, about 2 minutes. If the batter is too watery, add a small amount of chickpea flour to thicken it.

Before shaping the nuggets, oil 1 or 2 trays or baking sheets. With a lightly oiled hand, form grape-size nuggets, and drop them on the tray. Place the nuggets close together, but not so they are touching. Cover the tray with cheesecloth and place in the full sun. The *titauraa* should be completely dried in 1 to 2 days, depending on the amount of sun. Always bring the tray indoors after sunset. Once they are set and slightly firm on top, gently turn them over to expose the bottom sides. Make sure there is no moisture present before storing them. (You may also use a food dehydrator to dry the nuggets, which should not take more than a couple of hours.) Store them in an airtight container at room temperature for up to 6 months.

FLAVORFUL DAAL
Jhaaneko Daal

Makes 4 to 6 servings

Here is a delicious, rich, and filling daal prepared from whole urad and mung beans. This dish tastes even better the next day, as the aromatic spices gently infuse the daal, adding more flavor.

1½ cups whole black urad beans (*singo maas ko daal*)
½ cup whole green mung beans (*singo moong ko daal*)
4 small cloves garlic, minced
1½ teaspoons minced fresh ginger
1 teaspoon ground coriander
1 teaspoon salt, adjust to taste
½ teaspoon ground turmeric
2 cassia leaves
1 tablespoon fresh lemon or lime juice

¼ cup finely chopped cilantro
2 to 3 green onions (white and pale green parts), thinly sliced

Tempering spices:
¼ cup clarified butter (*gheu; page 314*)
2 dried red chilies, stemmed
Small pinch ground asafetida
1 medium onion, halved lengthwise and thinly sliced
1 medium tomato, chopped (about 1 cup)

Combine the urad beans, mung beans, garlic, ginger, coriander, salt, turmeric, cassia leaves, and 6 cups of water in a deep, heavy pot. Bring the mixture to a boil over medium-high heat, uncovered, stirring occasionally to make sure the beans do not boil over. When they come to a full boil, lower the heat, cover, and simmer gently until the mixture is soft and the beans are tender, about 1 hour. Add more water if the liquid evaporates. The beans are cooked when they break easily and flatten when pressed between your fingers. Remove the pot from the heat and set aside, covered.

Prepare tempering spices: In a separate small skillet, heat the clarified butter over medium-high heat. When hot, add the chilies and fry until lightly browned and fragrant, about 5 seconds. Add the asafetida, then immediately add the onion slices and cook until light brown, about 7 minutes. Add the tomatoes and stir until soft, about 2 minutes. Remove the skillet from the heat and immediately pour the entire mixture into the cooked beans and stir well. Bring the pot back to a simmer, covered, for 10 minutes to bring out the flavors. Add more water if the mixture has thickened, to attain a moderately thick consistency.

Mix in the lemon juice. Transfer the daal to a serving dish, sprinkle the cilantro and green onions on top, and serve.

SOYBEAN AND GUNDRUK SOUP

Makes 4 to 6 servings

Gundruk re Bhatmaas ko Jhol

Gundruk ko jhol is a traditional thin soup prepared from fermented dried greens and dried soybeans. It is served with plain boiled rice, millet, or cornmeal porridge (*dhindo, page 179*). The following recipe is particularly flexible, and any ingredients (meat, fish, lentil nuggets, or potatoes) can be added.

1 cup *gundruk* (store bought or *see recipe in sidebar next page*)	1 teaspoon ajowan seeds
2 tablespoons vegetable oil	1 medium tomato, chopped (about 1 cup)
½ cup dried soybeans, yellow or brown (*bhatmaas*)	3 medium cloves garlic, finely chopped
	1½ teaspoons minced fresh ginger
2 dried red chilies, halved and seeded	½ teaspoon ground turmeric
	1 teaspoon salt, adjust to taste

In a medium bowl, soak the *gundruk* in water to cover, for about 10 minutes. Drain thoroughly, chop, and set aside.

Heat the oil in a medium saucepan over medium-low heat. When the oil is hot, but not smoking, add the soybeans and cook, stirring constantly, until light brown, about 2 minutes. Remove them with a slotted spoon and set aside.

In the same pan in the remaining hot oil, fry the dried chilies and ajowan seeds until lightly browned and fragrant, about 5 seconds. Mix in the drained *gundruk* and cook, stirring constantly, for 1 minute. Then add the tomatoes, garlic, ginger, turmeric, and salt and cook until the tomatoes are soft, about 2 minutes.

Mix in 3 cups of water and bring the mixture to a boil. Add the soybeans, reduce the heat to medium-low, cover, and simmer until the soybeans are soft and the liquid has slightly reduced, about 10 minutes. Transfer the soup to a bowl and serve hot.

HOW TO MAKE GUNDRUK (FERMENTED DRIED GREENS)

Makes 1 cup

Gundruk, or fermented dried greens, are a traditional staple in Nepali cuisine. The dish is common in the hilly and mountainous regions of Nepal, where vegetables are difficult to grow due to infertile soil and harsh climates. Gundruk has a slightly sour taste and its flavor varies according to the type of greens used. It can be served plain or with a combination of vegetables, such as soybeans, potatoes, onions, and tomatoes. One of the most popular ways of serving *gundruk* is in a delicious vegetable soup (*see previous page*) served with *dhindo* (millet or cornmeal porridge).

Gundruk is prepared during harvesting time, typically in October and November, when these greens are abundant. The leaves are packed into earthenware pots with narrow necks and a wooden ladle. The pots are then placed in the sun to ferment for several days. The fermented greens are removed and spread on a bamboo or straw mat and dried completely before storing for future use.

Gundruk is sometimes pickled by soaking and gently crushing the leaves and mixing them with pickling spices. It can also be mixed with shredded meat to serve as an appetizer.

Gundruk is rarely found in Kathmandu restaurants, but it is popular in many homes. It is certainly an acquired taste. It can be purchased from Nepali stores, but making *gundruk* is not as complicated as it might seem. In fact, it is quite easy, requiring only a large quantity of greens, a wide-mouth, heavy, clean jar, a spoon, and plenty of sunshine.

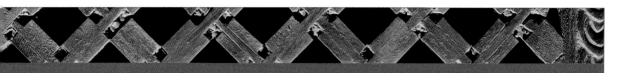

1 large bunch mustard greens or any leafy vegetable*
Nylon netting or cheesecloth
Kitchen twine

To prepare the greens, cut off and discard the thick and tough stem ends and any yellow leaves. Wash the leaves thoroughly and drain. Tear the large leaves into two to three pieces, but keep the small leaves whole. Spread them on a large tray lined with cloth or paper towel. Cover the tray with nylon netting or cheesecloth and secure with kitchen twine. Place the tray in the full sun outdoors or in a well-ventilated indoor area. Turn frequently until the moisture is completely removed and the greens are wilted, 2 to 3 hours.

Using a wooden spoon or your hand, pack the wilted greens into a large clean jar, by placing a small amount of the dried greens at a time in the jar, pushing firmly between layers. Make the leaves as compact as possible, and press down firmly until the pot is filled and has no air bubbles or moisture. Cover with a clean cloth and then a plate or a heavy board. Place the jar outside in the direct sun, or if sun is not present, place it in a warm area (above 70 degree F). Bring the jar indoors in the evening.

The next day, uncover the jar, further compress the greens, cover tightly, and allow it to continue to ferment. Fermentation is usually completed in 6 to 7 days, depending upon the temperature. The first signs of fermentation are yellow-brown bubbles and a sour odor.

Once the greens are fermented, remove them from the jar and drain off any excess water. Spread them out on a clean cloth and let them dry completely in the full sun for 3 to 4 days. Make sure there is no moisture present before storing them in an airtight container.

*Note: *Gundruk* can be made from many leafy green vegetables, including mustard greens (*raayo ko saag* or *tori ko saag*), radish leaves (*mulaa ko paat*), cauliflower leaves (*phool govi ko paat*), cabbage leaves (*banda govi ko paat*), kohlrabi leaves (*gyanth govi ko paat*), and turnip leaves (*shalgam ko paat*).

Chapter 6

FLATBREADS
ROTI

Roti is the generic term for flat unleavened bread in Nepal. These breads are prepared from a variety of ground grains, including wheat, rice, corn, millet, soybean, legumes, and buckwheat. In Nepal, the flour is traditionally ground in a *jaato*, a circular milling or grinding stone on a pivot. Stone grinding is still common in many parts of Nepal, although it has largely been replaced by machine grinding. Nepali bread is as diverse as the country itself and many ethnic groups have their own specialties. There are many ways to prepare *roti*, but it is most commonly griddle-cooked, pan-fried, or deep-fried. Nepali breads range from crispy deep-fried rice-flour bread to flat corn breads, puffed *poori* bread, and thin wheat-flour flatbreads. Their texture varies, ranging from very thin, to thick, chewy, and stuffed. Homemade Nepali breads are easy to make and are usually prepared fresh for each meal. They are served with various gravy-based dishes, such as meat and vegetable curries, lentil dishes, chutneys and pickles, sweet dishes, and yogurt. They can be eaten with almost anything. There is no hard and fast rule as to which bread accompanies which dish. Much depends upon one's taste, the amount of rice served, and how elaborate the meal is.

Most of the flat, unleavened breads are cooked in a heavy cast-iron skillet known as a *taabaa* or *taawaa*, which when heated on a stovetop absorbs heat quickly and distributes it evenly, so the bread will cook thoroughly. Its concave shape holds the oil at the bottom of the pan where it is needed, so the griddle-cooked bread can be cooked with a small amount of oil. If you do not have a *taabaa* you may use a cast-iron griddle or skillet.

Rolling *roti* into a perfect circle is a challenge at first. However, your skill will improve with practice. The dough is usually rolled out on a round wood, stone, or marble platform, known as a *chaukaa*. The *belnaa*, a rolling pin, is usually made of wood. Nepalese rolling pins usually have tapered ends, and are suited for rolling out thin and round breads. They provide a good grip and are the perfect weight, but a regular rolling pin will work fine.

For my everyday simple *roti* recipes, I prefer to use *atta* or chapatti flour (durum wheat), which is a finely ground whole wheat flour made from a low-gluten wheat. This flour makes dough that is easy to knead and roll, and bread with a light texture. In the US it is found in Indian grocery stores, some supermarkets, and on-line stores. If it is not available, you can substitute a mixture of all-purpose white flour and whole wheat flour as indicated in the recipes.

Whole-Wheat Rotis / *Sukkhaa-Roti*

WHOLE-WHEAT FLATBREAD

Makes 12 *roti*

Sukkhaa-Roti

Sukkhaa-roti, also called *phulkaa-roti*, or just *roti*, is a thin unleavened flatbread prepared from durum whole-wheat flour. It is the most basic Nepali bread, very light textured, easy to prepare, and usually cooked just before serving. Typically, the dough is rolled into thin circles and cooked on a dry Nepali cast-iron griddle (*taabaa*), but any regular griddle that has even heat distribution can be used. Expert cooks can roll and cook the bread at the same time, but the dough can also be rolled and kept covered before cooking. The bread usually puffs up during cooking and should be immediately basted with butter to maintain moistness. It is served with almost any combination of vegetables, gravy-based meat curries, lentils, and pickles.

2½ cups chapatti (*atta*) flour; or 1 cup whole wheat flour mixed with 1½ cups all-purpose white flour, plus ½ cup for rolling	½ teaspoon salt 1 tablespoon vegetable oil 3 to 4 tablespoons clarified butter (*gheu*)

In a medium-size bowl, combine the flour and salt. Add the oil and mix by hand until all ingredients are well-combined. Gradually add ¾ to 1 cup of water, a little at a time, to form a dough that holds together. Knead well in the bowl until the dough is smooth and elastic, about 5 minutes. The dough should be soft but not sticky. If it is too sticky, sprinkle some flour over the dough and knead some more. Cover with plastic wrap or a damp towel and set aside at room temperature for 25 to 30 minutes.

Remove the dough from the bowl and knead on a flat surface until soft and pliable, about 5 minutes. Divide the dough into fifteen portions, shape each into a ball, and coat each with a little flour. With a rolling pin, flatten out one of the balls and roll it into a 6-inch circle about ¼-inch thick, using only enough flour to keep the dough from sticking (adding too much flour will toughen the bread). Repeat with the remaining dough. Cover the unused balls and rolled circles with damp kitchen towels while working.

Heat a cast-iron griddle over medium-high heat. Test for readiness by sprinkling a few drops of water on the griddle. If the drops bounce and sputter, it is ready, but if the water evaporates immediately, it is too hot, so adjust the heat accordingly. Place the circles of dough on the griddle, one at a time and cook until the top is slightly dry, and small bubbles begin to form, moving it frequently. When the underside is dotted with light brown dots, turn it over. At this stage, the bread will slowly start to puff up. Take a kitchen towel and gently press down on the surface of the bread until the whole bread puffs up. Turn it over again and cook the other side until light brown spots starts to appear. The entire process should take less than 3 minutes. Spread the *roti* with clarified butter, transfer to a covered dish, and keep warm while you cook the rest of the *roti*.

FLAKY FLATBREAD

Makes 10 *roti*

Tinkune-roti

Tinkune-roti, also called *patre-roti* or *parauthaa-roti*, is a triangular-shaped flatbread with multiple layers. During preparation, clarified butter is added in three stages of the cooking process. First, a small amount of butter is added to the dough; in the second stage, butter is applied during the rolling and folding of the dough; finally, the bread is basted in clarified butter while cooking. *Tinkune-roti* has a slightly crispy crust outside and very soft layer inside. This variety of bread is richer, slightly thicker, and more filling than most flatbreads.

3 cups chapatti (*atta*) flour or 1½ cups whole wheat flour mixed with 1½ cups all-purpose white flour, plus an extra ½ cup for rolling	1 teaspoon salt 6 tablespoons clarified butter (*gheu; page 314*), at room temperature

In a medium-size bowl, combine the flour and salt. Add 1 tablespoon of the clarified butter and mix well by hand until all ingredients are well combined. Gradually add 1 to 1¼ cups of water to form a dough that holds together. Knead well in the bowl until the dough is smooth and elastic, about 5 minutes. The dough should be soft but not sticky. If it is too sticky, sprinkle some flour over it and knead some more. Cover with plastic wrap or a damp kitchen towel and set aside at room temperature for 25 to 30 minutes.

Remove the dough from the bowl and knead on a flat surface until it is soft and pliable, about 5 minutes. Roll the dough into a rope about 2 inches in diameter and divide it into 10 equal portions. Roll each portion into a ball and coat it with a little flour. Flatten a ball of dough and, with a rolling pin, roll it into a 6- to 7-inch circle. Lightly brush the top with melted clarified butter (do not use too much butter, as it will make the dough too slippery and the butter will leak out when the bread is re-rolled). Fold the circle into a half-circle and apply more clarified butter. Fold in half again to form a small triangle. With the rolling pin, roll the triangle 6 to 7 inches long, taking care to maintain its triangular shape. Place each rolled piece of dough in a single layer on a tray and cover with damp kitchen towels. Repeat until all the dough is used up.

Heat an ungreased cast-iron griddle over medium-high heat. Test for readiness by sprinkling a few drops of water on the griddle. If the drops bounce and sputter, it is ready, but if the water evaporates immediately, it is too hot, so adjust the heat accordingly. Place a piece of rolled-out dough

on the griddle and cook until the top is dry and the bottom is dotted with brown spots, about 1 minute. Turnover, brush 1 teaspoon of melted clarified butter around the edges and on the surface, and rotate frequently. Flip again and add another teaspoon of the butter. At this stage, the flaky layers will separate, puff up slightly, and the outer layers will become crispy. Rotate and flip the bread frequently until it is light golden brown on both sides. The entire process should take less than 3 minutes per *roti*. When cooked, transfer the bread to a covered dish and keep warm while you cook the remaining roti.

POORI BREAD

Makes 12 to 14 5-inch *poori*

Poori, pronounced *"poo-ree,"* is a deep-fried puffed bread, generally prepared from wheat flour. The dough can be prepared in advance, but rolling and frying should be done just before serving. *Poori* are fried in bubbling hot oil and puff up into steam-filled, light-brown balloons. *Poori* tastes best if eaten piping hot, puffed up with a crispy outside and a moist inside. Though it starts to lose its puffiness and becomes somewhat chewy and tough when cold, *poori* is still quite tasty when eaten that way. It is one of the most popular breads and a classic accompaniment to any Nepali meal. It is also eaten during family celebrations and religious festivals including for *Naivedya*, sacred food that is ritualistically offered to deities during worship. At the same time, it is often packed for picnics and long journeys as a good traveling bread.

2½ cups chapatti flour (*atta*) or 1½ cup whole wheat flour mixed with 1½ cups all- purpose white flour, plus an extra ½ cup for rolling	½ teaspoon salt 2 to 3 cups vegetable oil

In a medium-size bowl, combine the flour and salt. Add 1 tablespoon of oil and mix by hand until all ingredients are well combined. Gradually add ¾ to 1 cup of water to form a dough that holds together. Knead in the bowl until the dough is smooth and elastic, about 5 minutes. The dough should be moderately stiff. If the dough is too sticky, add 1 or 2 tablespoons of flour; if it feels too firm, add a little water and knead some more. Cover with plastic wrap or a damp kitchen towel and set aside at room temperature for 25 to 30 minutes.

When the dough is well rested, place it on a flat surface and knead it until pliable, about 5 minutes. Roll the dough into a rope about 2 inches in diameter and divide it into twelve to fourteen equal portions. Roll each portion into a ball and coat it with a little flour. Flatten the balls with a rolling pin and roll into 4- to 5-inch circles, about ¼ inch thick. Keep the dough covered with damp towels while working. Place the circles on a tray so they are not touching each other.

Heat the oil in a deep skillet over medium-high heat until it reaches 350 to 375 degrees F (*see Note below*). Test for readiness by placing a small piece of dough into the hot oil. If it bubbles and rises to the surface immediately, it is ready. Place the dough circles into the oil, one piece at a time. The dough will sink to the bottom, but will immediately rise up. Use light pressure with the back of a slotted spoon to submerge the dough until it puffs. Then, turn it over to brown the second side. The second side of *poori* is slightly heavier, so fry it longer until golden. Remove the *poori* with a slotted spoon and drain on paper towels. Repeat the procedure with the remaining dough. Serve immediately, if possible, or keep warm, covered, until ready to serve.

Note: While frying, be careful to keep the oil at 350 to 375 degrees F for even cooking. If the oil is too hot, the *poori* will brown too fast and may remain doughy and uncooked inside. If the oil is not hot enough, it will not puff up and the dough will absorb a lot of fat.

Variation:
SPINACH POORI
Add ½ teaspoon cayenne pepper, ¼ teaspoon turmeric, ¼ teaspoon ground coriander, and ¼ teaspoon ground cumin to the flour and salt. When you add the tablespoon of oil, stir in 1½ cups chopped fresh spinach, 2 chopped mild green chilies, and 1 tablespoon minced fresh ginger. Proceed as directed above.

SWAARI FLATBREAD

Swaari Roti

Makes 12 to 14 *rotis*

Swaari is a delicious, soft, fried bread prepared from all-purpose white flour. The thin bread is white in color, very chewy and prepared with just three ingredients: flour, oil, and water. It is hand-stretched, fried in hot oil and removed promptly before it starts to get crispy, brown, or over fried. It is served at room temperature, folded in half or into a triangle. This bread is usually made for celebrations and festivals and bought from sweet shops. *Swaari* is often eaten with *jilphi* (pretzel-shaped syrup-filled loops, *page 286*). When served with *Manbhog Haluwaa* (Wheat Flour *Pudding, page 277*) it becomes a delicious breakfast or snack food.

> 2½ cups all-purpose white flour (*maida ko pitho*)
> 2 to 3¼ cups vegetable oil

In a medium-size bowl, combine the flour and 3 tablespoons of the oil and mix by hand until thoroughly combined. Gradually add ¾ to 1 cup of water, until the dough holds together. Knead well in the bowl until the dough is smooth and elastic, about 5 minutes. The dough should be soft but not sticky. If it is too sticky, add a tablespoon of flour; if it feels too firm, add a little water and knead some more. Cover with plastic wrap or a damp kitchen towel and set aside at room temperature for 1 hour or more.

When the dough is well rested, knead it on a flat surface with the heel of your hand until you have a pliable and smooth dough, about 5 minutes. Roll the dough into a rope about 2 inches in diameter and divide it into 12 to 14 equal portions. Roll each portion into a ball. Lightly oil your hands and stretch the dough balls between your palms to create 5-inch uneven circles about ⅛-inch thick. (Alternatively, place the dough on a greased work surface and use a rolling pin.) Keep the dough covered with damp towels while working. As you work, place the stretched dough in a single layer on a tray.

Heat the remaining 2 to 3 cups of oil in a deep skillet over medium-high heat until it reaches 350 to 375 degrees F. Test for readiness by placing a small piece of dough into the hot oil. If it bubbles and rises to the surface immediately, it is ready. Gently place the circles of dough into the oil, one at a time. The dough will sink at first, and when it rises, turn it quickly and fry for 30 to 40 seconds more. Remove from the oil with a slotted spoon while still white and soft, and drain on paper towels. Fold it in half and keep covered until ready to serve. Repeat with the remaining dough.

MUNG BEAN FLATBREAD
Moong Daal ko Roti

Makes 10 to 12 *rotis*

This crisp, griddle-cooked bread prepared from split yellow mung beans is both filling and nutritious. It is easy to prepare, but it requires some practice to make into perfect round shapes. Nepali cooks usually use their fingers to spread the batter on the griddle.

> 2½ cups split yellow mung beans, without skins (*pahelo moong ko daal*)
> 2 fresh mild green chilies, minced to a fine paste
> 1 tablespoon minced fresh ginger
>
> ¼ teaspoon ground turmeric
> Salt, adjust to taste
> Small pinch ground asafetida
> ¾ cup clarified butter (*gheu, page 314*)

In a large bowl, soak the mung beans for at least 4 hours or overnight. Place the drained beans in a food processor or blender and process, adding up to 1 cup of fresh water to make a semi-thick puree with no grainy bits. (You may have to do this in two batches.) Transfer the puree to a bowl and mix it with the chilies, ginger, turmeric, salt, and asafetida. The batter should be easily spreadable. If the batter is too thick, add 1 to 2 tablespoons more water and beat with a fork or your hand until fluffy. Cover the bowl and allow to rest at room temperature for at least 10 minutes.

Heat a cast-iron griddle over medium-high heat. Test the griddle for readiness by splashing on a few drops of water. If the drops bounce and sputter, it is ready. If the water evaporates immediately, it is too hot. Adjust the heat accordingly. Melt ½ teaspoon of clarified butter on the griddle. Pour ½ to ¾ cup of batter onto the center of the griddle. Moving the back of a spoon or your fingers in a circular motion, spread the batter evenly into a 5-inch circle. The batter should cover the griddle in a thin layer. Cook until the edges start to crisp and the underside starts to brown, about 2 minutes. Turn the *roti* over and drizzle 2 teaspoons of butter around the edges and top. Rotate and turn the *roti* frequently, adding more butter, until it is browned on both sides and slightly crispy. Transfer to a serving dish and keep warm. Repeat with the remaining batter. If the batter starts to dry up while you are cooking, add teaspoons of water until smooth. Serve warm or at room temperature.

POTATO-STUFFED FLATBREAD

Makes 12 *rotis*

Aalu-Roti

Aalu-roti is a delicious stuffed bread cooked on a griddle. The filling consists of spiced mashed potato, but any combination of vegetables, such as cauliflower, peas, spinach, radish, and homemade paneer cheese can also be used. This flatbread is not difficult to make, but it does take time. Experts can roll the dough, stuff, and cook simultaneously and this can be mastered with a little practice. However, the task can be simplified if you have someone to cook while you roll and assemble. These flatbreads can be prepared ahead of time and reheated just before serving. They are served as part of a meal or as part of a light lunch with a variety of chutneys, pickles, and yogurt.

Dough:
3 cups chapatti flour (*atta*) or 1½ cups whole
   wheat flour mixed with 1½ cups all-purpose
   white flour, plus an extra ½ cup for rolling
½ teaspoon ajowan seeds
½ teaspoon salt
1 tablespoon vegetable oil
½ cup melted clarified butter (*gheu; page 314*)

Potato Stuffing:
3 to 4 medium potatoes
1 tablespoon vegetable oil
1 medium onion, finely chopped (about 1 cup)

2 fresh mild green chilies, finely chopped
1 tablespoon minced fresh ginger
2 large cloves garlic, minced
1 teaspoon ground cumin
Salt, adjust to taste
½ teaspoon Nepali garam masalaa (*page 310*)
¼ teaspoon turmeric powder
½ cup finely chopped cilantro
3 to 4 green onions (white and pale green
   parts), finely chopped
2 tablespoons fresh lemon or lime juice

Make the dough: In a medium-size bowl, combine the flour, ajowan seeds, and salt. Add the oil and mix by hand until thoroughly combined. Gradually add 1 to 1¼ cups of water, a little at a time, to form a dough that holds together. Knead well in the bowl until the dough is smooth and elastic, about 5 minutes. The dough should be moderately stiff. If the dough is too sticky, add 1 or 2 tablespoons of flour; if it feels too firm, add a little water and knead it some more. Cover with plastic wrap or a damp kitchen towel and set aside at room temperature for 25 to 30 minutes or until ready to use.

Make the potato stuffing: Place the potatoes in a medium-size saucepan with enough water to cover, and bring to boil over high heat. Reduce the heat to low, cover the pan, and cook until the potatoes are tender, about 20 minutes. Drain, and when cool enough to handle, peel and mash the potatoes completely. Set aside. Heat the oil in a saucepan over medium-high heat. When the oil is hot, but not smoking, add the onions and cook until soft, about 5 minutes. Add the green chilies, ginger, garlic, cumin, salt, garam masalaa, and turmeric and cook for 1 more minute. Stir in the mashed potatoes, and cook until the moisture has evaporated. Remove the pan from the heat and stir in the cilantro, green onions, and lemon juice. Transfer the mixture to a bowl and let it cool to room temperature before using.

Assemble the flatbreads: When the dough is well rested, knead it on a flat surface until pliable. Divide the dough into twenty-four equal portions. Roll each piece into a ball, coat it with a little flour, and flatten slightly on the work surface. Using a rolling pin, roll each dough piece into a 4-inch circle, making sure the middle is thicker than the edges. Set aside on a tray.

Place 2 to 2½ tablespoons of the potato mixture in the center of one circle of dough and gently spread it over the dough leaving a ½-inch margin. Place another circle on top and press the edges together, pinching to seal, making sure the filling is secure inside. Gently reroll the stuffed dough into a 7-inch circle of even thickness. Make sure the stuffing does not come out while rolling. If it pokes out, seal it with a piece of dough. Repeat the process with the remaining dough and stuffing. As you assemble the breads, keep them on a tray covered with a kitchen towel.

Cook the flatbreads: Heat an ungreased cast-iron griddle over medium-high heat. Test for readiness by placing a few drops of water on the griddle. If they bounce and sputter, it is ready, but if the water evaporates immediately, it is too hot, so adjust the heat accordingly. Carefully place one of the stuffed breads on the griddle and cook for about 1 minute. Turn it over, brush 1 teaspoon of clarified butter on the edges and top. Flip and cook the underside until it is dotted with light brown spots. Brush 1 teaspoon of clarified butter over the surface. Rotate and turn the bread frequently until it is lightly browned on both sides. The entire process should take less than 3 minutes. Transfer the bread to a covered dish and keep it warm while you cook the remaining breads. Serve warm or at room temperature.

BUCKWHEAT FLATBREAD

Makes 8 to 10 *rotis*

Phaapar ko Roti

Phaapar ko Roti is a delicious light gray-colored bread prepared with buckwheat flour. The flatbread is made from a smooth batter that is spiced and cooked on a griddle similar to the way pancakes are cooked. It is delicious by itself, or can be served as part of a light lunch accompanied with a combination of vegetables, yogurt, and buttermilk.

---

2 cups buckwheat flour
2 to 3 fresh mild green chilies, minced
1½ teaspoons minced fresh ginger
1 small clove garlic, minced
1 teaspoon salt, adjust to taste

⅛ teaspoons timmur (Nepali pepper; *see page 31*), finely ground with a mortar and pestle
½ cup clarified butter (*gheu; page 314*)

In a medium-size bowl, combine the flour, chilies, ginger, garlic, salt, and timmur. Gradually add ¾ to 1 cup of water, and beat well with a fork to make a smooth batter without lumps. Continue beating with a fork until fluffy. Cover and set aside at room temperature for 10 to 15 minutes. If the batter thickens, add more water. The batter should have a semi-thick consistency, and should spread evenly when poured on the griddle.

Heat a heavy griddle or nonstick skillet over medium-high heat. Test the griddle for readiness by splashing on a few drops of water. If the drops bounce and sputter, it is ready. If the water evaporates immediately, it is too hot. Adjust the heat accordingly. Pour about ½ cup of the batter onto the hot griddle. Tilt the pan to distribute the batter, forming a circle. Cook until the edges start to brown and the top is covered with air bubbles. Pour 1 teaspoon of the clarified butter around the edges and over the top. Gently flip and cook the other side. Add 1 more teaspoon of butter and continue cooking until golden brown. Remove from the heat and serve immediately. Repeat with the remaining batter.

BUCKWHEAT / PHAAPAR

Phaapar is a very important food crop in Nepal and commonly grown in the higher mountainous regions and to some extent in the Middle Hills, Inner Terai, and Sub-Terai areas. Buckwheat is also grown in regions where rice cultivation is impossible due to high altitudes. In the most remote mountain regions of Nepal such as Humla, Manang, Mustang, Jumla, Dolpa, and Baitadi, local people have been using buckwheat as a traditional diet staple for centuries. Buckwheat is also widely grown in the mid-hill area such as Lamjung, Gorkha, Myagdi and Parbat.

This photo of fields of buckwheat was captured when I visited the Chitwan National Park area (Terai) of Nepal.

Although the name buckwheat sounds like a wheat crop, it is not related to wheat; instead, it is related to rhubarb and sorrel. According to Nepal Agriculture Research, buckwheat is an annual fast-growing herbaceous plant that is ready to harvest within 90-100 days of seeding. The plant bears bright green heart shaped leaves, hollow stems with beautiful pink and white flowers, and when pollinated it produces seeds. The seeds are triangular in shape with rounded bottoms and upon maturity, change from green to red-brown. The outer husks are removed and ground into flour. Generally, the buckwheat grain produced in the mountains are larger than those produced in the Terai area. Buckwheat crops are not susceptible to disease or damaged by insects.

There are two types of buckwheat cultivated in the hills and mountains of Nepal:

Common buckwheat

Botanical name: *Fagopyrum esculentum*   Nepali name: *Mithe Phaapar*

The flour from common buckwheat is used preparing bread (pancake-like phaapar ko roti), buckwheat dhindo (Nepali-style polenta), *puwaa*, *phulaura* (buckwheat fritters), buckwheat finger chips, unleavened flatbread, thick bread (pancake-style *pahadi* bread), beverages, and medicinal food. The dried leaves of the plants are used in soup. The young green buckwheat leaves (*phaapar ko saag)* are also cooked as green vegetables.

Tatary buckwheat

Botanical name: *Fagopyrum tataricum Geartn*   Nepali name: *Tite Phaapar*

Tatary buckwheat is capable of growing under very cold climate condition in the higher hills. Although the seeds are bitter in taste, they can serve as food for people living in the hills during scarcity days. It is believed that the leaf and flower play a role in treating intestinal problems, hemorrhages, and high blood pressure.

Sweet Rice Flatbread / Sel-Rot

SWEET RICE FLATBREAD

Makes 10 to 12 *rotis*

Sel-Roti

Sel-Roti does not need any introduction in Nepali cuisine—it is one of the most "uniquely Nepali" dishes, a sweet rice bread, distinct from any other breads of the world. *Sel-Roti* resembles a large thin puffed-up doughnut and has a crispy texture and reddish-brown color. It is popular as a festive bread for many different occasions.

Traditional Nepali cooks grind the soaked rice in a heavy rectangular stone mortar and pestle (*silauto-bacchaa*), which produces a perfectly textured batter, because it provides the right pressure while grinding. I grind the rice in a blender for convenience. Traditional versions of *Sel-Roti* require the batter to be deep-fried in pure clarified butter (gheu), but now vegetable oil has replaced gheu for a lighter version. Sel-Roti is delicious by itself, but can also be served with plain yogurt, fried vegetables, and pickles. It tastes best fresh, and becomes tough and chewy once it gets cold, although it still tastes good.

3 cups white rice	¾ cup unsalted butter, melted
1 medium very ripe banana	¼ cup rice flour, or as needed
1 cup sugar, or to taste	4 to 5 cups vegetable oil

In a large bowl, soak the rice in water to cover for at least 4 hours or overnight. Drain and place in a blender or food processor with the banana, sugar, and butter and process, adding up to 1¼ cups of water to make a semi-thick puree with no grainy bits. (You may have to do this in two batches.) Transfer the batter to a mixing bowl, and beat with a fork until fluffy, 2 to 3 minutes. Cover with plastic wrap or a damp towel and set aside to rest for 20 to 25 minutes.

When the batter is well-rested, mix it again. The consistency should be similar to heavy cream. If it seems too thick, gradually add 1 to 2 tablespoons of water; if it feels too thin, add 1 to 2 tablespoons of rice flour and mix well.

Heat the oil in a skillet over medium-high heat until it reaches 350 to 375 degrees F (*see Note*). Test for readiness by placing a small drop of the batter into the hot oil. If it bubbles and rises to the surface immediately, it is ready. Pour about ¼ cup of batter into the oil slowly, making a large circle (pour the batter from a cup or a pastry bag with a medium-size opening). Stretch and move the batter using a wooden spoon or chopstick to create the circle. As the *sel-roti* puffs and rises, push it into the oil with the back of a spoon until it is light golden brown. Flip and fry the second side until golden brown. Remove with a slotted spoon and drain it on paper towels. Repeat with the rest of the batter.

Note: While frying *sel-roti*, be careful to keep the oil at 350 to 375 degrees F for even cooking. If the oil is too hot, the batter will brown too quickly and the insides may remain undercooked and doughy. If the oil is not hot enough, the batter will absorb a lot of oil. Occasionally check the batter as it may thicken while you are cooking. Add a small amount of water to adjust the consistency.

STEAMED RICE BREAD

Yomari

Makes 10 to 12 breads

Yomari or *yohmari* is a delicious stuffed and steamed bread. The fillings can change according to family preference, varying from milk fudge (*khuwaa*) or spicy ground meat and bean paste, to sesame seeds or coconut. The stuffed bread is molded into different shapes that often resemble animals, fruits, ceremonial lamp stands, and figurines of gods and goddesses. The most popular shape is the dough formed like a pointed fig fruit. The preparation of *yomari* is a family affair and even small children help to mold the dough. It is eaten warm or at room temperature, by itself or with beverages.

---

3 cups rice flour
1 to 1½ cups boiling water, or as needed
¾ cup sesame seeds
3 tablespoons unsweetened shredded
   coconut

¾ cup dark brown sugar
Vegetable oil

In a large bowl, combine the rice flour and 1 cup of boiling water. When cool enough to handle, knead the dough until smooth and pliable. If the dough is too firm, knead in 1 teaspoon of water. Cover with plastic wrap or a damp towel and set aside to rest at room temperature for 20 to 25 minutes.

While the dough is resting, prepare the filling. Heat a small skillet over medium-low heat. Toast the sesame seeds, stirring and shaking the skillet, until lightly browned and aromatic. Remove from the heat and cool. Use a spice grinder to grind the sesame seeds into a fine powder. Pour into a small bowl. Add the coconut to the grinder and grind into a fine powder. In the small bowl, mix the ground sesame seeds with the ground coconut, brown sugar, and 1 cup of water. Place the mixture in a small saucepan over medium-low heat and simmer, stirring frequently, until the mixture thickens, about 5 minutes. Remove from the heat and set aside.

When you are ready to proceed, place the rested dough on a flat surface and knead for 1 to 2 minutes. With lightly oiled hands, divide the dough into ten to twelve equal portions. Shape each piece into an oval and form a small pocket with your finger. Place about 2 teaspoons of the filling inside each and pinch the dough to seal tightly. Once sealed, you can create any shape.

YOMARI ORIGINS AND TRADITIONS

Yomari is a delicious steamed bread with mouth-watering filling made from a new harvest rice flour dough. According to my good friend and cookbook writer, Hind M. Vaidya, in her book, *Nepalese Cookery*, this steamed bread plays a very important role in many auspicious ceremonies in the Newar community. Newars are one of the oldest ethnic groups in the capital valley of Kathmandu, and they have an important cultural connection to Nepal. They are well known for their festivities and preparing unlimited sumptuous feasts. The name *yomari* originates from the Newari language: "*yoh*" means "to love" or "to like," and "*mari*" means "bread dish." Ms. Vaidya says, "Literally as the name says, it is one of the most loved and liked steamed bread with stuffing."

She also highlights a popular teasing song, where a group of young children go around their neighborhood from house-to-house asking for steamed bread and singing a *yomari* song on the special festival of *Yohmari Punhi*. The customary traditional song is, "*yoh mari chwamu, ukke dunne chakku, byuma lyassi, mabyuma buricha*" ("the bread is pointed, the filling is sweet, if you give me a bread, you will be a pretty lady, if you don't, ugly ...").

Yomari is a very popular festive dish, traditionally prepared during post-harvest celebration of *Yomari Punhi* or *Dhanya Purnima*. The celebration is observed during the full moon from December to January. During the festival, the people of Kathmandu worship the goddess of grains, Annapurna, for good harvest and enjoy a grand feast after all the hard work of the harvesting season. *Yomari* is prepared and offered ritualistically to the gods. Although the festival has its roots in the Newar farming community, today it is observed in almost every Newari home in Kathmandu and surrounding areas. *Yomari* is also prepared during the celebration of children's birthdays, where a *yomari* garland is used to honor the child. *Yomari* is widely prepared and served at many other auspicious occasions, such as the rice feeding ceremony of a child (*paasne*), *Dhau-Baji* (celebration of expectant mother before childbirth), as a *sagun* food (auspicious food representing good luck, fortune, and good health), Janku celebrations (celebration of old age), Indra Jatra (*samay baji* food tower festival), new house moving celebrations, and many more.

If there are any cracks in the surface, be sure to seal them. Cover with plastic wrap or a damp kitchen towel while forming the remaining breads.

Fill the bottom of a vegetable steamer with water and bring it to a boil over high heat. Grease the steamer tray with oil. Arrange the *yomari* on the steamer tray(s), making sure that there is ½ inch of space between each, allowing the steam to circulate. You may have to do this in batches. Place the steamer trays on the steamer, cover, and steam for 8 to 10 minutes or until cooked and they appear glazed. Carefully transfer the *yomari* to a serving dish and serve hot.

RICE FLOUR FLATBREAD WITH VEGETABLES

Chataamari Roti

Makes 10 to 12 *rotis*

Chataamari is a traditional Newari rice flour bread, made from a rice flour batter topped with seasoned ground meats, eggs, vegetables, or just plain sprinkled with sugar. It is also referred to as Newari pizza, rice pancake, or Newari crepe. It has become a popular snack food or can be served as a light lunch. The bread is delicious plain or can be served with vegetables, pickles, and chutney. Here is my version with a vegetable topping.

---

2 cups rice flour (*chaamal ko pitho*)
¾ cup urad bean flour (*maas ko pitho*)
1 teaspoon salt, adjust to taste
2 medium tomatoes, chopped (about 2 cups)
1 medium red onion, finely chopped (about 1 cup)

1 small red or green bell pepper, cored and finely chopped (about 1 cup)
4 to 5 green onions (white and pale green parts), finely chopped
½ cup finely chopped cilantro
2 to 3 fresh hot green chilies, chopped
½ cup clarified butter (gheu), melted

In a medium-size bowl, combine both flours and the salt. Gradually add ¼ to ½ cup of water, beating well to make a smooth batter. Beat with a fork to make it fluffy. Cover with plastic wrap or a damp towel and set batter aside at room temperature for 15 to 20 minutes.

If the rested batter has thickened, stir in 1 or 2 tablespoons of water. It should be thin and spread evenly when poured on the griddle. In a separate bowl, combine the tomatoes, onions, bell pepper, green onions, cilantro, and green chilies and set aside.

Heat a cast-iron griddle over medium-high heat. Test the griddle for readiness by splashing on a few drops of water. If the drops bounce and sputter, then it is ready. If the water evaporates immediately, it is too hot. Adjust the heat accordingly. Brush the griddle lightly with butter. For each *chataamari*, pour about ½ cup of the batter into the center of the griddle. Swirl the pan and spread the batter into a 5-inch circle. Sprinkle ½ cup of the mixed vegetables evenly over the batter and press lightly with a spoon. Cover the pan with a lid, adjust the heat to medium-low, and cook until the edges start to crisp and the underside starts to brown, about 3 minutes. Drizzle 2 teaspoons of clarified butter around the edges. Rotate the bread frequently and cook, covered, until lightly browned and slightly crispy, about 2 minutes. *Chataamari* are only cooked on one side, so remove it from the heat, fold in half, and serve immediately or transfer it to a covered dish to keep warm while you cook the remaining batter.

FRIED BREAD BALLS

Makes about 20 balls

Gwaramari

Gwaramari is a smooth, fluffy, soft and deep-fried bread that goes very well with a warm milky cup of morning tea. These round breads are a very popular Newari breakfast dish. *"Gwaramari"* literally means "a round bread" in the Newari language. If you are walking around Kathmandu valley during morning hours, you will see every local *haluwai pasal* (sweet shop) and street food vendors busy preparing and serving piping hot *gwaramari* bread.

1¼ cups all-purpose flour
1 teaspoon baking powder
¼ teaspoon salt

1 tablespoon sugar
¼ teaspoon ground turmeric
3 to 4 cups vegetable oil, for frying

In a medium-size mixing bowl, whisk together flour, baking powder, salt, sugar, and turmeric. Gradually add ¾ to 1 cup of lukewarm water, stirring continuously, until the mixture has become a thick smooth paste. Cover the bowl and refrigerate overnight. When the dough is well rested, it will thicken slightly, mix again.

Heat the oil in a large skillet over medium-high heat until it reaches 350 degree F. Test the readiness of the oil by dropping a little dough into the hot oil. If it rises to the surface immediately, it is ready. Form the soft dough into balls using 1½ tablespoons of mixture for each. Drop the balls into the hot oil, five or six at a time. Flip them over a few times, until they are cooked through, puffed, golden brown and crisp outside, about 4 minutes. Remove with a slotted spoon, draining excess oil, and place on a paper towel-lined plate. Repeat with the remaining batter.

Chapter 7

VEGETABLE DISHES

TARKAARI

Nepal has a complex topography with hills and flatlands, and the Kathmandu valley is renowned for the seasonal vegetables grown in its fertile soil. Vegetables (*tarkaari*) are one of the most important foods in the daily Nepali diet, and a typical Nepali meal consists of rice, lentils, and some kind of side vegetable dish.

The most common vegetables include green beans, cauliflower, cabbage, eggplant, greens, okra, potatoes, Nepali radish, squash, and tomatoes along with many other seasonal local vegetables. Generally, green leafy vegetables such as spinach and mustard greens are eaten daily in large quantities whenever available. Vegetables are also made into pickles, salads, snacks, and even desserts.

Due to the scarcity of cultivated land in many rural and hilly areas in different parts of Nepal, fresh vegetables are limited, so locals tend to consume root vegetables as well as dried and fermented vegetables.

During the peak growing season, you may see a local farmer heading to the market balancing a bamboo pole across his shoulders, holding two wicker woven baskets full of freshly picked vegetables. In Nepali *tarkaari* bazaars (vegetable markets) one can witness the proud skills of vendors arranging every tiny space with a dramatic display

of vegetables and fruits. Greens, such as spinach, mustard, fresh coriander, and garden cress are neatly tied in small bundles and piled up in a beautiful way. A variety of dry vegetables such as potatoes, onions, and shallots are skillfully arranged in wicker trays, baskets, or jute-burlap sacks. On many street corners, vendors set up small stands with fresh fruits and vegetables such as green gooseberries, lapsi fruit (hog plum), guava, or tangerines. The vegetables sold in the markets are weighed in a hand-held local scale known as a *taraaju*, which comes in a variety of sizes and forms. Measurements are done in kilograms. Most Nepali households do not store vegetables, so they are bought fresh every day.

SPINACH WITH GARDEN CRESS

Makes 4 to 6 servings

Chamsoor-Paalungo Saag

Spinach (*paalungo ko saag*) has long been one of the most beloved vegetables in Nepal and is served with almost every Nepali meal. *Chamsoor-Paalungo Saag*, a mild flavored spinach cooked with peppery garden cress, is a favorite combination. Garden cress (*chamsoor*) has long tender stems, pointed narrow leaves, and a spicy flavor. Cress can be cooked by itself, like any green, but tastes best when combined with other greens. If garden cress is not available substitute watercress, which is available in the produce section of regular grocery stores or at Asian markets.

3 tablespoons mustard oil	2 small bunches (1 pound) garden cress or
1 dried red chili, halved and seeded	watercress, trimmed and washed
⅛ teaspoon fenugreek seeds	1½ teaspoons minced fresh ginger
2 to 3 bunches (about 1½ pounds) fresh	2 large cloves garlic, minced
spinach, stemmed, washed, and coarsely	½ teaspoon salt, adjusted to taste
chopped	

Heat the mustard oil in a skillet over medium-high heat until the oil faintly smokes. Add the dried chili and fenugreek seeds and fry until dark brown and fully fragrant, about 5 seconds. Add the spinach, cress, ginger, garlic, and salt. Cook until the greens are tender and most of the liquid has evaporated. Transfer the greens to a serving dish and serve warm.

Vegetable Dishes

SPICED MUSTARD GREENS

Makes 4 to 6 servings

Sit le Khaeko Raayo ko Saag

Young tender mustard greens (*raayo ko saag*) are one of the most common and popular vegetables in Nepal and are grown in abundance. In winter months, when the pungent leaves are exposed to frost, they become very tender and delicate. *"Sit le khaeko raayo ko saag"* literally translates as "mustard greens tenderized by frost," and are among the most tender and delicious greens. You may also use the mustard shoots (*raayo ko duku*) that form as the mustard plant matures.

---

2 to 3 bunches fresh mustard greens (about 2 pounds)

3 tablespoons mustard oil

¼ teaspoon ajowan seeds

2 dried red chilies, halved and seeded

2 medium cloves garlic, minced

1½ teaspoons minced fresh ginger

Salt to taste

To prepare the mustard greens, discard any wilted, insect-damaged, or yellowing leaves and fibrous stems. Tear the leaves into bite-size pieces. Rinse the torn mustard greens in cold water. Drain and reserve.

Heat the mustard oil in a heavy saucepan over medium-high heat, until faintly smoking. Add the ajowan seeds and dried chilies and fry until lightly browned and fragrant, about 5 seconds. Add the mustard greens, garlic, ginger, and a sprinkling of salt. Cover the pan and cook, stirring occasionally, until the greens become tender and most of the liquid evaporates, 10 to 12 minutes. Taste for seasoning and add more salt if needed. Transfer the greens to a serving dish and serve immediately.

ABOUT MUSTARD GREENS

Mustard greens (Nepalese: *raayo ko saag*; botanical name: *Brassica Juncea (L.) Czen. & Cos*; family: *cruciferae*) are one of the most common and popular winter vegetables in Nepal, grown in abundance November through April. This cool-season annual vegetable grows quickly and thrives in chilly weather. Mustard leaves have rich dark-green colors and a pungent mustard flavor with a biting taste. But the greens are pungent and bitter only when eaten raw and become soft and delicious when cooked. The leaves from the plants are harvested one-by-one as they mature; this allows the plants to continue producing. As the mustard plant matures, it starts to form flowering shoots that are known as *raayo ko duku*. The young mustard shoots are also eaten as a vegetable and appreciated by many Nepalese.

What is *sit le khaeko saag*? In the winter months, when the pungent leaves of mustard plants are exposed to frost, they become very tender and delicate. *Sit le khaeko saag* literally translates as "mustard greens tenderized by frost" and are among the most tender and delicious greens.

Mr. Puskal P. Regmi in his book, *An Introduction to Nepalese Food Plants* (1982) writes, "The several types of leaf mustard so far believed to be met with in Nepal are as follows: broad-leaved mustard (*B.Juncea,* var. *folicosa Bailey*), curled mustard, Ostrich plume (*B. Juncea,* var. *crispifolia Bailey, B. Juncea,* var. *multisecta Bailey, B. Juncea,* var. *auneifolia Roxb.) Kitam, B. pekinensis, Rupr* – chinese cabbage."

Traditionally, mustard greens are cooked as simply as possible with very little seasoning. They are just cooked by themselves in a little oil, flavored with ajowan seeds, dried red chilies, and ground fresh ginger-garlic until completely tender but still bright green. How long you allow the greens to cook is a matter of taste. Some people cook until the liquid has evaporated and dried out. No matter how you cook it, it is important not to overcook because you want to preserve the fresh flavor of the greens. Nepalese never add water while cooking greens. They are cooked only with the water that clings to the leaves after washing.

SAUTÉED ASPARAGUS WITH POTATOES

Kurelo-Aalu Taareko

Makes 4 to 6 servings

Asparagus is one of the most delectable of spring vegetables and is considered the king of vegetables in Nepal. This recipe is best when prepared with the young, freshest asparagus of the season, as freshly harvested spears are so tender they hardly need cooking at all. The most popular way of cooking asparagus in Nepal is sautéing it in a little oil. This brings out a depth of flavor that boiling and steaming do not.

3 tablespoons vegetable oil
⅛ teaspoon fenugreek seeds
2 medium red potatoes, peeled and cut into ¼-inch pieces
¼ teaspoon ground turmeric
Small pinch ground asafetida
2 fresh mild or hot green chilies, cut into long slivers
3 medium cloves garlic, minced

1 teaspoon minced fresh ginger
1½ teaspoons ground coriander
1 teaspoon ground cumin
1 teaspoon cayenne pepper powder
1 teaspoon salt, adjust to taste
½ teaspoon freshly ground black pepper
2 pounds asparagus, trimmed and sliced diagonally into 1-inch pieces (about 6 cups)

Heat the oil in a skillet over medium-high heat. When the oil is hot, but not smoking, add the fenugreek seeds and fry until dark brown and fully fragrant, about 5 seconds. Add the potatoes, turmeric, and asafetida and cook, stirring frequently, until the potatoes brown, 6 to 7 minutes.

Add the green chilies, garlic, ginger, coriander, cumin, cayenne pepper powder, salt, and black pepper and mix well. Add the asparagus and cook for 1 minute. Reduce the heat to medium, cover and cook, stirring occasionally, until the vegetables are tender and the liquid has evaporated, 6 to 8 minutes. Do not overcook! When you think they are done, sample a piece. It should be firm with a bit of crunch. Transfer the vegetables to a serving dish and serve warm.

SAUTÉED BALSAM APPLE

Barelaa re Aalu ko Tarkaari

Makes 4 to 6 servings

Balsam apples (*Barelaa*) are a late summer vegetable that measure between 1 to 2 inches long. They are slightly curved at one end with a soft, delicate texture. This pale green juicy fruit is a relative of bitter melon. Balsam apples are cooked only when young and tender and still green. Since this vegetable is delicate, it cooks quickly.

2½ tablespoons vegetable oil
1 dried red chili, halved and seeded
¼ teaspoon fenugreek seeds
¼ teaspoon ground turmeric
3 medium red potatoes, peeled and sliced
  ¼-inch thick

25 to 30 fresh green balsam apples, trimmed,
  halved lengthwise, and mature seeds
  removed
1½ teaspoons minced fresh ginger
½ teaspoon ground cumin
Salt to taste

Heat the oil in a wide skillet over medium-high heat. When the oil is hot, but not smoking, add the dried chili and fenugreek seeds and fry until dark brown and highly fragrant, about 5 seconds. Sprinkle in the turmeric, and then add the potatoes. Cook, stirring frequently, until the potatoes are halfway cooked and beginning to brown.

Add the balsam apples, ginger, cumin, and a sprinkling of salt. Cook, stirring frequently, until the balsam apples are crisp-tender and potatoes are cooked, about 10 minutes. While cooking, the balsam apples will release some water. Adjust the heat to high, and cook until the liquid evaporates, about 4 minutes. Taste and adjust salt to taste. Transfer to a serving dish and serve hot.

SAUTÉED PUMPKIN VINE SHOOTS

Makes 4 to 6 servings

Pharsi ko Muntaa

Pumpkin vine shoots (*pharsi ko muntaa*) are the young, uppermost tender shoots, tendrils, leaves, and delicate stems from pumpkin plants. They are considered a delicacy. The shoots are harvested from the growing end of the vine (the top 3 to 4 inches) by pinching off the tender ends. The plant will put out a new shoot or growth after the vine has been harvested. Pumpkin vine shoots have a distinct light flavor that can be described as a cross between squash and spinach. They should be cooked within a day of picking or they will lose their freshness and flavor. Like any leafy green, the volume of this vegetable reduces by half during cooking. Look for these shoots at your local farmer's market or at Indian markets. However, the best way to get them is to grow your own.

1 large bunch pumpkin vine shoots (8 cups after trimming)	1 large clove garlic, minced
¼ cup clarified butter (gheu)	1½ teaspoons minced fresh ginger
1 dried red chili, halved and seeded	½ teaspoon ground cumin
¼ teaspoon fenugreek seeds	½ teaspoon ground turmeric
	Salt to taste

Pick through and discard any tough, large stems and matured leaves from the vine shoots. Use only the young shoots with crisp stems and fresh leaves. Snap or bend each stem, remove the fuzzy outer covering and fiber from all sides and discard. When the fuzzy covering is removed the stems should be shiny. Break the stems into 1½-inch pieces. Separate and tear the leaves into small pieces. Some cooks prefer to remove the tendrils from the pumpkin vine shoots, but I like to include them. Wash, drain, and set the greens aside.

Heat the clarified butter in a heavy saucepan over medium-high heat. When hot, add the dried chili and fenugreek seeds and fry until dark brown and fully fragrant, about 5 seconds. Reduce the heat to medium-low and add the garlic, ginger, cumin, turmeric, a sprinkling of salt, and pumpkin shoots. Cover the pan and cook, stirring occasionally, until the shoots are tender and have reduced to half of their original volume, 12 to 15 minutes. Taste for seasoning and transfer the shoots to a serving dish and serve.

160

ROASTED EGGPLANT
Bhantaa Saandheko

Makes 4 to 6 servings

This delicious Nepali eggplant dish, also called *bhanta ko chokhaa*, will compliment any Nepali meal. Choose a variety of eggplant with a lot of pulp, rather than the slim Asian variety, making sure that they are plump, firm, and glossy.

¼ cup sesame seeds
1 large or 2 medium eggplants (about 2½ pounds total)
½ cup finely chopped cilantro
1½ tablespoons fresh lemon or lime juice
1 teaspoon cayenne pepper powder or to taste
Salt to taste
2 tablespoons vegetable oil

⅛ teaspoon fenugreek seeds
½ teaspoon jimbu (Nepali aromatic herb; *see page 30*)
2 fresh hot or mild green chilies, julienned
4 medium cloves garlic, thinly sliced
1 tablespoon peeled and finely julienned fresh ginger
½ teaspoon ground turmeric

Heat a small cast-iron skillet over medium heat and toast the sesame seeds, stirring constantly to prevent the seeds from flying all over, until they give off a pleasant aroma and darken, 2 to 3 minutes. Pour the sesame seeds into a bowl to halt the toasting and let them cool. Once cool, transfer the seeds to a spice grinder, grind to a fine powder, and set aside.

Preheat a charcoal or gas grill to medium-high heat or preheat the broiler. Prick the eggplants all over with a fork or the tip of a knife to speed the cooking and to allow the steam to escape. Roast the eggplants over the grill, turning frequently, to cook on all sides. The eggplants are done when the skin wrinkles, the juice seeps out, and they release a pleasant smoky aroma, 30 to 40 minutes, depending on the size of the eggplants. Set the cooked eggplants aside until cool enough to handle. Once cool, peel off the charred skin and remove and discard as many seeds as possible. The skins should come off easily. Mash the pulp by hand or with a fork and mix it with the ground sesame seeds, cilantro, lemon juice, cayenne pepper powder, and some salt to taste and set aside.

Heat the oil in a small skillet over medium-high heat until hot but not smoking. Add the fenugreek seeds and jimbu and fry until dark brown and fully fragrant, about 5 seconds. Add the green chilies, garlic, ginger, and turmeric and fry until crisp, but not brown, about 7 seconds. Immediately pour the entire contents into the eggplant mixture. Stir well, cover the bowl, and allow the seasoning to develop for 20 minutes or more. Taste for seasoning and add more salt if needed. Transfer the eggplant to a serving dish and serve.

CAULIFLOWER WITH POTATOES AND PEAS
Cauli-Aalu-Keraau Tarkaari

Makes 4 to 6 servings

Cauliflower is one of the most beloved vegetables in Nepal. Combined with potatoes and peas, it makes this classic Nepali vegetable dish, the flavors complimenting each other perfectly. This recipe can be served with almost all Nepali meals, with pressed rice flakes (*cheuraa*), with roti bread as a snack dish, or as a side dish with a main meal. The golden rule is not to overcook cauliflower or it will become mushy.

---

1 medium-size head cauliflower (about 6 to 7 cups when prepped)

½ cup mustard oil

2 dried red chilies, stemmed

¼ teaspoon fenugreek seeds

¼ teaspoon cumin seeds

¼ teaspoon jimbu (Nepali aromatic herb; *see page 30*)

2 small red potatoes, peeled and cut into 1-inch cubes

2 green cardamom pods, crushed

1 (1-inch) cinnamon stick, halved

½ teaspoon ground turmeric

1 cassia leaf

2 whole cloves

1 tablespoon minced fresh ginger

1½ teaspoons ground coriander

1 teaspoon ground cumin

1½ teaspoons salt, adjust to taste

½ teaspoon cayenne pepper powder

1 cup shelled fresh peas

1 small red or green bell pepper, cored and cut into 1-inch pieces (about 1 cup)

½ cup finely chopped cilantro

3 to 4 green onions (white and pale green parts), finely chopped

1 teaspoon Nepali garam masalaa (*page 310*)

Break the cauliflower into 1½-inch florets. Discard any yellow leaves, but reserve the tender green leaves attached to the stem. Peel the stem and cut into ½-inch pieces.

Heat the mustard oil in a wide, heavy saucepan over medium-high heat until faintly smoking. Add the dried chili, fenugreek seeds, cumin seeds, and jimbu and fry until seeds are several shades darker and fully fragrant, about 5 seconds. Immediately add the potatoes, cardamom pods, cinnamon stick, turmeric, cassia leaf, and cloves. Cook, stirring frequently, until the potatoes are light brown, 5 to 7 minutes.

With a slotted spoon, transfer the potatoes to a bowl, draining as much oil as possible. Add the cauliflower florets, leaves, and stems to the pan and cook for 5 minutes, stirring frequently. Stir in the ginger, coriander, cumin, salt, and cayenne pepper powder. Reduce the heat to medium, cover the pan, and cook, stirring gently, until the cauliflower is lightly browned and half cooked, about 15 minutes.

Mix in the reserved potatoes, peas, and bell pepper and cook, covered, until the vegetables are tender, 10 to 12 minutes.

Stirring gently to avoid breaking the florets (see Note) add in the cilantro, green onions, and garam masalaa. Transfer to a serving dish and serve.

Note: Cauliflower can go from being undercooked to overcooked very quickly. Since cauliflower has a tendency to become mushy, stir gently by lifting and tossing the ingredients in the pan without the use of utensils.

MUSHROOM CURRY
Chyau ko Tarkaari

Makes 4 to 6 servings

Many Nepalese consider mushrooms (*chyau*) a delicacy. This recipe works best with oyster mushrooms, which offer a delicate, mild, and velvety texture, but it can be made with any variety of mushrooms.

1 pound fresh oyster mushrooms	1½ teaspoons minced fresh ginger
2 tablespoons mustard oil	½ teaspoon ground turmeric
¼ teaspoon fenugreek seeds	Small pinch ground asafetida
⅛ teaspoon jimbu (Nepal aromatic herb; see page 30)	1 teaspoon ground coriander
	½ teaspoon ground cumin
1 medium onion, finely chopped (about 1 cup)	Salt to taste
	½ teaspoon cayenne pepper powder
2 fresh mild or hot green chilies, halved lengthwise	⅛ teaspoon timmur (Nepali pepper; see page 31), finely ground with a mortar and pestle
2 medium cloves garlic, minced	

Rinse the mushrooms under running cold water and drain (do not leave them in the water for a long time, as they become water logged). Cut off about 1 inch from the bottom of the stems and discard. Break the mushrooms into bite-size pieces and set aside.

Heat the mustard oil in a wide skillet over medium-high heat until faintly smoking. Add the fenugreek seeds and jimbu and fry until dark brown and highly fragrant, about 5 seconds. Add the onions, green chilies, garlic, ginger, turmeric, and asafetida and fry until the onions soften, about 5 minutes.

Add the mushrooms, coriander, cumin, a sprinking of salt, cayenne pepper powder, and timmur and cook, uncovered, stirring frequently until most of the liquid has evaporated, about 10 minutes. Taste for seasoning and add more salt if needed. Transfer the mushrooms to a serving dish and serve.

SPICED CHAYOTE SQUASH

Makes 4 to 6 servings

Ishkush ko Tarkaari

In Nepal, we call chayote squash "*ishkush*," probably derived from the word "squash." It is a type of squash that grows on a climbing vine. The plant produces a light green fruit, resembling a pear, with crispy white flesh and a single large, soft seed. Its shoots, roots, and fruits are widely used for different varieties of curries. Be sure to select young unblemished chayote for the freshest flavor. Chayote squash is available at Asian markets and some large supermarkets.

*Important: When cutting chayote squash, place it under running water to prevent skin irritation from the sticky substance that it releases.

2 tablespoons vegetable oil
¼ teaspoon fenugreek seeds
½ teaspoon brown mustard seeds
4 medium fresh chayote squash, peeled, seeded, and thinly sliced*
2 medium cloves garlic, minced

1 tablespoon minced fresh ginger
1 teaspoon ground cumin
Salt to taste
½ teaspoon cayenne pepper powder
¼ teaspoon ground turmeric
Small pinch ground asafetida

Heat the oil in a medium-size saucepan over medium-high heat. When the oil is hot, but not smoking, add the fenugreek seeds and mustard seeds and fry until the fenugreek seeds darken, the mustard seeds pop, and they are fully fragrant, about 5 seconds. (You may want to cover the pan, as mustard seeds splatter when heated.)

Add the chayote squash, garlic, ginger, cumin, a sprinkling of salt, cayenne pepper powder, turmeric, and asafetida and cook, stirring constantly, for 5 minutes. Reduce the heat to medium-low, cover the pan, and cook, stirring as needed, until the vegetables are tender but not mushy, about 20 minutes. Taste for seasoning. Transfer the chayote squash to a serving dish and serve.

TEMPERED TARO LEAVES

Makes 4 to 6 servings *Jhanako Karkalo ra Gaabaa ko Tarkaari*

Karkalo is the Nepali name for taro leaves. Nepalese use all three parts of the taro plant: the leaves (*karkalo*), the young stalks (*gaabaa*), and the underground tuber (*pidhaalu*). In this recipe, the tender stalks and young leaves are cooked together, producing a delicate flavor and silky texture, similar to spinach. The secret to this dish is to use fresh taro leaves and stems. Avoid the wilted, yellowing, and dried-out ones, as the tough and mature leaves and stems are inedible and unsuitable for cooking.

*Important: When cleaning the taro plant, the sap secreted by the stem can cause skin irritation and the temporary discoloration of your fingers so wear rubber gloves or rub your hand with oil, or wash your hands frequently. Taro is never eaten raw because it causes an itchy, stinging, and very irritating sensation to the throat called *kokyaoone* in Nepali. Once cooked, the irritating aspect is gone and lemon juice helps further.

---

1 large bunch (10 to 15) fresh, young taro leaves, stalks, and young shoots*
2 tablespoons mustard oil
1 dried red chili, halved and seeded
⅛ teaspoon fenugreek seeds

⅛ teaspoon ajowan seeds
Salt, adjust to taste
2 tablespoons fresh lemon or lime juice, or as needed

Separate the taro leaves and stalks with a knife and rinse thoroughly. Place each leaf on a work surface, roll it into a tight cylinder, and tie the ends together to form a loose knot. Bend each stem and peel off the outer covering by pulling the fiber from all sides until you have smooth and silky stems. Cut them into ⅛-inch pieces and rinse them thoroughly. Set aside.

Heat the mustard oil in a small skillet over medium-high heat. When the oil is hot, but not smoking, add the dried chili, fenugreek seeds, and ajowan seeds and fry until dark brown and fragrant, about 5 seconds. Add ½ cup of water and bring it to a rolling boil. Add the taro and a sprinkling of salt and reduce the heat to medium-low. Cover the pan, and cook until the taro softens, the excess water evaporates, and the taro is reduced to a silky, smooth paste, 10 to 12 minutes. While cooking, stir frequently to make sure the taro does not burn.

Remove the pan from the heat, add the lemon juice, and mix thoroughly. Taste and add more lemon juice and salt as needed. Transfer the mixture to a serving dish and serve hot.

Variation:
TARO LEAVES WITH GINGER AND GARLIC
Prepare the fresh taro leaves as directed above. Heat 2 tablespoons vegetable oil over medium-high heat and sauté ⅛ teaspoon fenugreek seeds until dark, 5 seconds. Stir in 4 mild green chilies (slit lengthwise), 1 chopped onion, 1 chopped red or green bell pepper, 8 chopped cloves garlic, and 1 teaspoon minced fresh ginger. Cook for 5 minutes. Reduce the heat and add the taro leaves, 2 chopped tomatoes, 1 teaspoon ground cumin, 1 teaspoon ground coriander, and ½ teaspoon salt. Cook until the taro softens and the liquid evaporates, 10 to 12 minutes. Remove from the heat and stir in 2 tablespoons lemon juice.

*Note: Fresh taro leaves are available at Indian markets under the name *arbi patta*. They are also sold prepackaged in plastic bags.

SPICED BOTTLE GOURD

Makes 4 to 6 servings

Laukaa ko Tarkaari

Bottle gourd (*laukaa*) is also known as long melon or opo squash. The musky-scented gourd has a smooth skin and is pale to deep green in color. It resembles a large zucchini, has a mild flavor, and releases a lot of liquid when cooked. It is edible only when young and tender, because as it matures, it becomes bitter. Its mild taste makes it easy to blend with many other vegetables and dried legumes. Bottle gourd is available during the summer and early fall in Asian or Indian grocery stores and some specialty produce markets.

3 tablespoons vegetable oil	1 small bottle gourd (2½ to 3 pounds),
4 fresh hot green chilies, halved lengthwise	peeled, halved lengthwise, seeded, and cut
4 medium cloves garlic, thinly sliced	into ½-inch pieces
1 tablespoon peeled and finely	Salt to taste
julienned fresh ginger, plus 1 teaspoon	1 teaspoon ground brown mustard seeds
minced	1 teaspoon ground cumin
½ teaspoon ground turmeric	½ teaspoon cayenne pepper powder
Generous pinch ground asafetida	⅛ teaspoon freshly ground black pepper

Heat the oil in a heavy saucepan over medium-high heat. When the oil is hot, but not smoking, add the green chilies, garlic, and julienned ginger and fry until crisp, about 30 seconds. Stir in the turmeric and asafetida, followed by the gourd and a sprinkling of salt, and cook, stirring occasionally, for 7 minutes.

Add the minced ginger, mustard seeds, cumin, cayenne pepper powder, and black pepper and mix well. Reduce the heat to medium-low, cover the pan, and cook, stirring and mashing the gourd with the back of the spoon from time to time, until the gourd is very soft and most of the juice has evaporated, 30 to 35 minutes. Taste for seasoning and add more salt as needed. Transfer the mixture to a serving dish and serve.

BITTER MELON CHIPS

Makes 4 to 6 servings

Taareko Tito Karelaa

Bitter melon is one of the most popular vegetables in Nepal as well as in many other Asian countries. They are availbale in the US at Asian/Indian markets. The Nepali variety of *tito karelaa* is somewhat skinny and dark green in color, pointed at the blossom end with very bumpy skin. It is much more bitter than the Chinese variety, which is larger, plumper, and pale green. This vegetable is certainly an acquired taste because of its bitterness, but loved by Nepalese people. It is believed to have medicinal value and acts to cure stomach ailments, as an appetite stimulant, and to purify the blood and improve circulation. Serve these chips alongside any Nepali main dish or as an appetizer.

6 to 8 medium bitter melons (enough to make 8 cups sliced) Salt, adjust to taste	¼ cup vegetable oil Fresh lemon or lime juice, adjust to taste

Wash the bitter melons thoroughly, but do not peel. Slice off one inch from the top and bottom ends. Rub the cut pieces against the cut surfaces of the melon in a circular motion to release a white, foamy substance. This will reduce the bitterness. Discard the ends and wash the bitter melons. This process will extract some of the bitterness. With a spoon, remove any mature seeds and spongy pulp (like coring an apple) and discard. Slice the melons into ⅛-inch rounds.

In a colander, toss the melon slices with 1 teaspoon of salt and set aside for 30 minutes in the sink. Squeeze the bitter juice from the melons, rinse, drain, and pat dry. This will further remove the bitter flavor.

Heat the oil in a nonstick skillet over medium-high heat. When the oil is hot, but not smoking, add half of the bitter melon slices and fry, stirring constantly, until golden brown and crunchy, about 5 minutes. With a slotted spoon, transfer them to a paper towel-lined platter, draining as much oil as possible. Repeat the process with the remaining melon slices. Sprinkle them with salt and lemon juice to taste and serve at room temperature.

Sauteed Fiddlehead Ferns / *Neuro ko Tarkaari*

SAUTÉED FIDDLEHEAD FERNS

Makes 4 to 6 servings

Neuro ko Tarkaari

Fiddlehead ferns (*neuro*) are the young shoots of edible ferns. They resemble the spiral end of a fiddle, for which they are named, and taste similar to asparagus and okra. They are extremely perishable and need to be cooked shortly after picking. The shoots only remain coiled for a few days before they uncurl into lacy leaves that cannot be cooked as they become stringy and bitter. Fiddlehead ferns are available neatly bundled in specialty food stores or occasionally at well-stocked larger supermarkets.

1 to 2 bunches young fiddlehead ferns (6 cups chopped)
2 tablespoons clarified butter (gheu)
¼ teaspoon fenugreek seeds
2 fresh mild green chilies, halved lengthwise
2 medium cloves garlic, chopped

1½ teaspoons peeled and julienned fresh ginger
¼ teaspoon ground turmeric
Salt, adjust to taste
½ teaspoon ground cumin
½ teaspoon ground coriander

Remove the fuzzy coatings of the fiddleheads by rubbing them between your hands. Trim and discard the tough ends and cut the fiddleheads into 1-inch pieces. Rinse under cold water, drain, and set aside.

Heat the clarified butter in a heavy-bottomed wide skillet over medium-high heat. When hot, but not smoking, add the fenugreek seeds and fry until dark brown and highly fragrant, about 5 seconds. Add the green chilies, garlic, ginger, and turmeric and stir well. Add the fiddleheads and a sprinkling of salt, and cook uncovered, stirring frequently, for 5 minutes. Add the cumin and coriander and cook, covered, until the fiddleheads are tender, 5 to 7 minutes. Taste for seasoning and add more salt if needed. Transfer the fiddleheads to a serving dish and serve.

GREEN JACKFRUIT CURRY

Makes 4 to 6 servings

Rukh-Katahar ko Tarkaari

Jackfruit (*rukh-katahar*) is a large, oblong tree-born fruit with bumpy, hard green skin. It is eaten as a vegetable when green and a dessert when it is ripe. In this recipe, the young green fruit is cut into chunks and simmered with yogurt and spices. In the US fresh jackfruit is available at Asian food stores, and is also available canned at Indian, Asian, and specialty food markets. This recipe can be prepared from the canned variety, but make sure they are rinsed in several changes of water before using.

2 dried red chilies, halved	¼ teaspoon freshly ground black pepper
¼ cup hot water	¾ cup vegetable oil
1 small fresh green jackfruit (about 8 cups after trimming); or 2 cans (20-ounces each) jackfruit packed in water or brine, drained and rinsed	1 (2-inch) cinnamon stick, halved
	4 green cardamom pods, crushed
	4 whole cloves
	2 bay leaves
1 medium onion, coarsely chopped (about 1 cup)	3 medium tomatoes, chopped (about 3 cups)
1½ tablespoons peeled and coarsely chopped fresh ginger	Salt, adjust to taste
	1 cup plain yogurt, stirred
4 medium cloves garlic, peeled	1 teaspoon Nepali garam masalaa (see page 310)
1 tablespoon ground coriander	
1½ teaspoons ground cumin	½ cup finely chopped cilantro
½ teaspoon ground turmeric	

Soak the chilies in the hot water until soft.

Before handling the fresh jackfruit, rub your hands and knife with oil (when the fruit is cut, a copious gummy latex accumulates that may irritate bare skin). Peel the exterior covering off the fruit and cut the fruit into 1½-inch pieces and set aside.

Place the chilies and soaking water, onion, ginger, garlic, coriander, cumin, turmeric, and black pepper in a food processor or blender and process, adding 1 to 2 tablespoons of water if needed, to make a smooth paste. Transfer the paste to a small bowl and set aside.

GREEN JACKFRUIT & HINDU WEDDINGS

In Nepal, green jackfruit is considered a festive vegetable. In Hindu marriage ceremonies of some Brahmin families, the bride's family does not serve meat when a daughter gets married. Instead, unripe jackfruit is substituted and cooked as "vegetarian meat" called *kahatahar ko maasu* and served during the wedding feast. It is believed that the texture and flavor of cooked jackfruit is similar to meat.

Heat the oil in a heavy saucepan over medium-high heat. When the oil is hot, but not smoking, add the cinnamon stick, cardamom pods, cloves, and bay leaves and fry until they begin to puff up, darken, and give off a pleasant aroma, about 5 seconds. Reduce the heat to medium, add the spice paste, and fry, stirring constantly, until it is light brown, 3 to 4 minutes. Add the tomatoes and cook until they soften and all the juices evaporate, about 5 minutes.

Add the jackfruit and cook, stirring for 5 minutes. Add ½ cup of water and some salt and bring the mixture to a boil. Reduce the heat to medium-low, cover the pan and continue cooking, stirring occasionally, until the jackfruit is soft and most of the water has evaporated, about 15 minutes.

Mix in the yogurt 1 tablespoon at a time, stirring vigorously and constantly until well combined. Add the garam masalaa and continue cooking until the liquid has evaporated and the sauce has thickened and coats the jackfruit, about 5 minutes. Taste for seasoning and add more salt if needed. Transfer the jackfruit to a serving dish and sprinkle with the cilantro. Serve hot.

SPICY POTATOES
Aalu Taareko

Makes 4 to 6 servings

In this recipe, I leave the potato skins on because they add an earthy flavor, but you can peel them. For best results, use a wide, deep skillet to give the potatoes enough room to brown. Serve as a side dish or a snack with pressed rice flakes (*cheuraa*) or warm roti bread.

2 fresh hot green chilies, minced	1 teaspoon jimbu (Nepali aromatic herb; *see page 30*)
4 medium cloves garlic, minced	
1 tablespoon minced fresh ginger	¼ teaspoon fenugreek seeds
1 teaspoon ground cumin	8 medium red potatoes (about 2½ pounds), sliced ½-inch thick
1 teaspoon ground coriander	
⅛ teaspoon freshly ground black pepper	½ teaspoon ground turmeric
½ cup mustard oil	Small pinch ground asafetida
1 dried red chili, halved and seeded	Salt to taste

In a small bowl, mix together the green chilies, garlic, ginger, cumin, coriander, and black pepper. Stir in 2 tablespoons of water to make a paste and set aside.

Heat the mustard oil in a cast-iron or nonstick skillet over medium-high heat until the oil faintly smokes. Add the dried chili, jimbu, and fenugreek seeds and fry until seeds are dark brown and fully fragrant, about 5 seconds. Add the potatoes, turmeric, and asafetida and cook, stirring constantly, until lightly browned and firm, about 7 minutes. Stir in the spice paste and some salt. Reduce the heat to medium, cover the pan, and continue cooking, stirring gently, until the potatoes are tender and golden, and 7 to 8 minutes. Taste for seasoning and add more salt if needed. Transfer the potatoes to a serving dish and serve.

SPICY LONG BEANS

Makes 4 to 6 servings

Tane Bodi ko Tarkaari

These long beans (*tane bodi*) are also called yard beans, asparagus beans, or Chinese long beans. Long beans should be cooked just before serving to preserve their crispy texture. For better flavor, use only tender, slim, and evenly colored beans, as over-mature beans tend to taste bitter. In the US they are available and neatly packaged at Asian, Indian, specialty food stores, and some well-stocked supermarkets.

3 tablespoons vegetable oil	½ teaspoon ground turmeric
1 dried red chili, halved and seeded	Salt, adjust to taste
⅛ teaspoon fenugreek seeds	1 teaspoon Nepali garam masalaa (see page
1½ pounds long beans, trimmed and cut into	310)
1-inch to 2-inch pieces	1 tablespoon minced fresh ginger
2 medium cloves fresh garlic, finely chopped	½ teaspoon cayenne pepper powder

Heat the oil in a heavy-bottomed wide saucepan over medium-high heat. When the oil is hot, but not smoking, add the dried chili and fenugreek and fry until dark brown and fully fragrant, about 5 seconds. Add the long beans, garlic, turmeric, and a sprinkling of salt and cook, stirring frequently, for 5 minutes.

Add the garam masalaa, ginger, and cayenne pepper powder and mix well. Adjust the heat to medium-low, cover the pan, and cook, stirring from time to time, until the beans wrinkle and shrink slightly, but are still crisp, 15 to 20 minutes. Taste for seasoning and add salt as needed. Transfer the beans to a serving dish and serve.

BAMBOO SHOOT STEW

Makes 6 to 8 servings

Taamaa-Aalu

Bamboo shoots (*taamaa*) are the underdeveloped, young, edible shoots of the bamboo plant. They have a unique flavor and texture, are considered a delicacy in traditional Nepali cuisine, and are a favorite wild vegetable for many. The young, tender shoots are mild-flavored and can be pickled, fermented, dried, or cooked with any combination of vegetables and other ingredients.

The fermented bamboo shoots are made into a popular stew-like dish combined with black-eyed peas, potatoes and several herbs and spices called *"taamaa-aalu-bodi ko tarkaari."* An exotic bamboo flavor dominates the whole dish, which is usually accompanied by freshly boiled rice as part of an everyday Nepali traditional meal. To make fermented bamboo, the fresh bamboo shoots are sliced into thin pieces, mixed with salt, mustard seeds, turmeric, and mustard oil, and fermented in the sun until they become slightly sour and flavorful. The authentic flavor of the dish comes from the selection of bamboo shoots you use. Some people prefer fresh *taamaa*, but some like fermented *taamaa*. No matter what your preference is make sure to enjoy one of the most traditional wild vegetables that Nepalese have been eating for centuries.

For this recipe, you may substitute packaged bamboo shoots, readily available in many forms (fresh, canned, bottled, packed in brine, or vacuum-packed in plastic) at Asian markets.

2 tablespoons vegetable oil	1 tablespoon minced fresh ginger
¼ teaspoon fenugreek seeds	1½ teaspoons salt, adjust to taste
1 medium onion, finely chopped (about 1 cup)	1 teaspoon cayenne pepper powder
½ teaspoon ground turmeric	3 medium tomatoes, chopped (about 3 cups)
½ cup dried black-eyed peas (*bodi*), soaked and drained	1 small red or green bell pepper, cored and diced (about 1 cup)
2 medium red potatoes, peeled and sliced ½-inch thick	2 cups (bottled or canned) bamboo shoots, well rinsed, drained, and cut into bite-size pieces
2 fresh hot green chilies, halved lengthwise	½ cup finely chopped cilantro
1 tablespoon brown mustard seeds, finely ground	2 tablespoons fresh lemon or lime juice

Heat the oil in a large saucepan over medium-high heat. When the oil is hot, but not smoking, add the fenugreek seeds and fry until dark brown and highly fragrant, about 5 seconds. Reduce the heat to medium, add the onions and turmeric, and cook, stirring frequently, until the onions soften, about 5 minutes.

Add the drained black-eyed peas and cook for 10 minutes.

Mix in the potatoes, green chilies, ground mustard seeds, ginger, salt, and cayenne pepper powder and stir for 1 minute. Stir in the tomatoes and bell peppers and continue cooking until the tomatoes soften, about 5 minutes. Increase the heat to high, add 3 cups of water, and bring the mixture to a boil for 7 minutes. Reduce the heat to medium-low, cover, and cook, stirring from time to time, until the black-eyed peas and potatoes are tender and the sauce has thickened, about 20 minutes.

Add the bamboo shoots and cook for another 5 minutes to allow the flavors to blend. If you prefer a thinner sauce, add some water and boil further. Transfer the mixture to a bowl and stir in the cilantro and lemon juice. Serve hot.

MIXED VEGETABLE MEDLEY

Makes 4 to 6 servings

Mismaas Tarkaari

This colorful vegetable medley can be made from any assortment of vegetables of your choice. I recommend using only fresh vegetables. The most common vegetables used are potatoes, peas, onions, cauliflower, beans, mushrooms, and tomatoes. Do not overcook the vegetables or overcrowd them in a small pan, as they will turn into mush.

¼ cup vegetable oil
½ teaspoon cumin seeds
½ teaspoon ground turmeric
Small pinch ground asafetida
2 medium potatoes, peeled and cut into
  1-inch pieces (about 2 cups)
2 medium red onions, quartered
1 small eggplant, cut into 1-inch piece (about
  1 cup)
2 small red and green bell peppers, cored and
  cut into 1-inch pieces
1 cup shelled fresh or frozen peas, thawed and
  thoroughly drained

3 medium tomatoes, quartered
2 fresh mild or hot green chilies, split
  lengthwise
2 medium cloves garlic, finely chopped
1 tablespoon minced fresh ginger
2 teaspoons ground coriander
1½ teaspoons ground cumin
1 teaspoon cayenne pepper powder
1 teaspoon salt, adjust to taste
½ cup finely chopped cilantro
3 to 4 green onions (white and pale green
  parts), cut into 1-inch pieces

Heat the oil in a wide, heavy saucepan over medium-high heat until hot. Add the cumin seeds and fry until light brown and fragrant, about 5 seconds. Add the turmeric and asafetida, followed by the potatoes, and cook, stirring frequently, for 2 minutes. Stir in the onions, eggplant, red and green peppers, and peas. Reduce the heat to medium, cover the pan, and continue cooking, stirring occasionally, until the vegetables are half cooked, about 10 to 12 minutes.

Add the tomatoes, chilies, garlic, ginger, coriander, cumin, cayenne pepper powder, and salt and stir for 2 to 3 minutes. Reduce the heat to medium-low, cover the pan and cook, stirring occasionally, until the vegetables are tender and the liquid has slightly thickened, about 15 minutes. The vegetables should cook in their own juices, but if the mixture is dry, add a little water.

Mix in the cilantro and green onions, transfer the vegetables to a serving dish, and serve.

CORNMEAL PORRIDGE
Makai ko Pitho ko Dhindo

Makes 4 to 6 servings

Dhindo is a thick porridge or mush, made by cooking stone-ground cornmeal or millet flour. It has been the staple food of most rural and middle mountain area people in Nepal, especially in dry areas where rice or wheat crops are difficult to grow. This hearty, nutritious food is eaten with homemade butter (*nauni*), curried vegetables (*jhol tarkaari*), pickles, buttermilk, or yogurt. Traditionally, *dhindo* is cooked in a cast-iron pan with a long handle and rounded bottom, called a *taapke*, that has excellent heat distribution qualities (*see pages 46-47*). It is typically stirred with a large iron spoon with a long handle (*panyu*). *Dhindo* should be eaten right away since it hardens once it cools.

> ½ teaspoon salt, or adjust to taste
> 1 cup coarse or medium-ground cornmeal
> 2 tablespoons clarified butter (gheu)

In a heavy saucepan, bring 4 cups of water and the salt to a boil over high heat. Once it comes to a full boil, pour in the cornmeal in a slow, steady stream with the left hand, while mixing vigorously and constantly with the right hand. Mix until it is well-combined, making sure there are no lumps. Reduce the heat to medium-low and continue stirring until the mixture thickens, about 20 minutes. It is ready when the porridge begins to pull away from the sides of the pan. Remove it from the heat and stir in the butter until melted. Pour it directly onto plates and eat piping hot.

Variations:

MILLET FLOUR PORRIDGE
Kodo ko Pitho ko Dhindo
Millet is an important source of food in the rural and hilly regions of Nepal because it is drought-tolerant and can be grown on slopes, in poor soil conditions, and even in high-elevation areas. It is a high-fiber grain, nourishing and wholesome, and especially suitable for people used to hard physical labor. Millet is also used to make breads and a popular alcoholic drink called *chhang*. This dish is eaten with vegetables and is often accompanied by buttermilk or yogurt.

To make this recipe, please follow the directions above using millet flour in place of the cornmeal.

GUNDRUK-DHINDO
Gundruk-Dhindo is the most common combination, served in farming communities in Nepal. It combines *dhindo* with fermented greens (*gundruk*). See page 130 on fermenting greens.

FOODS & FLAVORS FROM NEPAL

Chapter 8

MEAT, POULTRY & EGGS

MAASU, KUKHURAA & PHOOL

I n Nepal, meat is a high-status food and does not feature frequently in the regular diet of most people. Poorer people consume meat only on special occasions and festivities, while the urban middle class consumes meat more frequently. The most common and preferred meat is freshly slaughtered goat and the Nepali words for goat are the same as the generic words for meat—*khasi* or *boka*. All parts of the animal are eaten, including the liver, intestines, brain, kidney, tongue, tripe, and blood. Meat from castrated goats is called *khasi ko maasu*, young goat meat is called *boka ko maasu*, and both can be purchased at Indian or Middle Eastern grocery stores and some farms. Most butchers will cut meat according to your specifications, upon request.

Other common meats eaten in Nepal include lamb (*bheda*) and pork (*bangoor* or *banel*). The majority of Nepalese do not eat beef for religious, cultural, and legal reasons. The cow is considered a sacred and holy animal and a lot of religious sentiments are attached to it. Cows are considered a symbol of Goddess Laxmi and worshipped during the most auspicious festival of Tihaar.

In many areas of Nepal, certain ethnic groups eat water buffalo (*raango ko maasu*) as their primary source of meat. Water buffalo meat is extremely lean and tender. It is also versatile and lends itself to spicy cooking. Water buffalo was once a less expensive alternative to goat, but as a greater portion of the population is beginning to recognize its health benefits, it is becoming increasingly expensive. Game meats, such as boar (*banel*) and venison (*mirga*), are popular in some regions and usually signifies a family celebration. Venison is usually obtained by hunting. Due to a lack of refrigeration, on hunting trips it is sun-dried so that it doesn't spoil. In the high-altitude areas of Nepal near the Tibetan border, yak (*chamari gai*) is consumed fresh and dried. It is similar in flavor to water buffalo, but much leaner and juicier, with a strong, gamy odor.

Religious laws dictate that meat is prohibited on certain days and in combination with certain foods. For example, meat is not to be consumed during Ekaadasi (Auspicious Day), the eleventh day after the full moon, and the eleventh day after the new moon. During this time, meat is not sold in the local markets. During the most important religious festival of *Dashain*, however, a large number of animals are sacrificed and offered to the deities. After religious rites are performed, the animal is cooked and distributed among friends, relatives, and neighbors. At this time, great feasts are prepared in many homes and a large quantity of *prashad ko maasu* (blessed meat) is consumed. For many families, this is one of the few occasions during the year that they are able to eat meat. Many Nepali seniors stop meat consumption after reaching a certain age and switch to a plant-based diet. The main motivations behind these changes are spirituality and health concerns.

In Nepal, butchered animals are cooked and eaten right after slaughtering, rather than stored. The meat is usually prepared well done. Most frequently, it is cooked in a pressure cooker. **Note:** Most meats (goat, lamb, water buffalo, and pork) can be used interchangeably in the recipes in this chapter unless otherwise indicated.

Chicken (*kukhuraa*) was rare and high priced in Nepal until recently, but it is now more readily available and cooked more frequently. Traditionally chicken is cooked on the bone because it is more flavorful and succulent than boneless chicken. The skin is removed before cooking so that the spices can better penetrate the chicken. Recipes for chicken range from simple, lightly spiced curries to highly spiced dishes, and dishes cooked with vegetables. I prefer to purchase whole chickens rather than precut pieces because this results in more flavorful dishes, but you may use precut pieces for convenience.

Eggs are widely enjoyed in Nepal, although some orthodox Brahmins do not eat them. They are not limited to breakfast fare, but are served as snacks, appetizers, or part of a full meal. Farm-fresh hen eggs are most common, but some people prefer duck eggs, which are more flavorful and higher in fat. Duck eggs have a significant role in Nepal for religious, social, and culinary reasons. In Newar communities, they are used as a *sagun* (sacred) food to promote good luck and prosperity. Eggs are also offered to the gods during religious rituals.

GOAT CURRY WITH YOGURT

Makes 4 to 6 servings   *Dahi Haaleko Khasi ko Maasu*

This classic Nepali goat curry is marinated in tenderizing yogurt. This dish is best when cooked with leg of goat, but is also delicious with tender cuts of lamb, pork, or water buffalo. Serve it with rice and green vegetables.

2½ to 3 pounds bone-in young goat (preferably from the leg), cut into 1½-inch pieces	1 tablespoon ground coriander
¼ cup vegetable oil	2 teaspoons cayenne pepper powder, or to taste
1 teaspoon ground turmeric	4 to 6 green cardamom pods, crushed
1½ teaspoons salt, adjust to taste	1 black cardamom pod, crushed
2 medium onions, each cut into 6 wedges	1½ teaspoons ground cumin
2 medium tomatoes, each cut into 6 wedges	¼ teaspoon freshly ground black pepper
1 cup plain yogurt, stirred	⅛ teaspoon ground nutmeg
6 medium cloves garlic, minced	1 (1-inch) cinnamon stick, halved
2 or 3 fresh mild or hot green chilies, split lengthwise	2 or 3 cassia leaves
1½ tablespoons minced fresh ginger	4 whole cloves
	1 cup hot water
	½ cup finely chopped cilantro

Rinse the goat meat well under cold water and place it in a bowl with the oil, turmeric, and salt, rubbing to coat the meat. Add the onions, tomatoes, yogurt, garlic, green chilies, ginger, coriander, cayenne pepper powder, green cardamom, black cardamom, cumin, black pepper, nutmeg, cinnamon stick, cassia leaves, and cloves, rubbing again to coat the meat. Cover and marinate for at least 30 minutes at room temperature or refrigerate overnight, but return to room temperature before cooking.

Once the meat has marinated, place it in a large saucepan. Cook, uncovered, over medium-high heat, stirring from time to time, until the meat loses its pink color and comes to a boil, 7 to 8 minutes. Stir in the hot water and return to a full boil. Reduce the heat to medium-low, cover, and simmer, stirring occasionally, until the meat is tender and cooked through, and the sauce has thickened, about 1 hour. Transfer to a serving dish, sprinkle with cilantro, and serve hot.

GOAT CURRY
Khasi ko Maasu

Makes 4 to 6 servings

This is a basic recipe for cooking goat, but it works equally well with lamb, pork, water buffalo, venison, or even poultry. Traditionally, bone-in goat is used, which contributes more flavor, but boneless meat can also be used. In this recipe, goat is marinated for several hours before cooking. If the meat is tender and lean, it should cook in its own juice without additional water. Serve with rice, bread, and vegetables.

2½ to 3 pounds bone-in young goat (preferably from the leg), trimmed and cut into 1½-inch pieces	4 whole cloves
1 (1-inch) cinnamon stick	2 or 3 dried red chilies, halved, seeded, and soaked in ¼ cup hot water until soft
2 teaspoons coriander seeds	¼ cup vegetable oil
1½ teaspoons cumin seeds	4 to 6 medium cloves garlic, minced
4 to 6 green cardamom pods, crushed	1½ tablespoons minced fresh ginger
1 black cardamom pod, crushed	1 teaspoon ground turmeric
¼ teaspoon black peppercorns	1½ teaspoons salt, adjust to taste
⅛ teaspoon fennel seeds	⅛ teaspoon ground nutmeg
2 to 3 cassia leaves	½ cup finely chopped cilantro

Wash the meat thoroughly with cold water, drain, and place it in a medium-size bowl. Set aside while you prepare the spices.

Heat a small cast-iron skillet over medium-low heat and toast the cinnamon stick, coriander seeds, cumin seeds, green cardamom pods, black cardamom pod, peppercorns, fennel seeds, cassia leaves, and cloves, stirring constantly until they give off a pleasant aroma and are heated through, 2 to 3 minutes. Pour into a dry container to halt the toasting. Cool and remove the seeds from the cardamom pods and discard the pods. Place the toasted spices in a spice grinder or a mortar and pestle and grind to a fine powder.

Drain the chilies and coarsely grind them into a paste with a mortar and pestle or spice grinder. In a small bowl, combine chili paste with the oil, garlic, ginger, turmeric, salt, nutmeg, and ground toasted spices. Rub this spice mixture over the meat. Cover and allow the meat to marinate for 30 minutes at room temperature or refrigerate it overnight, but bring it back to room temperature before cooking.

Place the marinated meat in a large heavy-bottomed saucepan. Cook, uncovered, over medium-high heat, stirring from time to time, until the meat loses its pink color and comes to a boil, 7 to 8 minutes. Lower

the heat, cover, and simmer, stirring often to prevent scorching, until the meat is tender and cooked through and the juices are absorbed into the meat, about 1 hour. The cooking time depends on the quality and age of the goat. If the meat has not reached the desired tenderness after an hour, add ½ cup hot water and continue cooking until it is tender and most of the juices have evaporated. Transfer the meat to a serving dish, sprinkle the cilantro on top, and serve hot.

THREE-LAYER GOAT CURRY

Makes 4 to 6 servings

Tintaha ko Khasi Maasu

"Tintaha ko maasu" translates as "three layers of meat" and corresponds to how the meat is cut in this recipe. These layers consist of bone-in and boneless meat pieces with thick fat and skin attached. Nepalese call it *"boso, chaalaa re haad bhayoko maasu."* The meat that is attached to the bone is the most tender and flavorful. The skin is considered a delicacy, and the fat layer is left in because it helps to baste the meat and makes it tender as it cooks. Nepali cooks are very careful to balance the texture, flavor, and color of the meat and the result is a very flavorful meat dish with gravy. This recipe is perhaps one of the most popular ways of cooking goat meat during festive occasions in Nepal. The dish calls for a special cut of goat meat and some specialty butchers (or Indian meat markets) will prepare this cut of meat upon request.

2½ to 3 pounds young bone-in goat meat, cut into 1½-inch pieces (with skin and fat)
1 teaspoon ground turmeric
1 teaspoon salt, adjust to taste
2 medium onions, chopped (about 2 cups)
1½ tablespoons minced fresh ginger
4 to 6 medium cloves garlic, minced
¼ cup vegetable oil
1 tablespoon ground coriander
1 (1-inch) cinnamon stick, halved
2 teaspoons cayenne pepper powder, or to taste
1½ teaspoons ground cumin
¼ teaspoons ground black pepper
⅛ teaspoon ground nutmeg
2 or 3 cassia or bay leaves
1 bunch cilantro leaves with tender stems, finely chopped (½ cup)

Wash the goat pieces thoroughly with cold water and drain. Place the meat in a heavy-bottomed pan and add the turmeric, salt, onions, ginger, garlic, oil, coriander, cinnamon stick, cayenne pepper powder, cumin, black pepper, nutmeg, and cassia leaves. Rub the spices into the meat vigorously by hand for 1 to 2 minutes, making sure they are well coated.

Cook the seasoned meat, uncovered over medium-high heat, stirring from time to time, until it loses its pink color and comes to boil, about 10 minutes. Reduce the heat to medium-low, cover, and simmer, stirring occasionally, until the meat is tender and cooked through, and the gravy has thickened. If the meat starts to dry out but has not reached desired tenderness, add ½ cup of water and cook until the meat is tender. Transfer the meat to serving dish, sprinkle with cilantro and serve hot.

SOUPY GOAT MEAT

Suruwaa Maasu

Makes 4 to 6 servings

This dish is also called *jhol*, *ras*, or *umaaleko maasu*, which simply means "soupy boiled meat." The term *suruwa* refers to meat that is gently simmered with fresh herbs and spices to produce a thin soup. This slow-cooking method tenderizes the meat and brings out the flavor of the spices at the same time. The dish is even better the next day when the flavors have more fully developed.

---

3 tablespoons clarified butter (gheu) or vegetable oil
½ teaspoon ajowan seeds
2½ to 3 pounds bone-in young goat (leg or shoulder), cut into 1½-inch pieces
1 teaspoon ground turmeric
Large pinch ground asafetida
1 medium onion, thinly sliced
6 medium cloves garlic, slivered
1 tablespoon peeled and finely julienned fresh ginger
1 large shallot, minced
2 or 3 fresh mild green chilies, split lengthwise

1 (1-inch) cinnamon stick, halved
1½ teaspoons ground coriander
1 teaspoon ground cumin
Salt, adjust to taste
1 teaspoon cayenne pepper powder, or to taste
¼ teaspoon freshly ground black pepper
⅛ teaspoon ground nutmeg
1 black cardamom pod, crushed
2 medium tomatoes, finely chopped or crushed (about 2 cups)
4 or 5 green onions (white and pale green parts), finely chopped
1 cup finely chopped cilantro

Heat the clarified butter or oil in a heavy saucepan over medium-high heat. When hot, add the ajowan seeds and fry until lightly browned and fragrant, about 5 seconds. Add the goat, turmeric, and asafetida and cook, stirring as needed, until the meat is well browned, 7 to 8 minutes.

Add the onion slices, garlic, ginger, and shallot and continue to cook, stirring constantly, until the onions soften, about 5 minutes. Mix in the green chilies, cinnamon stick, coriander, cumin, some salt, cayenne pepper powder, black pepper, nutmeg, and cardamom pod and stir for 1 minute. Add the tomatoes, green onions, half of the cilantro, and 4 cups of water and bring to a boil. Reduce the heat to medium-low, cover, and simmer, stirring from time to time, until the meat is falling off the bones and the liquid has slightly reduced and thickened, 50 to 55 minutes. Transfer to a serving dish, sprinkle with the remaining cilantro and serve piping hot.

LAMB WITH GRAVY
Masaledaar Maasu

Makes 4 to 6 servings

"Masaledaar" means a "delicate mixture of herbs and spices," and *"maasu"* means "meat" in Nepali, so this recipe blends spices and meat in aromatic gravy. The dish can be prepared one day in advance and then reheated on the stovetop by gently simmering. It is served piping hot with rice, lentils, sautéed vegetables, and warm Nepali breads. Traditionally this dish is made with goat on the bone, but this recipe uses boneless lamb.

2½ to 3 pounds boneless lamb (or goat), trimmed and cut into 1-inch pieces	4 to 6 green cardamom pods, seeds removed
2 medium onions, coarsely chopped (about 2 cups)	6 whole cloves
2 to 3 large shallots, chopped	½ cup vegetable oil
6 medium cloves garlic, peeled	2 medium cassia leaves
3 fresh mild green chilies, stemmed	Small pinch ground asafetida
1½ tablespoons peeled and coarsely chopped fresh ginger	8 blanched whole almonds, ground
3 dried red chilies, halved and seeded, or to taste	1 teaspoon ground turmeric
1 tablespoon coriander seeds	1 teaspoon salt, adjust to taste
1 (1-inch) cinnamon stick, halved	¼ teaspoon ground nutmeg
2 teaspoons cumin seeds	2 medium tomatoes, finely chopped (about 2 cups)
¼ teaspoon whole black peppercorns	1 cup plain yogurt, stirred
⅛ teaspoon fenugreek seeds	½ cup finely chopped cilantro
⅛ teaspoon fennel seeds	5 or 6 green onions (white and pale green parts), finely chopped

Wash the lamb thoroughly with cold water, drain, and set it aside.

Place the onions, shallots, garlic, green chilies, and ginger in a food processor or blender. Add just enough water to facilitate blending and process to a smooth paste.

Heat a small cast-iron skillet over medium-high heat and toast the dried chilies, coriander seeds, cinnamon stick, cumin seeds, peppercorns, fenugreek seeds, fennel seeds, cardamom seeds, and cloves, stirring constantly, until they give off a pleasant aroma, 2 to 3 minutes. Remove spices from the skillet and pour them into a dry container to halt the toasting. Cool, and then grind the spices in a spice grinder to a fine powder (a mortar and pestle can also be used).

Heat the oil in a heavy saucepan over medium-high heat. When the oil is hot, but not smoking, add the cassia leaves and asafetida, and then immediately add

the onion paste. Stir until golden, 5 to 7 minutes. Add the ground spice mixture, ground almonds, turmeric, salt, and nutmeg and mix well. Add the tomatoes and continue cooking until they are soft and all the juices evaporate, about 5 minutes. Add the yogurt, 1 tablespoon at a time, stirring constantly. Continue cooking until the liquid has evaporated in the spice mixture, about 2 minutes.

Add the lamb to the spice mixture and cook, uncovered, stirring from time to time, for 10 minutes. Add 1 cup of water and bring to a boil. Reduce the heat to medium-low, cover the pan, and continue cooking, stirring as needed, until the meat is tender, about 50 minutes. If the meat is not tender after 50 minutes and the gravy has started to stick to the pan, add ½ cup more water and continue cooking, covered. The dish will be ready when the oil begins to separate from the side of the pan and the gravy is rich, thick, and brown. Remove from the heat. Mix in the cilantro and green onions, transfer the lamb to a serving dish, and serve hot.

GRILLED LAMB KEBABS

Makes 4 to 6 servings

Sekuwaa Maasu

Here is a recipe for boneless lamb marinated in yogurt and spices. The yogurt helps to tenderize the lamb and makes the spices stick to the meat during grilling. This is a wonderfully flavorful meat dish that is quick and easy to prepare. Leftovers can be shredded and made into *chowelaa*, a Nepali meat salad dish. It can be served as an appetizer, mid-afternoon snack, or as a supplement to any lunch or dinner menu.

8 to 10 grilling skewers (if wooden, soak for 30 minutes before use)

2½ to 3 pounds boneless lamb (preferably from the leg), trimmed and cut into 1½-inch pieces

2 tablespoons melted butter or vegetable oil

1 medium red onion, sliced ⅛-inch thick and separated into rings

⅛ teaspoon salt

1 teaspoon fresh lemon or lime juice

1 small cucumber, peeled, halved lengthwise, seeded, and sliced ¼-inch thick

2 medium tomatoes, each cut into 6 wedges

10 fresh green chilies

Marinade

1 teaspoon salt, or adjust to taste

1 tablespoon fresh lemon or lime juice

½ teaspoon ground turmeric

1 teaspoon Nepali garam masalaa (*page 310*)

1 tablespoon peeled and minced fresh ginger

3 medium cloves garlic, minced

2 fresh hot green chilies, minced

½ cup plain yogurt, stirred

Combine all the marinade ingredients in a medium-size bowl, add the lamb and mix well, making sure that each piece is coated. Place the lamb with marinade in a heavy, sealable plastic bag, and refrigerate for at least 8 hours. Shake and turn the bag from time to time.

Preheat a charcoal or gas grill to medium-high heat. Remove the lamb from the marinade, and thread onto the skewers—for juicy meat, place the pieces close to one another on the skewers. Discard the marinade. Grill, turning frequently and basting with the melted butter, until the lamb is browned on all sides and cooked through, about 25 minutes. Remove the skewers from the grill and allow the meat to cool a little before removing it from the skewers.

While the lamb is cooking, combine the onion slices with the salt and lemon juice. Transfer the lamb to a platter. Surround it with the onions, cucumbers, tomatoes, and chilies, and serve immediately.

LAMB MEATBALLS
Maasu ko Bari

Makes 4 to 6 servings

This light, but filling, Nepali version of meatballs that we call *bari* are sometimes shaped into patties and deep-fried. They can be served as a mid-afternoon snack, appetizer, or as a supplement to a Nepali meal with any variety of chutney or garnish. This dish can also be made using ground pork, goat meat, water buffalo, turkey or chicken (*see variation below*).

2 pounds lean ground lamb	1 large shallot, minced
1 cup dry bread crumbs	2 teaspoons minced fresh ginger
1 medium onion, finely chopped (about 1 cup)	1 teaspoon ground turmeric
½ cup finely chopped cilantro	1 teaspoon ground coriander
2 or 3 green onions (white and pale green parts), finely chopped	1 teaspoon cayenne pepper powder
3 or 4 fresh mild green chilies, finely chopped	1 teaspoon salt, adjust to taste
2 eggs, lightly beaten	½ teaspoon ground cumin
4 medium cloves garlic, minced	¼ teaspoon freshly ground black pepper
	2 cups vegetable oil

In a large bowl, combine the ground meat with all the ingredients except the oil. Mix well with your hands until all the ingredients are thoroughly mixed. Cover the bowl and let it rest for 7 to 10 minutes at room temperature to allow the flavors to develop.

With moistened fingers, form the meat mixture into 1½-inch balls. Place them on a tray in a single layer.

Heat the oil in a wide nonstick skillet over medium-high heat until it reaches 350 to 375 degrees F. Test for readiness by placing a small piece of the meat mixture into the hot oil. If it bubbles and slowly rises to the surface, it is ready. Gently place the meatballs into the hot oil. Do not overcrowd. Fry the meatballs gently, turning carefully so they do not break or stick to the pan. Cook until firm, cooked through, and golden brown on all sides, 10 to 15 minutes. Remove with a slotted spoon and drain on paper towels. Repeat with the remaining meatballs. Serve warm or at room temperature.

Variation:
CHICKEN MEATBALLS *Kukuraa ko Bari*
Use 2½ pounds ground chicken in place of the lamb. Combine all the ingredients as directed above, reducing the garlic to 2 cloves, the turmeric to ½ teaspoon, and the cayenne pepper powder to ½ teaspoon. Omit the coriander and increase the black pepper to ½ teaspoon. Form meatballs and cook as directed above.

VENISON JERKY
Mirga ko Sukuti

Makes 3½ to 4 pounds

The term *sukuti* refers to any meat that has been preserved by drying or smoking. Such dried meat is very popular in Nepal and is usually made from deer, water buffalo, yak, or fish. Deer meat is an especially prized delicacy. It is considered upscale meat in Nepal because of its rarity, since it is obtained only through hunting. Due to the lack of refrigeration in hunting areas, the entire animal is dried before it spoils. The meat is cut into long thin strips, suspended on a rope and slowly dried in the air and sunlight or over a slow fire. This process may take several days depending on the sunlight, temperature, and humidity. When the moisture is completely removed from the meat and it becomes dry, Nepalese eat it as a chewable snacks or prepare it with other ingredients.

At home I use a food dehydrator to dry the meat, but you can also dry it in direct sunlight or in the oven. Sun-drying gives the meat a chewier texture compared with other drying method. However, the meat should be dried until all the moisture is completely removed or it will begin to spoil immediately. Jerky can be kept at room temperature in an airtight container, but I usually refrigerate it for longer storage.

10 to 12 pounds boneless venison, trimmed and cut into ½-inch-thick strips	1 teaspoon ground turmeric
	1 teaspoon ground ginger
1 tablespoon garlic powder	1 teaspoon cayenne pepper powder
2 teaspoons salt	¼ teaspoon freshly ground black pepper

In a medium-size bowl, combine the venison, garlic powder, salt, turmeric, ginger, cayenne pepper powder, and black pepper, rubbing to make sure the meat is well coated with spices. Set aside for at least 2 hours at room temperature.

Food-dehydrator method:
Arrange the venison evenly in a single layer on two to three dehydrator trays, without overlapping, to allow good circulation. Place the trays in the food dehydrator. Follow the manufacturer's instructions for the drying temperature. Do not over-dry. The finished jerky should be completely dry, but not brittle. To test for dryness, remove a piece of meat, allow it to cool, and check to see that it bends easily and does not break.

Oven-drying method:
Preheat the oven to the lowest temperature (140 to 160 degrees F). Place the venison directly on the oven racks (or place it on racks set on baking sheets). Do not overlap the strips, to allow them good circulation. Place a tray underneath to trap any dripping from the meat. Turn the meat occasionally. Continue until the meat is dry and all the moisture is removed. This process may take 8 to 10 hours depending on the cut of

meat. To test for dryness, remove a piece of meat and taste. It should be chewable. Remove it from the oven and place it on a tray in a well-ventilated sunny area to further remove any moisture for 1 to 2 days before storing.

Store the jerky in an airtight container in the refrigerator for up to 6 months.

SPICED VENISON SALAD
Mirga ko Sukuti Saandheko

Makes 4 to 6 servings

This dish is perfect to serve as a snack or appetizer garnished with tomato wedges. It also makes a spicy accompaniment to plain boiled rice. I use homemade venison jerky, but you can substitute any variety of purchased jerky. When adding the spices like red pepper and timmur, measure carefully because they have a distinct, strong flavor and may overpower the entire dish. A large quantity of spiced dried meat can be prepared ahead of time and stored in an airtight container in the refrigerator, but the fresh ingredients, such as green onions, cilantro, fresh chilies, and lemon should be added right before serving. Raw shelled green peas or peanuts can be mixed with the salad to give an extra crunchy texture.

---

2 tablespoons vegetable oil
2 pounds Venison Jerky (*see page 192 and *Note below*)
½ cup finely chopped cilantro
4 or 5 green onions (white and pale green parts), finely chopped
3 tablespoons fresh lemon or lime juice
2 fresh hot or mild green chilies, minced
3 large cloves garlic, minced

1½ teaspoons minced fresh ginger
1 teaspoon cayenne pepper powder, or adjust to taste
½ teaspoon ground cumin
¼ teaspoon ground turmeric
⅛ teaspoon timmur, (Nepali pepper; *see page 31*), finely ground with a mortar and pestle

---

Heat the oil in a medium-size nonstick skillet over medium heat until hot. Add the jerky and sauté, stirring constantly, until lightly browned and crispy, 5 minutes. Using a slotted spoon, remove the jerky, draining as much oil as possible, and place it in a bowl. When cool enough to handle, shred the meat into small pieces. If the meat is hard to shred by hand, place pieces in a mortar and pound them into shreds.

In the same bowl, combine the shredded meat with the cilantro, green onions, lemon juice, green chilies, garlic, ginger, cayenne pepper powder, cumin, turmeric, and timmur and mix well. Cover and set aside for 30 minutes for the seasonings to set. Transfer to a serving dish and serve at room temperature.

*Note: For convenience, many cooks purchase pre-packaged sun-dried venison or other dried meat from the store. If you use sun-dried meat, bring a small pot of water to boil over high heat. Add the dried meat and bring it to a rolling boil. Reduce the heat to medium-low, cover the pot, and cook until soft, about 20 minutes. Drain the meat and discard the water. When cool enough to handle, separate the meat into shreds, and follow the recipe above.

CHICKEN CURRY

Kukhuraa ko Pakku

Makes 4 to 6 servings

This is a simple recipe for chicken curry. To make this curry, purchase a whole young chicken and cut it into serving-size pieces, and remove the visible fat and skin so that the spices can penetrate directly into the chicken meat while cooking. Alternatively, you can purchase pre-cut chicken pieces, which will be much easier to handle. For best results, marinate these pieces in the morning to prepare an evening meal. The chicken cooks in its own juices without additional water.

2 or 3 dried red chilies, halved	1 teaspoon ground turmeric
¼ cup hot water	1½ teaspoons salt, adjust to taste
1 (3- to 3½-pound) chicken, skinned and cut into 8 to 10 pieces	⅛ teaspoon freshly ground black pepper
	⅛ teaspoon ground nutmeg
1 medium onion, finely chopped (about 1 cup)	1 (1-inch) cinnamon stick, halved
¼ cup vegetable oil	4 green cardamom pods, crushed
1½ tablespoons minced fresh ginger	1 black cardamom pod, crushed
4 medium cloves garlic, minced	6 whole cloves
2 teaspoons ground coriander	2 medium cassia or bay leaves
1½ teaspoons ground cumin	½ cup finely chopped cilantro

Soak the chilies in the hot water until softened. Drain and coarsely grind with a mortar and pestle.

Rinse the chicken well under cold water and drain. Prick the chicken all over with a fork or a sharp knife and place it in a large bowl.

In a separate small bowl, combine the ground chilies, onion, oil, ginger, garlic, coriander, cumin, turmeric, salt, black pepper, and nutmeg. Rub this spice mixture into the chicken with your hands, making sure it is well-coated. Add the cinnamon stick, green and black cardamom pods, cloves, and cassia leaves. Cover and marinate for at least 2 hours in the refrigerator.

Once the chicken is marinated, place it with all the marinade and whole spices in a large heavy-bottomed saucepan. Cook, uncovered, over medium-high heat, stirring from time to time, for 10 minutes. Reduce the heat to low, cover, and simmer, stirring often to prevent scorching, until the chicken is tender and cooked through, about 40 minutes. Transfer the chicken to a serving dish, sprinkle with cilantro, and serve hot.

CHICKEN WITH AROMATIC SAUCE

Masaledaar Kukhuraa

Makes 4 to 6 servings

This is a slightly more elaborate dish than the preceding chicken recipes as it is cooked in a spicy, seasoned yogurt sauce. This recipe can be prepared one day in advance and reheated on the stovetop by gently simmering until it is heated through. Serve this chicken with buttered rice, warm bread, vegetables, and pickles.

---

1 (3- to 3½-pound) chicken, skinned and cut into 8 to 10 pieces
1 teaspoon salt, adjust to taste
½ teaspoon ground turmeric
¼ cup vegetable oil plus 2 tablespoons
4 large onions, 3 coarsely chopped (about 3 cups) and 1 halved lengthwise and thinly sliced
4 fresh hot green chilies, split lengthwise
1½ tablespoons peeled and coarsely chopped fresh ginger
4 medium cloves garlic, coarsely chopped
1 tablespoon ground coriander
1½ teaspoons ground cumin
⅛ teaspoon freshly ground black pepper
⅛ teaspoon ground nutmeg
3 medium tomatoes, finely chopped (about 3 cups)
1 cup plain yogurt, stirred
1½ teaspoons fragrant garam masalaa (*see page 311*)
½ cup finely chopped cilantro
2 or 3 green onions (white and pale green parts), cut into ¼-inch pieces

---

Rinse the chicken pieces well under cold water and drain. Prick with a fork or a sharp knife and place in a large bowl. With your hands, rub the chicken with the salt and turmeric and set aside in the refrigerator.

Heat ¼ cup of the oil in a heavy saucepan over medium-high heat. When hot, but not smoking, add the chopped onion, green chilies, ginger, and garlic and cook until onions are soft but not browned, stirring frequently, about 5 minutes. With a slotted spoon transfer the onion mixture to a blender or food processor, reserving the oil in the pan. Blend the mixture to a smooth paste.

Sauté the onion slices in the oil remaining in the pan over medium-high heat until crisp and golden brown. With a slotted spoon transfer the crisp onions to a plate lined with paper towels to drain and set aside.

Return the onion paste to the pan. If there is only a little oil left, add the remaining 2 tablespoons oil. Stir in the coriander, cumin, black pepper, and nutmeg and cook over medium-high heat until lightly browned, about 2

minutes. Add the tomatoes and continue cooking, stirring, until the tomatoes are soft and the juices evaporate, about 5 minutes. Add the yogurt 1 tablespoon at a time, mixing after each addition, and cook until it is well incorporated.

Add the chicken and 1 cup of water, stir well, and cook, uncovered, for 10 minutes. Reduce the heat to medium-low, cover the pan, and cook until the chicken is tender and the sauce has thickened, about 25 minutes.

Stir in the garam masalaa. Transfer the chicken to a serving dish, add the fried onions, cilantro, and green onions, and serve piping hot.

TANDOORI CHICKEN
Tandoori Kukhuraa

Makes 4 to 6 servings

Tandoori chicken is originally from northern India, but it is also very popular in Nepal. Traditionally, the marinated chicken is cooked in a *tandoor*, a cylindrical clay oven sunk in the earth that is heated to a very high temperature with a charcoal fire. The chicken cooks very quickly in the intense heat, which seals in the juices and flavor. Although the authentic flavor of a *tandoor* cannot be duplicated in a regular oven or on an outdoor grill, this is my simplified version, especially adapted for Nepali palates, which is equally delicious.

1 (3- to 3½-pound) chicken, skinned and cut into 8 to 10 pieces

First Marinade:
¼ cup fresh lemon or lime juice
1½ teaspoons salt, or adjust to taste
1 teaspoon ground turmeric

Second Marinade:
1 medium onion, chopped (about 1 cup)
3 fresh mild green chili peppers, stemmed
¼ cup finely chopped cilantro
4 large cloves garlic, peeled
1 tablespoon peeled and coarsely chopped fresh ginger
2 dried red chilies, coarsely broken and seeded

2 teaspoons coriander seeds
1 teaspoon cumin seeds
1½ cups plain yogurt, stirred
¼ cup tomato paste
2 tablespoons vegetable oil
1 tablespoon paprika
1 teaspoon fragrant garam masalaa (*see page 311*)
¼ cup butter, melted

Garnish:
1 medium red onion, thinly sliced
1 medium cucumber, thinly sliced
2 medium tomatoes, cut into wedges
1 lemon, cut into wedges
3 or 4 whole fresh green chili peppers
2 or 3 cilantro sprigs

Rinse the chicken well under cold water and drain. Prick the pieces all over with a fork or sharp knife, making diagonal slits in the fleshy parts to allow the marinade to penetrate. Place the chicken in a bowl and add the first marinade ingredients: the lemon juice, salt, and turmeric. Rub over the chicken, and set aside to marinate in the refrigerator for at least 2 hours.

Meanwhile make the second marinade: Combine the onion, green chilies, cilantro, garlic, ginger, dried chilies, coriander seeds, and cumin seeds in a blender or food processor and process until the mixture forms a smooth paste. Add 1 or 2 tablespoons of water to facilitate blending, if necessary. Transfer the mixture to a bowl and stir in the yogurt, tomato paste, oil, paprika, and garam masalaa.

After the the chicken has marinated for 2 hours, pour the second marinade over the chicken and mix well, making sure that each piece is coated. Place the chicken and marinade in a sealable heavy plastic bag, secure it, and refrigerate for at least 8 hours. Shake and turn the chicken occasionally during the marinating process.

When you are ready to proceed, bring the chicken back to room temperature. Preheat a charcoal or gas grill or broiler to medium-high heat. Place the chicken pieces coated with the marinade on a wire rack and grill or broil them, turning frequently and basting with the melted butter, until well browned on all sides and cooked through, about 30 minutes.

Transfer the chicken to a platter, garnish it with the red onion slices, cucumber slices, tomato wedges, lemon wedges, chili peppers, and cilantro, and serve hot.

JOMSOM CHICKEN CURRY

Jomsom Kukhuraa Curry

Makes 4 to 6 servings

Here is another easy-to-prepare chicken dish that does not require marinating but has a delicious spicy flavor. Serve it with the traditional Nepali accompaniments of rice, lentils, and vegetables or with warm bread.

This chicken curry gets its name from a beautiful small village, Jomsom, situated in the Mustang District of Nepal. About ten years ago, when my daughter and I were trekking from Pokhara-Jomsom en route to Muktinath, the highlight of our trek was stopping at one of the Thakali restaurants in Jomsom. We were served a spicy chicken curry cooked in a delicious blend of fresh herb and spices. We loved the dish so much and started to call it *Jomsom ko khukuraa* curry. This is my simplified version of the chicken curry eaten there.

¼ cup vegetable oil

1 (1-inch) cinnamon stick

2 green cardamom pods, crushed

4 whole cloves

2 small cassia leaves

2 medium onions, finely chopped (about 2 cups)

1 (3- to 3½-pound) chicken, skinned and cut into 8 to 10 small pieces

1½ teaspoons salt, adjust to taste

1½ teaspoons ground cumin

1½ teaspoons ground coriander

½ teaspoon ground turmeric

2 medium tomatoes, finely chopped (about 2 cups)

2 fresh hot green chilies, split lengthwise

1 tablespoon minced fresh ginger

3 cloves garlic, minced

1 teaspoon Nepali garam masalaa (*see page 310*)

4 or 5 green onions (white and pale green parts), finely chopped

½ cup finely chopped cilantro

Heat the oil in a large heavy saucepan over medium-high heat. When the oil is hot, but not smoking, add the cinnamon stick, cardamom pods, cloves, and cassia leaves and fry until they begin to puff up, darken, and give off a pleasant aroma, about 5 seconds. Add the onions and cook until lightly browned, 5 to 7 minutes.

Adjust the heat to high, add the chicken, and cook, stirring occasionally, until lightly browned. Add the salt, cumin, coriander, and turmeric and stir for another minute. Then add the tomatoes and cook until they are slightly soft, about 2 minutes. Add 1 cup of water and bring the mixture to a boil, uncovered. Reduce the heat to medium-low, cover, and continue cooking for 10 minutes, stirring from time to time to make sure the sauce does not burn or stick to the bottom of the pan.

Uncover and add the green chilies, ginger, garlic, and garam masalaa and continue cooking until the chicken is tender and well coated with the smooth sauce, about 25 more minutes. Transfer the chicken to a serving dish, sprinkle the green onions and cilantro on top, and serve hot.

GRILLED CHICKEN

Makes 4 to 6 servings

Kukhuraa ko Sekuwaa

Sekuwaa is the term used to describe any meat dish that is cooked directly under or over a heat source, such as a broiler or grill. In this easy-to-prepare dish, boneless, skinless chicken is tenderized by yogurt and aromatic spices and then cooked by the *sekuwaa* method. The secret is to not overcook the meat, especially the breast, which tends to dry out very quickly. Chicken *sekuwaa* is served as an appetizer with a spicy chutney or it can supplement any lunch or dinner menu.

2½ to 3 pounds skinless, boneless chicken breasts, cut into 1½-inch pieces

1½ tablespoons plus 1 teaspoons fresh lemon or lime juice

1⅛ teaspoons salt, adjust to taste

2 medium red onions, 1 chopped (about 1 cup), and 1 sliced ⅛-inch thick and separated into rings

12 fresh mild green chilies

1 tablespoon peeled and coarsely chopped fresh ginger

3 large cloves garlic, peeled

1 cup plain yogurt, stirred

2 tablespoons vegetable oil

1 teaspoon ground paprika

1 teaspoon Nepali garam masalaa (*see page 310*)

½ teaspoon ground cumin

½ teaspoon ground turmeric

1 lemon or lime, cut into wedges

2 medium tomatoes, cut into 6 wedges

2 or 3 sprigs of cilantro

8 to 10 grilling skewers (if wooden, soak for 30 minutes before use)

Place the chicken in a large bowl with 1½ tablespoons of the lemon juice and 1 teaspoon of the salt. Mix thoroughly and set aside for 10 minutes. Put the chopped onion, 2 of the green chilies, the ginger, and garlic in a blender or a food processor and process until they are minced. Transfer the mixture to a small bowl and stir in the yogurt, oil, paprika, garam masalaa, cumin, and turmeric. Combine the mixture with the chicken, making sure that each piece is well coated. Cover the bowl and marinate for at least 2 hours in the refrigerator.

Meanwhile, marinate the onion rings in the remaining 1 teaspoon of lemon juice and ⅛ teaspoon of salt.

Preheat a charcoal or gas grill to medium-high heat. Thread the marinated chicken onto the skewers, place them over the rack, and grill, turning frequently, until they are lightly browned on all sides and cooked through, 20 to 25 minutes. Remove them from the grill and allow the chicken to cool a little before removing it from the skewers. Arrange the chicken on a serving dish and surround it with the marinated onion, lemon wedges, tomato wedges, remaining 10 green chilies, and the cilantro sprigs, and serve.

CHICKEN WITH CAULIFLOWER

Makes 4 to 6 servings

Cauli-Kukhuraa

In this dish, chicken and cauliflower are cooked together, lending each other flavor, and resulting in a delectable and textured dish. Add the cauliflower florets at the end of the cooking process, ensuring that they retain their shape but have enough time to absorb the spices and flavor of the chicken. This recipe uses bone-in chicken, which is more flavorful, but you can substitute skinless, boneless chicken and serve it as a one-dish meal with *cheuraa* (pressed rice flakes) for a mid-afternoon snack, or as part of a main meal with steamed rice.

---

1 (2½- to 3-pound) chicken, skin removed
  and cut into 12 to 14 pieces
¼ cup vegetable oil
⅛ teaspoon fenugreek seeds
1 cassia leaf
1 medium onion, finely chopped (about
  1 cup)
2 fresh mild green chilies, chopped
1 tablespoon minced fresh ginger
2 large cloves garlic, finely chopped

1 tablespoon Nepali garam masalaa *(see
  page 310)*
2 teaspoons cayenne pepper powder, or to
  taste
½ teaspoon ground turmeric
Salt, adjust to taste
½ head cauliflower, cut into 1½-inch florets
  (about 4 cups)
¼ cup finely chopped cilantro

Wash the chicken pieces thoroughly with cold water and drain completely. Prick with a fork or a sharp knife and set aside.

Heat the oil in a large heavy saucepan over medium-high heat. When hot, but not smoking, add the fenugreek seeds and fry until dark brown and highly fragrant, about 5 seconds. Add the cassia leaf, then immediately add the onions, green chilies, ginger, and garlic and cook until they are lightly browned, stirring frequently, 5 to 7 minutes.

Stir in the chicken pieces, garam masalaa, cayenne pepper powder, and turmeric and cook, uncovered, stirring from time to time, until the chicken is lightly browned, about 10 minutes. Add some salt and stir well. Reduce the heat to medium-low, cover the pan, and cook until the chicken is almost tender, about 15 minutes.

Add the cauliflower and mix well until the florets are evenly coated with spices. Cover the pan and continue cooking, gently stirring as needed, until the chicken is tender and cooked through, the cauliflower is crisp-tender,* and the spice mixture is boiled down and absorbed, about 20 minutes.

Taste for seasoning and add additional salt if needed. Transfer the mixture to a serving dish, sprinkle with the cilantro, and serve.

*Note: It is important to note that cauliflower goes from being undercooked to over-cooked very quickly. Since cauliflower has a tendency to become mushy, stir gently.

EGG AND CHICKEN ROTI

Makes 4 to 6 servings

Phool ko Roti

This versatile dish can be made with almost any combination of additions, including chopped leftover meat, vegetables, paneer cheese, or tofu. The ingredients are first cooked in a skillet, then covered with well-beaten eggs and cooked until it resembles thin flatbread. Egg *roti* is served with any spicy condiments as a snack or a light lunch.

6 eggs
¼ teaspoon salt, or adjust to taste
¼ teaspoon freshly ground black pepper
2 tablespoons vegetable oil
1 cup finely chopped cooked chicken or
  turkey
1 small onion, finely chopped (about ½ cup)
½ small red or green bell pepper, cored and
  finely chopped (about ½ cup)

½ cup fresh or frozen peas, thawed and
  drained
½ cup fresh or frozen corn kernels, thawed
  and drained
3 or 4 green onions (white and pale green
  parts), finely chopped
1 cup thinly sliced mushrooms

In a medium-size bowl, whisk together the eggs, salt, and black pepper until thoroughly mixed, but not foamy. Set aside.

Heat the oil in a large nonstick or cast-iron skillet over medium-high heat. When the oil is hot, add the chicken, onions, bell pepper, peas, corn, green onions, and mushrooms and cook until they are soft, 5 to 7 minutes.

Slowly pour the egg mixture into the skillet, covering the vegetables evenly. Lower the heat to medium, cover the skillet, and continue cooking, undisturbed, until the eggs are well set, about 4 minutes. Carefully flip the roti, and cook the other side until it is lightly browned, about 1 minute. Transfer the roti to a platter, cut it into wedges, and serve.

SPICY SCRAMBLED EGGS

Makes 4 to 6 servings

Phool ko Bhujuri

Bhujuri, the Nepali version of scrambled eggs, is made with herbs, spices, and chopped vegetables or cooked meat. For this recipe, any vegetables can be used. *Bhujuri* goes well with rice or roti, or as a snack with *cheuraa* (pressed rice flakes).

---

3 tablespoons vegetable oil
1 medium onion, finely chopped (about 1 cup)
2 fresh mild green chilies, finely chopped
2 or 3 green onions (white and pale green parts), finely chopped
1 teaspoon minced fresh ginger
1 medium clove garlic, finely chopped
1 medium tomato, chopped (about 1 cup)

¼ cup finely chopped cilantro
1½ cups thinly sliced mushrooms
¼ teaspoon salt, or adjust to taste
¼ teaspoon ground cumin
¼ teaspoon cayenne pepper powder, or to taste
⅛ teaspoon freshly ground black pepper
6 eggs, lightly beaten

Heat the oil in a large nonstick or cast-iron skillet over medium-high heat. When the oil is hot, add the onion, green chilies, green onions, ginger, and garlic and cook, stirring constantly, until the onions are soft, 5 to 7 minutes. Add the tomatoes, cilantro, mushrooms, salt, cumin, cayenne pepper powder, and black pepper and continue cooking until all the liquid has evaporated and the mixture is dry, about 7 minutes.

Pour in the beaten eggs and cook until the eggs are almost set. Then scramble them until they firm up and are lightly browned. Transfer the *bhujuri* to a platter and serve immediately.

NEPALI OMELET
Phool ko Saada Amlet

Makes 4 to 6 servings

A classic Nepali omelet consists simply of eggs, salt, and pepper, cooked in fragrant mustard oil, which imparts a particularly delicious flavor. Mustard oil is somewhat pungent and strong when raw, so it is heated well before using. Round cast-iron skillets called *taapke* are generally used for cooking omelets in Nepal to produce an attractive final dish. Omelets can be served at any time as a snack and are an easy food to make when the unexpected guest drops by. A combination of *cheuraa* (pressed rice flakes) and omelets is a popular snack.

6 eggs	¼ teaspoon freshly ground black pepper
¼ cup finely chopped cilantro	1½ tablespoons mustard oil or vegetable
2 fresh mild green chilies, finely chopped	oil
¼ teaspoon salt, or adjust to taste	

In a medium-size bowl, whisk together the eggs, cilantro, green chilies, salt, and black pepper until thoroughly mixed, but not foamy.

Heat the oil in a large nonstick or cast-iron skillet over medium-high heat. When the oil is hot, add the egg mixture, shaking the pan back and forth to spread the mixture evenly, and cook for 3 to 4 minutes, occasionally lifting the edges with a metal spatula to allow the uncooked egg to run underneath. When the eggs are almost set, carefully flip the omelet and cook the other side until it is well set, about 1 minute. Fold the omelet in half, transfer it to a platter, cut into wedges, and serve immediately.

Variation
VEGETABLE OMELET
Add 1 finely chopped small red onion, 1 finely chopped small tomato, ¼ cup finely chopped cilantro, 3 or 4 finely chopped green onions, and 1½ cups thinly sliced mushrooms. Cook the omelet as directed above, replacing the oil with 2 tablespoons of butter.

EGG CURRY
Phool ko Tarkaari

Makes 4 to 6 servings

Simple but elegant, this egg curry has a distinctive flavor, with an onion- and tomato-based gravy. It pairs perfectly with rice, roti and fresh salad on the side served for a light lunch or dinner.

6 eggs	2 teaspoons Nepali garam masalaa *(see page 310)*
¼ cup plus 1 tablespoon vegetable oil	1 teaspoon salt, adjust to taste
1 medium onion, coarsely chopped (about 1 cup)	½ teaspoon ground turmeric
2 fresh mild or hot green chilies	½ teaspoon cayenne pepper powder
4 medium cloves garlic, peeled	½ cup plain yogurt, stirred
1 tablespoon peeled and coarsely chopped fresh ginger	3 or 4 green onions (white and pale green parts), finely chopped
1 medium tomato, finely chopped (about 1 cup)	¼ cup finely chopped cilantro

Using a pin, make a tiny hole in the rounder end of each egg (this helps prevent the shell from cracking or leaking while boiling). Place the eggs in a large pot in a single layer and cover with cold water. Bring them to a boil over high heat. Reduce the heat to medium-low, cover the pan, and cook until the eggs are hard-boiled, about 10 minutes. Drain the water and run the eggs under cold water. Crack them gently and remove the shells.

Heat ¼ cup of the oil in a heavy saucepan over medium-high heat and fry the whole eggs, turning them gently, until they are lightly browned on all sides. Remove them with a slotted spoon, draining as much oil as possible and leaving oil in pan, and transfer to a platter. When they are cool enough to handle, halve each egg lengthwise, and set aside.

Place the onion, green chilies, garlic, and ginger in a blender or food processor and process to make a smooth paste. Add enough water just to facilitate blending. Transfer the blended mixture into the saucepan with the oil. Add the remaining 1 tablespoon of oil and cook over medium-high heat until the mixture is lightly browned, about 5 minutes.

Add the tomato, garam masala, salt, turmeric, and cayenne pepper powder and cook, stirring from time to time, until the tomatoes are soft and all the juices evaporate, 5 to 7 minutes. Mix in the yogurt, 1 tablespoon at a time, stirring constantly. Continue cooking until the yogurt has been absorbed into the sauce, about 2 minutes. Add 1½ cups of water and bring the mixture to a boil. Reduce the heat to medium-low, cover the pan, and continue cooking until the sauce has thickened slightly, 7 to 10 minutes.

Carefully place the egg halves in the sauce one at a time, cover the pan, and cook, stirring gently a few times, for 7 minutes. Try to avoid too much stirring, as the egg yolks may separate from the whites. Transfer the curry to a serving dish, sprinkle with the green onions and cilantro, and serve.

Spicy Deviled Eggs / *Saandheko Phool*

SPICY DEVILED EGGS
Saandheko Phool

Makes 4 to 6 servings

Saandheko phool is similar to American deviled eggs, but much spicier. It is a delicious party dish with a simple spicy seasoning that gives the boiled eggs a unique flavor and texture. This dish is best served at room temperature as an appetizer or as part of a meal.

---

8 to 10 eggs
¼ cup sesame seeds
1 dried red chili, halved and seeded
1 teaspoon cumin seeds
4 whole timmur (Nepali pepper, *see page 30*)
3 tablespoons plain yogurt
1 teaspoon fresh lemon or lime juice
½ teaspoon salt, adjust to taste
2 tablespoons vegetable oil

¼ teaspoon fenugreek seeds
¼ teaspoon jimbu (Nepali aromatic herb; *see page 30*)
2 fresh mild green chilies, julienned
½ teaspoon ground turmeric
3 or 4 green onions (white and pale green parts), finely chopped
¼ cup finely chopped cilantro

Using a pin, make a tiny hole in the rounder end of each egg. This helps prevent the shell from cracking and leaking while boiling. Place the eggs in a large pot in a single layer, and cover with cold water. Bring to a boil over high heat. Reduce the heat to medium-low, cover the pan, and cook until the eggs are hard-boiled, about 10 minutes. Drain the water and run the eggs under cold water. Crack them gently and remove the shells. Halve each egg lengthwise and place them on a platter.

Heat a small cast-iron skillet over medium heat and toast the sesame seeds, dried chili, cumin seeds, and timmur, stirring constantly with a wooden spoon to prevent the seeds from flying all over, until they give off a pleasant aroma and the sesame seeds are a few shades darker, about 5 minutes. Pour the spices into a dry container to halt the toasting. Let them cool, then transfer to a spice grinder and grind to a fine powder. (A mortar and pestle can also be used.) Place the ground spices in a small bowl and combine with the yogurt, lemon juice, and salt to make a paste.

Heat the oil in a small skillet over medium-high heat. When the oil is hot, but not smoking, add the fenugreek seeds and jimbu and fry until dark brown and highly fragrant, about 5 seconds. Add the green chilies, turmeric, and the prepared spice paste and mix well. Transfer everything to a small bowl and cool.

Very carefully, dip each egg half into the paste to coat it well. Place the eggs on a tray, sprinkle them with the green onions and cilantro, cover, and refrigerate until ready to serve.

Chapter 9

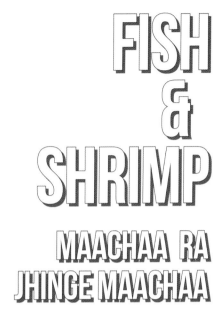

FISH & SHRIMP

MAACHAA RA JHINGE MAACHAA

Fish play a significant role in Nepali society for religious, social, and culinary reasons. Fish symbolize good luck, prosperity, and happiness. In the Newar community, dried fish is offered to friends and family as *sagun* (blessed) food to bring good luck, success, and good fortune. It is also considered sacred and is offered to various deities during festivals.

Because Nepal is a landlocked country, most fish comes from Himalayan rivers. They are caught by local fishermen using old-fashioned fishing techniques with bamboo poles, rods, and fishing traps. The most common fish available are carp, trout, and catfish. In many remote areas of Nepal where there is no transportation or processing facilities, smoking or sun-drying is used to preserve fish. Small dried fish known as *sidraa maachaa* are very popular and used extensively in Nepali cooking. Until recently, most other fish were imported from India, but the Nepali government has successfully encouraged commercial fish farming to meet local needs.

No matter what kind of fish one uses, the most important factor is that the fish should be absolutely fresh before cooking, keeping in mind that spoilage starts as soon as it is caught if the fish is not kept cold. Nepali techniques for cooking fish are very simple. It is usually marinated and deep-fried or curried. Fish is usually cooked as steaks, and fillets are not a usual custom. Most of the recipes in this chapter use fish steaks, but you can substitute fish fillets if you prefer.

FOODS & FLAVORS FROM NEPAL

FISH IN YOGURT SAUCE
Dahi-Maachaa

Makes 4 to 6 servings

This is one of my favorite methods of cooking fish and one of the most-loved dishes in my family. Here the fish is sautéed and then simmered in a spiced yogurt sauce resulting in a very flavorful dish.

10 to 12 (1-inch-thick) fish steaks or fillets (any kind), rinsed and patted dry	3 small cassia leaves
1 tablespoon fresh lemon or lime juice	4 whole cloves
2 teaspoons yellow mustard seeds, ground	2 medium onions, sliced (about 2 cups)
1 teaspoon salt	4 fresh hot or mild green chilies, chopped
½ teaspoon ground turmeric	1 tablespoon peeled and finely chopped fresh ginger
1½ cups plus 3 tablespoons vegetable oil	3 medium cloves garlic, finely chopped
1 (1-inch) cinnamon stick, halved	3 medium tomatoes, chopped (about 3 cups)
4 green cardamom pods, crushed	1 cup plain yogurt, stirred

In a bowl combine the fish with the lemon juice, ground mustard seeds, salt, and turmeric; mix well to coat. Heat 1½ cups of the oil in a large cast-iron skillet over medium-high heat until it reaches 350 to 375 degrees F. Test the oil by placing a small piece of fish into the oil—if it bubbles and rises to the surface immediately, it is ready. Fry half the fish steaks in the oil, placing one at a time in a single layer and not crowding the pan. Turn as needed, until light brown, about 4 minutes. Remove with a slotted spoon and transfer to a paper towel-lined platter to drain. Repeat with the remaining fish.

To make the sauce, heat the remaining 3 tablespoons of oil in a wide saucepan over medium-high heat until hot, but not smoking. Add the cinnamon stick, cardamom pods, cassia leaves, and cloves and fry until they begin to puff up, darken, and give off a pleasant aroma, about 5 seconds. Add the onions and cook until lightly browned, 5 to 7 minutes. Add the green chilies, ginger, and garlic and stir for 1 minute. Add the tomatoes and some salt to taste and cook until the tomatoes are soft and the juices evaporate. Mix in the yogurt, 1 tablespoon at a time and cook until blended, 2 to 3 minutes. Add 1 cup of hot water and bring to a boil. Reduce the heat to low, add the fish and stir gently. Cover and cook for 5 minutes to blend the flavors. Remove the pan from the heat and set aside, covered for at least 10 minutes before serving.

FISH IN AROMATIC GRAVY

Makes 4 to 6 servings

Ledo Maachaa

Here is a simple, mildly spiced fish curry that can be prepared a day in advance, as the fish will soak up the gravy, making it even more delicious the next day. Reheat it on the stovetop by gently simmering, but add the lemon, cilantro, and green chili just before serving.

2 dried red chilies, halved and seeded
¼ cup hot water
10 to 12 (1-inch-thick) fish steaks (trout, bass, carp or any fish of your choice), well rinsed and patted dry
1 teaspoon salt, adjust to taste
½ teaspoon ground turmeric
2 medium onions, chopped (about 2 cups)
1 tablespoon peeled and chopped fresh ginger
4 small cloves garlic, peeled
3 tablespoons vegetable oil
1 (1-inch) cinnamon stick, halved
2 cassia leaves
3 medium tomatoes, finely chopped (about 3 cups)
1½ teaspoons ground brown mustard seeds
1 teaspoon ground cumin
1 teaspoon ground coriander
⅛ teaspoon freshly ground black pepper
2 tablespoons fresh lemon or lime juice
½ cup finely chopped cilantro
4 fresh hot or mild green chilies, cut into long slivers

Soak the dried red chilies in the hot water until softened. Gently rub the fish with the salt and turmeric to coat completely and set aside.

Place the chilies with the soaking water, onions, ginger, and garlic in a food processor or blender and process to make a smooth paste.

Heat the oil in a heavy saucepan over medium-high heat until hot, but not smoking. Add the cinnamon stick and cassia leaves and fry until fully fragrant, about 5 seconds. Add the onion paste and cook, stirring frequently, until lightly browned, about 5 minutes. Add the tomatoes, ground mustard seeds, cumin, coriander, and black pepper and continue cooking, stirring as needed, until the tomatoes are soft and the juices evaporate. Add 1 cup of warm water and bring the mixture to a boil. Reduce the heat to medium-low, cover, and cook, stirring as needed, until the sauce has thickened slightly, about 15 minutes.

Add the fish, placing in a single layer in the sauce, and cook covered, stirring gently from time to time, until cooked through, 6 to 8 minutes. Mix in the lemon juice, transfer to a serving dish, and garnish with the cilantro and green chilies. Serve hot.

MALEKHU-STYLE FRIED FISH

Makes 4 to 6 servings

Malekhu ko Maachaa

This recipe is named after Malekhu, a little village located in Dhading, halfway between Kathmandu and Pokhara, which overlooks the Trisuli River (*see pages 18-19*). Malekhu is famous for its just-caught fresh fish from the Trisuli River and the road-side restaurants serve delicious deep-fried, smoked, and curried fish. Local buses usually stop at Malekhu for lunch breaks for travelers to enjoy the fish. This is my Malekhu-inspired fish recipe that I tried to keep as authentic as possible.

2 pounds small whole smelt fish (or use any small fish of your choice), cleaned, well rinsed and drained	½ teaspoon cayenne pepper powder
	1 tablespoon minced fresh ginger
	1 clove garlic, minced
1 teaspoon salt, adjust to taste	2 tablespoons all-purpose white flour
2 tablespoons lemon or lime juice	2 cups vegetable oil
½ teaspoon ground turmeric	Lemon wedges for serving

In a mixing bowl, combine fish with salt, lemon juice, turmeric, cayenne pepper powder, ginger, garlic, and flour and mix well. Rub each piece gently by hand, making sure they are all well coated. Let them stand for 15 minutes in the refrigerator.

Heat the oil in a large cast-iron skillet over medium-high heat until it reaches 350 to 375 degrees F. Test the readiness of the oil by dropping a small piece of fish into the hot oil. If it bubbles and rises to the surface immediately, it is ready. Gently drop some of the fish into the oil, one at a time, keeping them in a single layer—do not crowd the pan. Deep-fry, turning them frequently, until they are firm and golden brown on all sides, 5 to 7 minutes. With a slotted spoon, remove the fish, draining as much oil as possible, and transfer them to a paper towel-lined platter to drain. Repeat the process with the remaining fish.

Transfer the fried fish to a serving dish, surround with lemon wedges, and serve.

NEPALI-STYLE FRIED FISH

Makes 4 to 6 servings

Maachaa Taareko

This is a quick and easy-to-prepare deep-fried fish recipe. The fish steaks are first rubbed with turmeric, salt, and lemon to remove any fishy smell before mixing in other spices. (For a spicier version, see Variation next page.) Nepalese like to cook fish with the bones and skin, because this way it keeps its shape and retains flavor, but you can substitute fish fillets. Serve this on its own as a snack accompanied by a spicy chutney or as a tasty part of any lunch or dinner menu. (See also recipe for Spicy Fish Soup, page 218, that uses this fried fish as an ingredient.)

10 to 12 (1-inch-thick) fish steaks (trout, bass, carp or any fish of your choice), well-rinsed and drained

2 tablespoons plus 1 teaspoon fresh lemon or lime juice

1¼ teaspoons salt, or adjust to taste

½ teaspoon ground turmeric

2 teaspoons ground yellow mustard seeds

1 clove garlic, minced

1 teaspoon cayenne pepper powder

1 medium red onion, sliced ⅛-inch-thick and separated into rings

2 cups vegetable oil

1 lemon or lime, cut into wedges

2 medium tomatoes, cut into 6 wedges

Place the fish steaks in a bowl with 2 tablespoons of the lemon juice, 1 teaspoon salt, and turmeric and mix well. Rub each piece gently by hand, making sure the steaks are well coated. Let them stand for 10 minutes to absorb the salt. Add the ground mustard seeds, garlic, and cayenne pepper powder and mix well. Cover the bowl and marinate the fish for 20 minutes in the refrigerator.

In the meantime, in a bowl, combine the onion rings with the remaining 1 teaspoon lemon juice and ¼ teaspoon salt. Set aside to marinate.

Heat the oil in a large cast-iron skillet over medium-high heat until it reaches 350 to 375 degrees F. Test the readiness of the oil by dropping a small piece of fish into the hot oil. If it bubbles and rises to the surface immediately, it is ready. Gently drop some of the fish steaks into the oil, one at a time, keeping them in a single layer—do not crowd the pan. Deep-fry, turning them frequently, until they are firm and golden brown on all sides, 5 to 7 minutes. With a slotted spoon, remove the fish, draining as much oil as possible, and transfer them to a paper towel-lined platter to drain. Repeat the process with the remaining fish.

Transfer the fried fish to a serving dish, surround with the marinated onions and lemon and tomatoes wedges, and serve.

Variation:
SPICY NEPALI-STYLE FRIED FISH
Soak 2 halved and seeded dried red chilies in ¼ cup hot water until softened.
Drain the chilies and grind to a paste in a mortar and pestle. Add the chili
paste to the spice rub in the first step, along with an additional clove of
minced garlic, 1 teaspoon minced fresh ginger, ½ teaspoon ground cumin,
½ teaspoon ground coriander, and ⅛ teaspoon black pepper, but omit the
cayenne pepper powder. Marinate and fry the fish as in recipe.

SPICY FISH SOUP
Maachaa ko Ras

Makes 4 to 6 servings

In Nepal, fish is often cooked with ground mustard seeds, and the two ingredients seem to compliment each other naturally. Brown mustard seeds (*raayo*) are more flavorful and pungent than yellow mustard seeds (*sarsyun*). This soup can be cooked with either variety.

2 dried red chilies, halved and seeded	1 tablespoon minced fresh ginger
¼ cup hot water	Salt, adjust to taste
2 medium tomatoes, finely chopped (about 2 cups)	1 tablespoon vegetable oil
	¼ teaspoon fenugreek seeds
5 medium cloves garlic, minced	2½ cups hot water
1½ tablespoons yellow or brown mustard seeds, ground	1 recipe Nepali-style Fried Fish (page 216), without garnishes
1 large shallot, minced	½ cup finely chopped cilantro

Soak the chilies in the hot water until softened. Drain and coarsely grind with a mortar and pestle. In a small bowl, combine the chili paste, tomatoes, garlic, ground mustard seeds, shallot, ginger, and salt to taste, and set aside.

Heat the oil in a medium-size saucepan over medium-high heat until hot, but not smoking. Add the fenugreek seeds and fry until dark brown and highly fragrant, about 5 seconds. Add the spice paste and cook, stirring frequently, until browned and all the liquid evaporates, about 5 minutes. Stir in 2½ cups of hot water, bring the mixture to a boil, and continue boiling until the liquid has reduced and thickened slightly, about 7 minutes.

Add the fried fish, reduce the heat to medium-low, cover the pan, and cook until the flavors blend, 8 to 10 minutes. Transfer to a serving dish, sprinkle with the cilantro, and serve hot.

MUSTARD OIL FRIED FISH

Makes 4 to 6 servings

Sarsyun Maachaa

Mustard oil (*tori ko tel*), a very important cooking oil in Nepal, has a nutty taste and aroma. It is always heated to the smoking point before adding any ingredients because the raw oil has a very bitter, sharp flavor. Heating it to a high temperature reduces its pungency.

3 fresh mild or hot green chilies, minced	½ teaspoon ground yellow mustard seeds
1 teaspoon minced fresh ginger	2 tablespoons fresh lemon or lime juice
1 large clove garlic, minced	10 to 12 (1-inch-thick) fish steaks (trout, bass,
1½ teaspoons salt, adjust to taste	carp or any fish of your choice), well-rinsed
½ teaspoon ground turmeric	and patted dry
⅛ teaspoon freshly ground black pepper	½ cup chickpea flour (besan)
1 teaspoon ground brown mustard seeds	1½ cups mustard oil

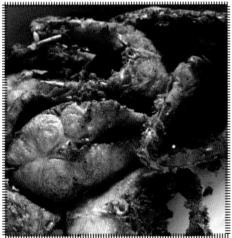

In a medium-size bowl, combine the green chilies, ginger, garlic, salt, turmeric, black pepper, and both ground mustard seeds. Add the lemon juice, mix into a paste, and set aside for 5 minutes. Place the fish steaks in the bowl and rub well to coat thoroughly with the spice paste. Cover and marinate for 20 minutes in the refrigerator.

Dredge the fish steaks in the chickpea flour, shaking off any excess, and place them on a tray. Heat the mustard oil in a large cast-iron skillet over medium-high heat. When the oil is faintly smoking, carefully place the fish in a single layer in the pan, about four pieces at a time. Do not crowd the pan. Fry, turning 2 to 3 times, until brown on both sides, 5 to 6 minutes. With a slotted spoon, remove the fish, draining as much oil as possible, and transfer to a paper towel-lined platter to drain. Repeat with the remaining fish, adding more oil if needed, and making sure the oil is heated well before adding the fish. Transfer the fried fish to a platter and serve hot.

LEMON-BUTTER FISH

Nauni Maachaa

Makes 4 to 6 servings

The following recipe is one of the easiest and fastest ways to cook fish. All you do is mix the spices with the fish fillets and then pan-fry everything. You can serve the fish with vegetables and the leftover fish can be used to make a quick lunch the next day. You can also use lime instead of the lemon for "Lime-Buttered Fish."

1 teaspoon garlic powder
½ teaspoon ground yellow mustard seeds
½ teaspoon cayenne pepper powder
1 teaspoon salt, adjust to taste
⅛ teaspoon freshly ground black pepper
2 tablespoons fresh lemon juice

2 pounds white fish fillets, cut into 2½-inch pieces, rinsed, and patted dry
8 to 10 tablespoons unsalted butter
1 lemon, cut into wedges
1 or 2 sprigs cilantro

In a medium-size bowl, combine the garlic powder, ground mustard seeds, cayenne pepper powder, salt, and black pepper. Add the lemon juice and mix it into a paste. Place the fish fillet pieces in the bowl and mix them with the spice paste, rubbing well to coat thoroughly. Set them aside for 10 minutes in the refrigerator.

Melt 8 tablespoons of the butter in a medium-size nonstick or cast-iron skillet over medium heat. Add some of the fish (without crowding) and cook, turning carefully, until golden brown on each side, 6 to 7 minutes. Put the fillets on a plate. Repeat the process with the remaining fillets, adding more butter if needed. Transfer the fish to a platter, garnish with the lemon wedges and cilantro, and serve.

TEMPERED DRIED FISH

Makes 4 to 6 servings

Maachaa ko Sukuti Saandheko

Dried fish are very popular in Nepal and are used extensively in various recipes, eaten as fish jerky, or used to make pickles. I usually make my own dried fish in a food dehydrator, but it is also available at Asian markets and specialty food stores where you can find small and medium-size whole dried fish. When selecting the fish, make sure it is freshly dried or smoked, as it tends to spoil quickly. Store-bought varieties may contain salt, so adjust the salt in this recipe accordingly. You can serve this dish as a spicy appetizer or as a side dish.

¼ cup vegetable oil
2½ to 3 pounds dried fish (any variety), skinned, boned, and separated into bite-size pieces
4 fresh hot or mild green chilies, julienned
4 large cloves garlic, thinly sliced
1 tablespoon peeled and finely julienned fresh ginger

½ cup finely chopped cilantro
4 or 5 green onions (white and pale green parts), finely chopped
2 tablespoons fresh lemon or lime juice
1 teaspoon cayenne pepper powder
⅛ teaspoon timmur (Nepali pepper, *see page 31*), finely ground with a mortar and pestle
Salt, adjust to taste

Heat the oil in a skillet over medium-low heat. When the oil is hot, fry the fish, stirring constantly, until lightly crispy, 1 to 2 minutes. Do not overcook. Using a slotted spoon, remove the fish, draining as much oil as possible, and place them in a bowl.

Add the green chilies, garlic, and ginger to the pan with the remaining oil and fry until crispy, about 1 minute. Mix them with the fish, along with the cilantro, green onions, lemon juice, cayenne pepper powder, and timmur. Taste and adjust the seasonings and add salt if needed. Cover the bowl and set it aside for 30 minutes to allow the flavors to develop. Transfer the mixture to a serving dish and serve at room temperature.

FISH PATTIES
Maachaa ko Bari

Makes 4 to 6 servings

Maachaa ko Bari are also called fish cutlets or fish cakes. They are crispy on the outside, soft, moist, and delicious inside. There are many ways to make fish patties, but this recipe uses whole fish, which are boiled first, separated from bones and skin, mixed with spices, formed into round patties and pan-fried. This is how my mother always prepared these traditional patties according to Nepali tradition, but you can substitute fish fillets for convenience. The fish patties can be served as a light snack or appetizer with chutney, or can supplement any Nepali meal.

---

1 or 2 whole trout or other fish of your choice (3½ to 4 pounds), cleaned and cut into 2 to 3 large pieces
1 cup finely chopped cilantro
2 medium red onions, 1 finely chopped (about 1 cup) and 1 sliced ⅛-inch thick and separated into rings
4 or 5 green onions (white and pale green parts), finely chopped
3 or 4 mild fresh green chilies, chopped
2 tablespoons plus 1 teaspoon fresh lemon or lime juice

2 teaspoons minced fresh ginger
2 medium cloves garlic, minced
1 teaspoon ground cumin
1 teaspoon cayenne pepper powder
Salt, adjust to taste
⅛ teaspoon freshly ground black pepper
2 eggs, lightly beaten
¼ cup dry bread crumbs
2 cups vegetable oil, plus more if needed
1 medium tomato, chopped
1 lemon or lime, cut into wedges

Bring a pot of water large enough to hold the fish to a rolling boil over medium-high heat. Add the fish and cook, uncovered, until the meat is falling off the bones, 10 to 15 minutes. Drain, and when cool enough to handle, carefully separate the meat from the bones, discarding the skin and bones.

Place the fish in a large bowl and mix in the cilantro, chopped onion, green onions, green chilies, 2 tablespoons of the lemon juice, ginger, garlic, cumin, cayenne pepper powder, ½ teaspoon salt, and the black pepper. Using a lightly oiled hand, shape the mixture into twelve 1-inch-thick patties.

Dip a patty into the beaten egg, let the excess drip off, roll it in the bread crumbs and shake off the excess, and put it on a platter. Repeat the procedure until all the patties are made. Set aside.

In a small bowl, combine the onion rings with the remaining 1 teaspoon lemon juice and ¼ teaspoon salt. Set aside to marinate while you cook the fish patties.

Heat the oil in a large nonstick or cast-iron skillet over medium-high heat. When the oil is hot, add some of the fish cakes and cook, turning carefully once or twice, until lightly browned and crispy on each side, 5 to 6 minutes. Remove them with a slotted spoon, draining as much oil as possible, and transfer them to a paper towel-lined platter to drain. Repeat the process with the remaining fish cakes, adding more oil if needed.

Transfer the cakes to a serving dish, surround them with the marinated onions and tomato and lemon or lime wedges, and serve.

NEPALI GARLIC BUTTER SHRIMP

Makes 4 to 6 servings

Lasoon, Nauni Haaleko
Jhinge Maachaa

A delicious, flavorful, and easy-to-cook shrimp dish, this can be served as an appetizer with chutney, or it can supplement any lunch or dinner menu.

1½ to 2 pounds large shrimp, shelled, deveined, washed and drained
1 teaspoon salt, adjust to taste
1 teaspoon garlic powder

½ cup unsalted butter
10 medium cloves garlic, chopped
1 tablespoon lemon or lime juice

Place the shrimp in a large bowl and season them with the garlic powder and salt. Cover the bowl and marinate the shrimp in the refrigerator for 15 minutes.

Melt the butter in a medium skillet over medium-high heat. Add chopped garlic and cook, stirring constantly, until it is light brown and crisp, 1 to 2 minutes. Using a slotted spoon, remove the garlic, draining as much butter as possible, and transfer to a small bowl. Add shrimp to the remaining butter, cook, stirring continuously, until they turn pink, 6 to 8 minutes. Add the lemon juice and mix well. Transfer everything to a serving dish, sprinkle the fried garlic on top, and serve.

SHRIMP WITH ONIONS AND TOMATOES
Jhinge Maachaa Masalaa

Makes 4 to 6 servings

This is an easy, delicious shrimp dish featuring a blend of spices that is perfect to serve with rice, or as an appetizer with chutney, and it can supplement any Nepali lunch or dinner menu. Do not overcook the shrimp because they tends to become dry and overly chewy.

¼ cup butter
1 medium onion, finely chopped (about 1 cup)
4 fresh mild green chilies, chopped
3 medium cloves garlic, minced
1½ teaspoons minced fresh ginger
2 medium ripe tomatoes, chopped (about 2 cups)

½ teaspoon ground turmeric
½ teaspoon ground cumin
⅛ teaspoon freshly ground black pepper
Salt, adjust to taste
1½ to 2 pounds large shrimp, shelled, deveined, washed, and patted dry
1 tablespoon fresh lemon or lime juice

Melt the butter in a wide nonstick or cast-iron skillet over medium-high heat. Add the onion, green chilies, garlic, and ginger and cook, stirring frequently, until they are soft, 4 to 5 minutes. Mix in the tomatoes, turmeric, cumin, black pepper, and salt to taste. Continue cooking, stirring from time to time, until the tomatoes are soft and the liquid evaporates, 5 to 7 minutes. Add the shrimp and cook, stirring continuously, until it turns pink, 6 to 8 minutes. Add the lemon juice and stir well. Transfer everything to a serving dish, and serve.

Chapter 10

STUFFED DUMPLINGS

NEPALI MOMOS

Momos, also known as *momo-cha*, are one of the most popular dishes enjoyed in Nepal. The *momo* is a bite-size dumpling made with a spoonful of stuffing wrapped in dough. The filling of meat becomes succulent as it produces an intensely flavored broth sealed inside the wrappers. *Momos* are usually steamed, though they are sometimes steam-fried or boiled. They can also be deep-fried until golden brown and crispy.

No one knows precisely how and when the *momo* traveled to Nepal and why they were named *momo*. Because this dish is popular among the Newar community of the Kathmandu valley, one prevalent belief is that Newari traders brought *momo* techniques from Lhasa, Tibet. They modified the seasoning of the dish with local ingredients, used water buffalo meat, and gave the dish a Nepali name. Others believe the dish was introduced to Nepali cuisine by Tibetans who settled in the mountains of Nepal. Though *momos* probably have a Tibetan or Chinese origin, they have since evolved to suit the Nepali palate.

Over the past several years, *momos* have become very popular and readily available on many restaurant menus. But it was not like that when my husband was growing up in Kathmandu. He remembers eating the most delicious and authentic *momos* in the run-down simple Momo House located near the Ranjana Cinema Hall alley in the old part of Kathmandu downtown. They were the pioneers of introducing the most authentic *momos* in town. I wonder how many people under the age of thirty would know about this place now—I am sure the older generation is still talking about *Ranjana galli ko raseelo momocha* (juicy *momos* from the alley).

In Nepal, the traditional *momo* is prepared with ground meat filling, but over the past several years, this has changed and they've become more elaborate. These days, momos are prepared with virtually any combination of ground meat, vegetables, tofu, and paneer cheese. They are also found in various sizes and shapes. *Momos* are also given fancy names such as *meetho momo* (delicious *momo*), *swaadista momo* (gourmet *momo*), *raseelo momo* (juicy *momo*), *jhol momo* (*momo* served with soup), *chilly momo* (spicy *momo*), *kothey momo* (steam-fried *momo*), *green momo* (blended with spinach), Himalayan *momo*, and the list goes on and on. For fillings, any variety of ground meat is used, such as goat, lamb, pork, water buffalo, yak meat, chicken, or turkey, and also seafood, combined with fresh herbs and spices. Sometimes two different kinds of meat and vegetables are used to give a different taste. Traditionally Nepalese prefer to use meat that has a lot of fat because it produces intensely flavored juicy *momos*. The best *momos* are always juicy, so sometimes a little oil is added to the leanest types of ground meat to keep the filling moist. All sorts of vegetables can be used to create vegetable fillings. The vegetables must be cut into very small pieces, flavored with fresh herbs and spices, and cooked lightly before being used for filling. The filling mixture should not be watery, as it will be difficult to seal the dough wrappers as the filling mixture will fall apart. Potatoes and cabbage are a popular vegetable combination.

Momo Making: A Family Affair

Making *momos* is an enjoyable affair. Family, friends and relatives often gather to spend joyful, leisurely time preparing *momos*. The dough is rolled very thin, the filling is placed in the center, and then the *momos* are shaped and sealed into small packets, leaving some space for them to fill with broth. Though *momo* shaping is an art, requiring patience, even young children can learn to enjoy the job. They can also help pound the herbs and spices in a mortar and pestle.

Serving Momos

Elderly relatives, friends, and the most respected family members are traditionally honored with a serving of the first batch of freshly steamed *momos*. Children are generally served a less spicy version. Instead of eating them all at once, guests are served *momos* in small quantities, which keeps them coming for second and third helpings. This way they can enjoy the steaming *momos* while they are still hot. The cook, host, and hostess always take pleasure serving others before they start eating their own *momos*.

Freshly steamed *momos* taste best served piping hot straight from the steamer pleated side up on a warm plate. If they are served as a meal, six to eight are a good serving. A meat-filled *momo* has to be eaten whole, as the flavorful juice in its steamed pocket will dribble out if it is broken. Though a well-seasoned juicy *momo* does not really need any condiments, it is traditionally accompanied by freshly made tomato chutney, or any other chutney of your choice.

Fresh Dough Wrappers or Store-Bought Wrappers

Fresh *momo* dough is made by mixing flour with water and kneading until the dough becomes smooth. Making dough is a matter of personal preference. Some cooks prefer white all-purpose flour to whole wheat flour because it makes a smooth and elastic dough, while others like to mix two parts white flour with one part whole wheat. Either way, the dough is kneaded until it is slightly sticky, then allowed to rest at room temperature for at least a half hour covered with a damp kitchen cloth, and then rolled out very thin and cut into three-inch circles. Making your own dough wrappers is time-consuming, but the result is rewarding. If you have the time you may find homemade wrappers a bit less fussy to work with, and your momos will be tastier than those made with purchased wrappers. Experienced Nepali cooks pride themselves on rolling the thinnest possible wrappers.

In the United States, my family sometimes makes *momos* with commercial dumpling wrappers, known as wonton wrappers or *gyoza*, found in the Asian sections of larger supermarkets or Asian markets. Commercial wrappers, which come in round or square shapes are convenient if you are in a hurry. If you decide to buy wrappers, make sure they are the paper-thin kind that become translucent when cooked. These wrappers tend to get soggy quickly, and should be steamed right after filling. If you use frozen wrappers, it is important to thaw them thoroughly and handle them very gently, as they become brittle and tear easily.

FRESH MOMO WRAPPERS

Makes 50 to 55 3-inch wrappers

Momo ko Pitho

This is a basic recipe for making momo wrappers from scratch. Though I use all-purpose flour, some people prefer to mix two-thirds of all-purpose flour with one-third whole wheat. Making your own wrappers takes time, but they are tastier than store-bought ones (see page 229).

> 3½ cups all-purpose white flour plus extra for kneading
> ½ teaspoon salt (optional)

In a medium-size bowl, combine the flour and salt. Make a well in the center and add ¾ to 1 cup of room temperature water, a little at a time, mixing with your fingers until the flour comes together in a crumbly mass. Transfer the dough to a floured surface and knead until it becomes smooth and elastic, about 5 to 6 minutes. If the dough is too stiff and dry, knead in a little more water to make it elastic and pliable. If the dough is too wet and sticks to your hands, knead in a little more flour until it just barely sticks to itself when folded. (It is easier to start too wet and adjust by adding flour than to add water to dough that is too dry.) Transfer the dough to a bowl, cover it with a damp kitchen towel, and let it rest for 30 minutes or more at room temperature.

Rolling out the Dough

After the dough has rested, knead it on a floured work surface just until smooth and elastic. Shape the dough into a 12-inch-long rope then cut the rope into 50 to 55 pieces and form them into balls. Flatten each ball on the floured surface. With a rolling pin, roll each one into a 3-inch circle. (When rolling the dough, leave the center a little thicker than the edges. This will make the wrapper easier to shape and seal around its filling, and will provide extra support to hold the juice that accumulates when steaming.) Arrange the disks in a single layer on a lightly floured tray and cover them with a damp towel to prevent them from drying out.

Rolling a Large Quantity of Dough: Rolling many wrappers individually can take a lot of time, but there is a faster method. Divide the prepared and rested dough into four or five pieces. With your hands, flatten each piece on a lightly floured surface, and roll it out ⅛-inch thick. With a 3-inch round cookie cutter (or the rim of a drinking glass), cut out as many rounds as you can fit from the sheet. Arrange them as above to keep them from drying out. Repeat the procedure with the rest of the dough. Gather up the dough scraps, roll them out, and continue cutting disks until all the dough is used. When rolling dough this way, use as little flour as possible, or else the wrappers cut from the re-rolled scraps will be tough.

Filling the Momos

Holding a wrapper in one hand, place about 1 tablespoon of filling in the center and use the other hand to gather the edges and seal the stuffing inside by squeezing the edges tightly, making small pleats to securely seal in the filling. Pleats make the momo pretty, like a bite-size bag closed tight with a drawstring. Take care not to stuff it too full or it will leak. Keep the filled *momos* and the unfilled wrappers covered with a damp cloth while working, as the wrappers can dry out and become brittle if exposed to air for too long. Brushing with cold water around the edges of the wrapper helps seal the edges.

Steaming the Momos

Grease a steamer tray with oil or cooking spray. You can also line the steamer tray with cabbage or lettuce leaves if you leave ½-inch margin at the edges so that steam can circulate. Arrange the *momos* on one or two trays, with the pleated sides up, close together, but not touching. Set aside.

Fill the base of the steamer with 3 to 4 inches of water and bring it to a full boil over medium-high heat. Place the *momo* tray(s) in the steamer. Cover tightly to prevent the steam from escaping. Steam until the dumplings are translucent and juicy, about 10 minutes. If you are using two stacked steamer trays, switch the top with the bottom halfway through the cooking so the *momos* cook evenly. Do not overcook, or they will dry out, leaving the filling tasteless. Remove them from the steamer and serve immediately. Repeat the procedure with the remaining dumplings. (Note: Always keep a kettle of boiling water handy to add to the steamer, as the boiling water evaporates quickly. Steam burns are very painful, so take care to protect your hands and wrists.)

Steam-fried Momos

Steam-fried *momos* are golden brown and slightly crunchy outside, while still juicy inside, they are first browned and then steamed. Heat 2 tablespoons of oil in a cast-iron or nonstick skillet over medium heat. Place the *momos* in the skillet pleated side up in one layer without touching each other. Fry until the bottoms are lightly browned, about 5 minutes. Add ¼ cup of cold water and cover the pan. Continue cooking until the liquid has been absorbed and the wrappers are slightly crispy. Transfer them to a platter and serve hot with dipping sauce. Repeat the procedure with the remaining dumplings.

Deep-Fried Momos

Heat 1 cup of oil. Add the *momos* and fry until golden brown.

The Next Best Thing to Fresh Momos

Leftover *momos* can be refrigerated or frozen. If you want to freeze them, let them cool first, then arrange them in a single layer without touching in a freezer bag and seal them airtight. Thaw the frozen *momos* and then steam-fry as directed above.

CHICKEN DUMPLINGS
Kukhuraa ko Momo

Makes 4 to 6 servings

Chicken *momos* have become popular among health conscious people because of their low fat content. You may also use ground turkey, but do not use ground turkey breast, as it tends to dry out. Serve chicken *momos* as a hot appetizer or as an entree with a tomato-based dipping sauce.

2½ pounds ground chicken	1 teaspoon salt
1 medium onion, finely chopped (about 1 cup)	1 teaspoon ground coriander
¼ cup finely chopped cilantro	½ teaspoon ground turmeric
2 tablespoons vegetable oil	½ teaspoon ground cumin
1 tablespoon minced fresh ginger	½ teaspoon cayenne pepper powder
2 medium cloves garlic, minced	1 recipe fresh Momo Wrappers (page 230)

In a large bowl, combine all the ingredients (except wrappers) and add ¼ cup of water. Working with your hands, mix well. Cover the bowl and let it rest for 10 minutes at room temperature for the flavors to blend. Following the directions on page 231, fill the *momo* wrappers and seal and steam them.

LAMB DUMPLINGS
Maasu ko Momo

Makes 4 to 6 servings

Any variety of ground meat, including lamb, goat, pork, or water buffalo, can be used for this recipe. Nepalese prefer meat that has a lot of fat, because it produces juicy *momos*. Traditionally, the spices are ground with water to a smooth paste in a mortar and pestle to bring out more flavors before adding them to the ground meat, though if you are in a hurry, pre-ground spices are almost as good. These *momos* are best served immediately after steaming, with any variety of freshly made tomato chutney.

2½ pounds ground lamb (preferably leg meat)	4 medium cloves garlic, minced
1 cup finely chopped cilantro	1 tablespoon minced fresh ginger
1 medium onion, finely chopped (about 1 cup)	1½ teaspoons Nepali garam masalaa (*see page 310*)
4 to 5 green onions (white and green parts), finely chopped	1 teaspoon salt
3 fresh mild or hot green chilies, chopped	1 teaspoon cayenne pepper powder
2 tablespoons vegetable oil (use only if the meat is very lean)	½ teaspoon ground turmeric
	1 recipe Fresh Momo Wrappers (*page 230*)

In a large bowl, combine all the ingredients (except wrappers) and add ½ cup of water. Cover the bowl and let it rest for 10 minutes at room temperature, for the flavors to blend. Following the directions on page 231, fill the *momo* wrappers and seal and steam them.

MUSHROOM AND TOFU DUMPLINGS

Makes 4 to 6 servings

Chyau ra Tofu ko Momo

My daughter Rachana learned the basics of momo cooking while working in Nepal after her college graduation. She experimented with a variety of vegetable fillings and came up with this recipe.

2 tablespoons vegetable oil	2 medium cloves garlic, minced
1 medium red onion, finely chopped (about 1 cup)	1 small red or green bell pepper, cored and finely chopped (1 cup) 1½ teaspoons minced fresh ginger
4 cups chopped fresh mushrooms (any variety; about 1½ pounds)	¼ cup finely chopped cilantro
2 cups firm tofu	¼ teaspoon ground cumin
2 medium red potatoes, boiled, peeled, and finely chopped (about 2 cups)	¼ teaspoon ground coriander
	Salt to taste
2 fresh hot green chilies, finely chopped	1 recipe Fresh Momo Wrappers (*page 230*)

Heat the oil in a wide saucepan over medium-high heat. When the oil is hot, but not smoking, add the onions and cook until they soften, 3 to 4 minutes. Add the mushrooms, tofu, potatoes, green chilies, garlic, bell pepper, and ginger and cook, stirring frequently, until the water from the vegetables has evaporated and the mixture is nearly dry. Add the cilantro, cumin, coriander and some salt to taste and mix well. Transfer the mixture to a bowl and let it cool. Following the directions on page 231, fill the *momo* wrappers and seal and steam them (but only steaming them for 7 to 8 minutes).

SPICY POTATO DUMPLINGS

Makes 4 to 6 servings

Aalu ko Momo

Here is a very simple vegetarian *momo* filling made from potatoes that are boiled in their skins, peeled, and mashed before they are seasoned with onion, ginger, garlic, and other spices.

2 pounds boiling potatoes	1 teaspoon ground cumin
¼ cup vegetable oil	1 teaspoon cayenne pepper powder
2 medium onions, finely chopped (about 2 cups)	½ teaspoon ground turmeric
	½ cup finely chopped cilantro
1 tablespoon minced fresh ginger	4 or 5 green onions (white and green parts), finely chopped
3 medium cloves garlic, minced	
1½ teaspoons ground coriander	2 fresh hot green chilies, finely chopped
1½ teaspoons Nepali garam masalaa (*see page 310*)	Salt, adjust to taste
	1 recipe Fresh Momo Wrappers (*page 230*)

Put the potatoes in a medium-size saucepan with enough water to cover, and bring to a boil over high heat. Reduce the heat to medium-low, cover the pan, and continue cooking until the potatoes are tender, 20 to 25 minutes. Drain, and when cool enough to handle, peel and mash the potatoes and set them aside.

Heat the oil in a wide saucepan over medium-high heat. When the oil is hot, but not smoking, add the onions and cook until they begin to soften, about 5 minutes. Add the ginger, garlic, coriander, garam masalaa, cumin, cayenne pepper powder, and turmeric and stir for 30 seconds. Add the mashed potatoes and mix well. Remove the pan from the heat and stir in the cilantro, green onions, and green chilies and taste and add salt as needed. Cool the stuffing to a temperature comfortable for handling. Following the directions on page 231, fill the *momo* wrappers and seal and steam them (but only steaming them for 7 to 8 minutes).

PORK AND VEGETABLE DUMPLINGS

Makes 4 to 6 servings   *Bangoor ra Tarkaari ko Momo*

In Nepal, traditional *momos* were made with only seasoned ground meat, but over the past several years, fillings have become more elaborate. The combination of vegetables and meat probably reflects the trend in Nepal towards health-conscious eating. This recipe was inspired by the Sthapit family, dear friends of my family, but I have modified it to suit my family's taste.

1 pound ground pork	1 teaspoon ground cumin
2 cups chopped fresh mushrooms (any variety)	1 teaspoon ground coriander
1 medium onion, finely chopped (about 1 cup)	1 teaspoon cayenne pepper powder
½ cup finely chopped cilantro	½ teaspoon ground turmeric
4 or 5 green onions (white and pale green parts), finely chopped	⅛ teaspoon freshly ground black pepper
2 fresh hot green chilies, finely chopped	½ head green cabbage, shredded (about 2 cups)
4 medium cloves garlic, minced	¼ head cauliflower, cut into ½-inch florets
1 tablespoon minced fresh ginger	1 cup shelled fresh peas
1 teaspoon salt, adjust to taste	1 recipe Fresh Momo Wrappers (*page 230*)

In a large bowl, place the ground pork, mushrooms, onions, cilantro, green onions, green chilies, garlic, ginger, salt, cumin, coriander, cayenne pepper powder, turmeric, and black pepper. Working with your hands, mix well until all the ingredients are thoroughly combined. Cover the bowl and let the mixture rest for 10 minutes at room temperature for the herbs and spices to absorb into the meat.

Bring a pot of water to a rolling boil over medium-high heat. Add the cabbage, cauliflower, and peas and cook just until they are tender, 2 to 3 minutes. Drain and run them under cold water to halt the cooking. Add them to the pork mixture and mix thoroughly. Following the directions on page 231, fill the *momo* wrappers and seal and steam them.

Mixed Vegetable Dumplings / *Tarkaari ko Momo*

MIXED VEGETABLE DUMPLINGS

Makes 4 to 6 servings

Tarkaari ko Momo

This is a basic vegetarian filling for *momos*. The ideal vegetable *momo* is delicate, with a balance of textures and the natural taste of fresh vegetables. The filling can be made of almost any vegetable, finely chopped and lightly cooked with fresh spices. Vegetable *momos* are a very popular appetizer, afternoon snack, or entree served with chutney or a dipping sauce.

2 tablespoons vegetable oil
1 medium onion, finely chopped (about 1 cup)
3 medium cloves garlic, finely chopped
1 tablespoon minced fresh ginger
1½ teaspoons ground coriander
1 teaspoon ground cumin
1 teaspoon cayenne pepper powder
½ teaspoon ground turmeric
⅛ teaspoon freshly ground black pepper
½ head fresh green cabbage, trimmed and shredded (about 2 cups)

1 small bunch fresh spinach, stemmed and coarsely chopped (about 2 cups)
1 medium carrot, peeled and shredded (about 1 cup)
1 cup ½-inch cauliflower florets
1 medium potato, boiled, peeled, and finely chopped (about 1 cup)
Salt, adjust to taste
1 recipe Fresh Momo Wrappers (*page 230*)

Heat the oil in a wide saucepan over medium-high heat. When the oil is hot, but not smoking, add the onions and garlic and cook until they begin to soften, 3 to 4 minutes. Add the ginger, coriander, cumin, cayenne pepper powder, turmeric, and black pepper and stir for 30 seconds.

Add the cabbage, spinach, carrots, cauliflower, potato, and salt and continue cooking, stirring until the liquid evaporates and the mixture is nearly dry. (This step is important so that the filling will not soak through its wrapper.) Taste for seasoning. Cool the stuffing to a temperature comfortable for handling. Following the directions on page 231, fill the *momo* wrappers and seal and steam them.

Chapter 11

SALADS, CHUTNEYS & PICKLES

ACHAARS

Nepalese use the term "*achaar*" for freshly-made chutney, cooked chutney, preserved pickles, fermented pickles, powdered-spice pickles, and freshly made salad-like pickle side dishes. Each of these varieties of *achaars* has distinct flavors, colors, and textures. They are an important component of any Nepali meal because they perk up and add tang to traditional dishes.

Achaars can be prepared from nearly any fruits and vegetables, dried legumes, herb and spices, and even some meat and seafood. Homemade Nepalese pickles are made on hot and sunny days throughout the year. The most common pickling spices are mustard seeds, fenugreek seeds, sesame seeds, turmeric powder, cayenne pepper powder, timmur pepper, and jimbu. They are preserved in oils, brine, and vinegar and also by natural fermentation. In Nepal, *achaars* are made seasonally when fruits and vegetables are in abundance. The shelf life of Nepali pickles depends on the process of pickling. Properly prepared pickles keep indefinitely and can be used year-round.

Chutneys are often made fresh for each meal, though they can be stored in the refrigerator and used within a few days. The most popular chutneys are made from tomatoes, cilantro, mint, and tamarind. Nepalese are very fond of tomato chutney, and it is prepared in countless ways. Chutneys range from mild to fiery hot and are eaten in small amounts with rice, daal, and vegetables.

A mild-flavored pickle is a nice accompaniment to any heavy or spicy food. Preserved and fermented pickles are bottled and can be stored at room temperature. The most common ones are made of cucumber, white radish, and lapsi fruit.

TOMATO-CUCUMBER-ONION SALAD

Makes 4 to 6 servings

Mismaas Salad

This light, refreshing salad is usually served as an accompaniment to a main dish, but you may also serve it with any variety of snacks. The vegetables can be chopped ahead of time, but the salt, pepper, and lemon juice should be added just before serving to maintain the salad's crunchy texture.

1 large ripe tomato, chopped (about 1½ cups)	1 medium red onion, finely chopped (about 1 cup)
2 medium cucumbers, peeled, halved, seeded, and finely chopped (about 2 cups)	3 tablespoons fresh lemon or lime juice
1 white radish, chopped (about 1½ cups)	Salt, adjust to taste
	⅛ teaspoon freshly ground black pepper

In a medium-size bowl, combine the tomatoes, cucumbers, radishes, and onions. Just before serving, toss with the lemon juice, salt, and black pepper. Transfer the salad to a serving dish and serve right away.

YOGURT CUCUMBER SALAD

Makes 4 to 6 servings

Dahi Haaleko Kaankro ko Salad

This refreshing salad goes well with any spicy Nepali meat or vegetable dish to create a cooling effect. For this recipe, I like to use whole milk yogurt, which has a very creamy texture.

2 medium cucumbers, peeled, seeded, and finely chopped (about 2 cups)	1 fresh mild or hot green chili pepper, finely chopped (any variety)
1¼ teaspoons salt, or adjust to taste	⅛ teaspoon freshly ground black pepper
1 teaspoon cumin seeds	¼ teaspoon cayenne pepper powder
3 cups whole-milk plain yogurt, stirred	

Place the cucumbers in a bowl and toss with 1 teaspoon of the salt. Set aside until the juices are released, 15 to 20 minutes, stirring a few times. Place the cucumbers in a colander and press to squeeze out as much liquid as possible.

Heat a small cast-iron skillet over medium heat and toast the cumin seeds, stirring constantly until they give off a pleasant aroma and are a few shades darker, about 1 minute. Remove the seeds from the skillet and coarsely grind them with a mortar and pestle.

In a bowl, combine the drained cucumbers, yogurt, green chili, ½ teaspoon of the toasted cumin seeds, remaining ¼ teaspoon salt, and black pepper. Transfer everything to a serving dish and sprinkle with the cayenne pepper powder and the remaining ground cumin seeds. Cover and refrigerate until ready to serve.

SPROUTED MUNG BEAN SALAD

Makes 4 to 6 servings   *Umaareko Moong ko Salad*

The healthy, wholesome, delicious salad is made with sprouted mung beans, which add a crunchy texture to the dish. Served chilled or at room temperature, this refreshing salad counteracts the effect of a spicy Nepali meal.

1 cup sprouted moong beans	1 large carrot, shredded
1 medium cucumber, peeled, halved, seeded and thinly sliced (about 1 cup)	3 or 4 green onions (white and pale green parts), chopped
1 medium tomato, chopped (about 1 cup)	¼ cup finely chopped cilantro
1 medium red onion, thinly sliced (about 1 cup)	1 fresh (mild or hot) green chili pepper, finely chopped
1 small white radish, chopped (1 cup)	3 to 4 tablespoons fresh lemon or lime juice
½ small green bell pepper, seeded and finely chopped (about ½ cup)	Salt, adjust to taste
	⅛ teaspoon freshly ground black pepper

In a medium-size bowl, combine the sprouted beans, cucumber, tomato, onion, radish, bell pepper, carrot, green onions, cilantro, and green chili and mix well. Just before serving, add the lemon juice, salt, and black pepper and mix well. Transfer everything to serving dish and serve right away.

POMELO AND ORANGE SALAD

Makes 4 to 6 servings

Bhogate-Suntalaa Saandheko

Here is a flavorful and delicious pomelo and orange salad dish dressed in Nepali spices and finished up with tempering spices. It is the most refreshing salad, full of immunity-boosting vitamin C— like sunshine in a bowl—and Nepalese enjoy it in the depth of winter.

¼ cup sesame seeds

4 medium white or red pomelos,* peeled and sectioned

4 medium navel oranges, peeled and sectioned

2 cups plain yogurt, stirred well

¾ cup sugar

2 tablespoons fresh lemon or lime juice

1 teaspoon cayenne pepper powder

½ teaspoon freshly ground black pepper

⅛ teaspoon timmur (Nepali pepper; *page 31*), finely ground with a mortar and pestle

Salt, adjust to taste

2 tablespoons mustard oil

½ teaspoon fenugreek seeds

½ teaspoon ground turmeric

Small pinch ground asafetida

Heat a small cast-iron skillet over medium heat and toast the sesame seeds for about 2 minutes, stirring constantly to prevent the seeds from flying out, until they give off a pleasant aroma and darken. Transfer the seeds to a dry container to cool. Place the cooled seeds in a spice grinder or mortar and pestle, and grind to a fine powder.

Put the ground sesame seeds, pomelos, oranges, yogurt, sugar, lemon juice, cayenne pepper powder, black pepper, timmur, and salt to taste in a bowl and mix gently.

Heat the mustard oil in a small skillet over medium-high heat. When the oil is hot, but not smoking, add the fenugreek seeds and fry until dark brown and fragrant, about 5 seconds. Remove the skillet from the heat and sprinkle in the turmeric and asafetida. Immediately pour these spices into the citrus mixture and stir well.

Taste and adjust the seasonings as needed. The finished dish should be spicy, sweet, tangy, and tart. Cover and set aside for 15 minutes to allow the seasonings and flavor to develop. Transfer the salad to a bowl and serve.

*Note: Pomelos are available at Asian food stores and occasionally in regular grocery stores. Be careful to select ripe pomelos. Immature pomelos can be very bitter, dry, and overpowering, and may not be suitable for this salad. When ripe, the fruit is slightly dry, the flesh is firm, and it has a slightly sweet-tangy taste. For this recipe you may substitute grapefruit if pomelos are not available.

CILANTRO CHUTNEY
Hariyo Dhaniya ko Chutney

Makes 4 to 6 servings

This bright green chutney has a tangy aroma and spicy refreshing taste. It is so versatile—serve with any fried snacks or it will be a perfect accompaniment to any Nepali lunch or dinner.

5 cups coarsely chopped cilantro
2 medium tomatoes, chopped (about 2 cups)
6 fresh hot green chilies, coarsely chopped
2 tablespoons fresh lemon or lime juice
2 medium cloves garlic, peeled

1 teaspoon peeled and coarsely chopped fresh ginger
½ teaspoon salt, or adjust to taste
⅛ teaspoon timmur (Nepali pepper; *page 31*), finely ground with a mortar and pestle

Place all the ingredients in a food processor or blender and process to a smooth consistency. Transfer the chutney to a bowl and serve. The chutney keeps in the refrigerator for up to 1 week in an airtight container.

MINT CHUTNEY
Baabari ko Chutney

Makes 4 to 6 servings

Mint (*baabari*) compliments any spicy dish and provides a cooling effect. This chutney can be made with any variety of mint, but select only young and tender sprigs with fresh leaves. Avoid wilted, matured, and dry leaves. Serve this with any fried or steamed appetizers or with a traditional Nepali meal.

4 cups young fresh mint leaves, coarsely chopped	½ cup plain yogurt
1 medium red onion, coarsely chopped (about 1 cup)	3 tablespoons fresh lemon or lime juice
	3 medium cloves garlic, peeled
4 fresh (hot or mild) green chilies, coarsely chopped	1 tablespoon peeled and coarsely chopped fresh ginger
	½ teaspoon salt, or adjust to taste

Place all the ingredients in a food processor or blender and process until you get a smooth consistency. Add 1 to 2 tablespoons of water, if needed. Taste and adjust salt and lemon juice. Transfer to a bowl and serve.

Note: This chutney keeps refrigerated for up to 1 week in an airtight container. It will change color to a pale green, but its flavor does not change, although lemon juice helps to preserve the green color to some extent.

TAMARIND CHUTNEY

Imili ko Chutney

Makes 4 to 6 servings

Tamarind (*imili*) is the reddish-brown fruit of the tamarind tree. The pulp of the fruit has a pleasant flavor with a distinct sweet-and-sour taste. The fibrous pulp is diluted in water and the strained juice is used to make chutney. Dried tamarind pulp is available at Indian and Asian markets or specialty food stores.

2 cups compressed tamarind pulp	1 tablespoon cayenne pepper powder, or
4 cups boiling water	adjust to taste
2 tablespoons vegetable oil	2 teaspoons salt, or adjust to taste
1 teaspoon cumin seeds	1 teaspoon ground ginger
1½ cups dark brown sugar	

Break the compressed pulp into small pieces in a bowl. Add the boiling water and soak until the pulp softens, about 1 hour. (The tamarind will swell and its volume will increase.) Mash the mixture and pour it through a fine-mesh strainer set over a bowl, pressing with the back of a spoon to collect the puree and juice in the bowl. Discard the fiber and seeds. Set the puree aside.

Heat the oil in a medium-size saucepan over medium-high heat. When the oil is hot, but not smoking, add the cumin seeds and fry until lightly browned and fragrant, about 5 seconds. Add the tamarind puree, brown sugar, cayenne pepper powder, salt, and ground ginger and bring to a boil. Reduce the heat to medium-low and cook, stirring occasionally, until the sauce reduces by half and the color becomes a rich brown, 15 to 20 minutes.

Remove the pan from the heat and let the chutney cool. It will thicken as it cools. Taste for tartness and adjust the seasonings and sugar. Serve the chutney immediately or transfer it to a clean jar. This chutney keeps refrigerated for up to 6 months.

ROASTED CHERRY TOMATO CHUTNEY

Makes 4 to 6 servings   *Poleko Saano Golbhedaa ko Chutney*

Roasted tomato chutney is a Nepali classic, prepared fresh daily in small quantities. Traditionally, the tomatoes are roasted in a small clay pot (*makkal*) over a charcoal fire, resulting in a smoky flavor. The roasted tomatoes are then crushed in an oval-shaped stone mortar and pestle (*khal*), and their tangy taste is enhanced by the addition of Nepali timmur.

---

2 pounds ripe cherry tomatoes, stemmed
6 to 8 medium cloves garlic, unpeeled
4 fresh hot green chilies
½ teaspoon salt, or adjust to taste

⅛ teaspoon timmur (Nepali pepper; *see page 31*)
¼ cup finely chopped cilantro

Preheat a charcoal or gas grill to medium-high heat. Loosely wrap the tomatoes in heavy-duty foil and roast them on the grill, turning often with tongs. The tomatoes are ready when the skins are blistered, blackened, and separate easily from the pulp. Remove them from the heat and transfer to a bowl.

Roast the unpeeled garlic in the same way, turning occasionally, until blackened on all sides and soft. Remove them and set aside. Roast the green chilies until slightly blistered and then set aside. When cool enough to handle, peel and remove the blackened skins from the tomatoes and garlic, but not from the chilies.

Place the roasted garlic, roasted green chilies, salt, and timmur in a mortar. Use the pestle to grind the mixture to a smooth paste. Add the roasted tomatoes and grind until smooth. You may have to do this in batches. (This process can also be done in a food processor or a blender.)

Transfer the chutney to a bowl and mix in the cilantro. Taste, adjust the seasonings, and serve immediately or cover and refrigerate until ready to serve.

HOT AND FIERY TOMATO CHUTNEY

Makes 4 to 6 servings

Piro Golbhedaa ko Chutney

This fiery tomato chutney will spice up any dish, including fried or steamed snacks or appetizers. Make sure to select succulent and fully ripe tomatoes for the best flavor.

6 medium tomatoes

6 medium cloves garlic, peeled

8 fresh hot green chilies

¼ cup finely chopped cilantro

2 teaspoons minced fresh ginger

¼ teaspoon timmur (Nepali pepper; *page 31*), finely ground with a mortar and pestle

Salt, adjust to taste

2 tablespoons mustard oil

3 dried red chilies, halved and seeded

½ teaspoon fenugreek seeds

⅛ teaspoon jimbu (Himalayan herb; *see page 30*)

Preheat the oven to 400 degrees F. In a roasting pan, arrange the tomatoes in a single layer and roast until they are soft, blistered, blackened, and most of the liquid has caramelized, about 30 minutes. Add the garlic and green chilies and roast for another 5 minutes.

Transfer the roasted vegetables to a food processor or blender and process into a smooth puree. Transfer the mixture to a bowl, mix in the cilantro, ginger, timmur and some salt to taste, and set aside.

Heat the oil in a small skillet over medium-high heat. When the oil is hot, but not smoking, add the dried chilies, fenugreek seeds, and *jimbu* and fry until dark brown and fragrant, about 5 seconds. Remove the skillet from the heat and immediately pour the mustard oil mixture over the tomato puree and mix thoroughly. Cover the bowl and let the tomato chutney stand for 10 minutes at room temperature to allow the flavors to blend.

Transfer the chutney to a bowl and serve. This chutney can be made up to 2 days in advance and kept covered and chilled.

Momo Tomato Chutney / *Momo ko Chutney*

MOMO TOMATO CHUTNEY
Momo ko Chutney

Makes 4 to 6 servings

I usually make this chutney when I am making *momos* (stuffed dumplings; *see Chapter 10*). When tomatoes, garlic, and dried chilies are roasted together, they add a wonderful smoky flavor to the chutney. There is no need to peel the blackened tomato skins because they add a deep, rusty, and rich color to the chutney. Make sure to select succulent and fully ripe tomatoes for the best flavor. Apart from serving it with *momos*, this chutney will spice up any dish, including fried or steamed snacks or appetizers.

¼ cup sesame seeds
1 teaspoon mustard seeds
1 teaspoon cumin seeds
6 medium tomatoes
6 medium cloves garlic, peeled
4 dried red chilies, halved and seeded
1 teaspoon minced fresh ginger

2 fresh hot green chilies
¼ cup finely chopped cilantro
¼ teaspoon timmur (Nepali pepper; *page 31*), finely ground with a mortar and pestle
1 teaspoon fresh lemon or lime juice
Salt to taste

Heat a small cast-iron skillet over medium heat and toast the sesame seeds, mustard seeds, and cumin seeds, stirring constantly, until they give off a pleasant aroma and darken, about 2 minutes. Remove them from the skillet and pour into a dry container to halt the toasting. When cool, transfer them to a spice grinder or a mortar and pestle and grind into a fine powder.

Preheat the oven to 375 degrees F. In a roasting pan, arrange the tomatoes in a single layer and roast until they are soft, blistered, blackened, and most of the liquid has caramelized, about 25 minutes. Add the garlic and red chilies and roast for another 5 minutes.

Transfer the roasted tomatoes, garlic, and red chilies, and the ground seeds, ginger, green chilies, cilantro, timmur, and lemon juice to a food processor or blender and process into a smooth puree. Taste and add salt as needed. Transfer the mixture to a bowl and serve. This chutney can be made up to 2 days in advance and kept covered and chilled.

TAMARILLO CHUTNEY

Makes 4 to 6 servings

Tyaamatar ko Chutney

Tyaamatar is the Nepali word for "tamarillo" or "tree tomato," an attractive egg-shaped fruit with meaty pulp and seeds. It has a tough, bitter skin and is very tart but flavorful when ripe. Although the tamarillo resembles a plum tomato in color and shape, it is not a true tomato. In Nepal, tamarillos are used primarily in chutneys such as this one. The flavorful and spicy chutney is made fresh in small quantities and is a delicious accompaniment to any meal. In the US, tamarillos are available at Asian markets, specialty produce stores, and well-stocked supermarkets.

5 medium ripe tamarillos (preferably red), stemmed

8 medium cloves garlic, 4 unpeeled and 4 thinly slivered

4 fresh hot green chilies, chopped

1/8 teaspoon timmur (Nepali pepper; *page 31*), finely ground with a mortar and pestle

Salt, adjust to taste

1½ tablespoons mustard oil

1/8 teaspoon fenugreek seeds

1/8 teaspoon jimbu (Himalayan herb; *see page 30*)

1¼ cups finely chopped cilantro

Preheat a charcoal or gas grill to medium-high heat. Roast the tamarillos over the grill, turning frequently, until the skins are blistered, blackened, and very soft. They are ready when the skins peel off easily and they release a pleasant aroma, 10 to 15 minutes. Roast the unpeeled garlic cloves in the same way, turning occasionally, until blackened and soft. Remove from the heat and cool to room temperature. Peel and discard the blackened skins from the tamarillos and garlic.

Place the tamarillo pulp, roasted garlic, green chilies, and timmur in a mortar. Use the pestle to grind the mixture to a coarse sauce. You may have to do this in batches. Transfer the sauce to a bowl. Taste and add salt as needed.

Heat the mustard oil in a small skillet over medium-high heat until faintly smoking. Add the fenugreek seeds and jimbu and fry until dark brown and fragrant, about 5 seconds. Add the slivered garlic and fry until golden, about 30 seconds. Remove the skillet from the heat, pour the contents into the tamarillo mixture and stir well. Cover the bowl and set it aside for at least 10 minutes to allow the flavors to blend.

Transfer the chutney to a serving dish and serve. This chutney will keep in the refrigerator for 2 to 3 days.

SHREDDED CUCUMBER ACHAAR

Makes 4 to 6 servings

Koreko Kaankro ko Achaar

The refreshing aroma of freshly shredded cucumber brings back warm memories of my childhood in Nepal. Cucumber *achaar* was prepared fresh daily at my home because it was my father's favorite, and he preferred garden-fresh cucumbers cut into matchsticks or julienned. This is my family's old recipe and you may adjust the spiciness to your liking. I prefer not to use bottled lemon juice because the preservatives in the bottled juice take away from the flavor of real lemon.

---

6 to 8 medium cucumbers, peeled, seeded, and shredded (about 8 cups)
1 tablespoon salt
½ cup sesame seeds
1 cup plain yogurt, stirred
¼ cup finely chopped cilantro
3 tablespoons fresh lemon or lime juice
2 fresh mild green chilies, cut into slivers

1 teaspoon cayenne pepper powder
⅛ teaspoon timmur (Nepali pepper; *page 31*), finely ground with a mortar and pestle
2 tablespoons mustard oil
½ teaspoon fenugreek seeds
½ teaspoon jimbu (Nepali aromatic herb; *see page 30*)
½ teaspoon ground turmeric

In a colander, combine the shredded cucumbers and salt. Let them rest in the sink, stirring occasionally, until the juices are released, 15 to 20 minutes. Press and squeeze out as much water as possible.

Heat a small cast-iron skillet over medium heat and toast the sesame seeds, stirring constantly to prevent the seeds from flying all over, until they give off a pleasant aroma and darken, about 2 minutes. Remove the seeds to a bowl to halt the toasting and let them cool. Transfer the seeds to a spice grinder and grind to a fine powder.

Place the cucumbers in a bowl. Add the ground sesame seeds, yogurt, cilantro, lemon juice, green chilies, cayenne pepper powder, and timmur and mix well.

Heat the mustard oil in a small skillet over medium-high heat. When the oil is faintly smoking, add the fenugreek seeds and jimbu, and fry until they turn dark brown and fragrant, about 5 seconds. Remove the pan from heat and add the turmeric. Pour the entire contents into the cucumber mixture. Mix well, cover, and set aside for 10 minutes to allow the seasonings to develop.

FIELD PEA AND RADISH ACHAAR

Makes 4 to 6 servings   *Saano Keraau re Mulaa ko Achaar*

This recipe is made with radishes and small Nepali field peas, known as *saano keraau*. Field peas are similar to common garden peas, except the pods are much narrower and longer, and the peas are green-gray in color and slightly larger than peppercorns. This *achaar* is a tangy accompaniment to a heavily spiced Nepali meal. Be sure to store this *achaar* in an airtight container.

1 cup dried small field peas (*sukeko hariyo saano kerau*)*	1 tablespoon minced fresh ginger
1½ pounds white radishes, peeled and julienned or grated (about 4 cups)	2½ tablespoons fresh lemon or lime juice
1½ teaspoons salt, or adjust to taste	⅛ teaspoon timmur (Nepal pepper; *page 31*), finely ground with a mortar and pestle
3 or 4 green onions (white and pale green parts), cut into ¼-inch pieces	1½ tablespoons mustard oil
¼ cup finely chopped cilantro	½ teaspoon fenugreek seeds
3 fresh mild green chilies, julienned	1 dried red chili, halved and seeded
	½ teaspoon ground turmeric

Place the dried field peas in a large bowl, cover them with cold water, and soak for at least 12 hours at room temperature until doubled in size. Drain and rinse the peas thoroughly and transfer them to a bowl.

In a colander, combine the radishes and 1 teaspoon of salt, and let them stand for 10 minutes in the sink. Press to squeeze the excess liquid from the radishes.

Transfer the radishes to a bowl and stir in the soaked field peas, green onions, cilantro, green chilies, ginger, lemon juice, and timmur. Set aside.

Heat the mustard oil in a small skillet over medium-high heat. When the oil is faintly smoking, add the fenugreek seeds and dried chili and fry until dark brown and fragrant, about 5 seconds. Remove the skillet from the heat, sprinkle in the turmeric, and immediately pour the entire contents over the pea and radish mixture and mix thoroughly. Taste and adjust the salt. Cover the bowl and allow the seasonings to develop, for at least 10 minutes. If not serving the *achaar* right away, cover and refrigerate until serving time. Serve cold or at room temperature.

*Note: Substitute regular dried peas (green or yellow) if field peas are not available.

POTATO AND YOGURT ACHAAR

Makes 4 to 6 servings

Palpali Chukauni Achaar

Chukauni achaar is one of the most popular dishes from the Western Palpa region of Nepal. The key to making this addictively delicious potato achaar is selecting any variety of thin-skinned small potatoes that can be easily peeled. Traditionally, the souring agent used for this *achaar* is *chook amilo* concentrate, which is made by boiling a special large Nepali variety of lemon (*nibua*) until it becomes a dark brown and thick liquid. This lemon concentrate can be stored for more than a year. For this recipe, I have used lemon juice instead of *chook amilo* concentrate. Although it is called an *achaar* dish (pickled), it is more like a side vegetable dish since it is served at room temperature.

---

8 to 10 small potatoes (about 3 pounds)
2½ cups plain yogurt, stirred
6 fresh (hot or mild) green chilies, each halved lengthwise
1 medium red onion, chopped
½ cup finely chopped cilantro
1 teaspoon cayenne pepper powder
Salt, adjust to taste

¼ teaspoon timmur (Nepal pepper; *see page 31*)
¼ cup fresh lemon or lime juice
3 tablespoons mustard oil or vegetable oil
½ teaspoon fenugreek seeds
2 dried red chilies, halved and seeded
½ teaspoon ground turmeric

Place the potatoes and water to cover in a medium-size saucepan and bring to a boil over high heat. Reduce the heat to medium-low, cover the pan, and continue cooking until the potatoes are tender, 20 to 25 minutes. Drain and allow to cool (do not pour cold water over the potatoes to cool them, as this will water down their flavor). When cool enough to handle, peel the potatoes and cut them into 1-inch cubes.

Place the potatoes in a large bowl and stir in the yogurt, green chilies, red onions, cilantro, cayenne pepper powder, salt, timmur and lemon juice. Set aside.

Heat the mustard oil in a small skillet over medium-high heat until faintly smoking. Add the fenugreek seeds and red chilies and fry until dark brown and fragrant, about 5 seconds. Remove the pan from the heat and sprinkle in the turmeric. Pour the entire contents over the potatoes and mix thoroughly. Taste and adjust the seasonings and lemon juice as needed. Cover the bowl and let the *chukauni achaar* stand for 30 minutes at room temperature to absorb the seasonings, stirring occasionally. Transfer the *achaar* to a serving dish and serve.

SPICY POTATO SALAD WITH SESAME SEEDS

Makes 4 to 6 servings

Aalu ko Achaar

This potato *achaar* is a popular, addictive, and refreshing potato salad. Only rarely have I come across a traditional Nepali meal that does not include potato *achaar*. For this recipe, use any variety of waxy potato that keeps its shape when boiled. Baking potatoes are not recommended because they produce a dry, starchy *achaar*. Although this is called an *achaar* dish (pickled), it is more like a side vegetable dish. It is served at room temperature.

8 to 10 small potatoes (about 3 pounds)	3 tablespoons mustard oil or vegetable oil
6 fresh (hot or mild) green chilies, each halved lengthwise	½ teaspoon fenugreek seeds
½ cup finely chopped cilantro	¼ teaspoon jimbu (Nepali aromatic herb; *see page 30*)
¼ cup fresh lemon or lime juice	1 medium red or green bell pepper, cored and diced (about 1½ cups)
1 teaspoon cayenne pepper powder	2 tablespoons fresh ginger, peeled and finely julienned
Salt, adjust to taste	
½ cup sesame seeds	½ teaspoon ground turmeric
2 dried red chilies, halved and seeded	Generous pinch ground asafetida
¼ teaspoon timmur (Nepali pepper; *page 31*)	

Place the potatoes and water to cover in a medium-size saucepan, and bring to a boil over high heat. Reduce the heat to medium-low, cover the pan, and continue cooking until the potatoes are tender, 20 to 25 minutes. Drain and allow to cool (do not pour cold water over the potatoes to cool them, as this will water down their flavor). When cool enough to handle, peel and cut the potatoes into 1-inch cubes. Place the potatoes in a large bowl and stir in the green chilies, cilantro, lemon juice, cayenne pepper powder, and salt to taste. Set aside.

Heat a small cast-iron skillet over medium heat and toast the sesame seeds, dried chilies, and timmur, stirring constantly to prevent the seeds from flying all over, until they give off a pleasant aroma and the sesame seeds darken, about 3 minutes. Pour the spices into a dry container to halt the toasting and let them cool. Transfer the cool spices to a spice grinder and grind to a fine powder. Stir the spices and ½ cup of water into the potato mixture.

AALU KO ACHAAR

Aalu ko Achaar can be served at any time of the day as a snack food with *cheuraa* (pressed rice flakes), *sel-roti* (fried rice bread), and *poori* (deep-fried puffed bread). It is often served during family gatherings, picnics, and other casual functions or festive gatherings. For a Nepali *bhoj* (feast), *aalu ko achaar* is a must item—a large quantity of potato *achaar* always accompanies other ceremonial food items.

I have prepared this dish often and experimented with many variations— I absolutely love it! There are many versions of *aalu ko achaar* throughout the country and each family has their own recipe depending upon their individual style and specialty. While preparing this traditional *achaar*, some add thinly sliced cucumbers, finely cut radish or carrot, refreshing crisp asparagus, spring onions, thinly sliced red onions, steamed banana blossoms, cubed bell peppers, field peas, green or yellow dried peas, and even sprouted mung beans. The dried, soaked, and dehydrated peas are incorporated raw for a crunch. There are endless variations.

The potatoes should not be overcooked or under-cooked. Try to use freshly squeezed lemon or lime juice, as the bottled lemon juice with the preservatives take away the flavor of *achaar*.

Heat the mustard oil in a small skillet over medium-high heat until faintly smoking. Add the fenugreek seeds and jimbu, and fry until dark brown and fragrant, about 5 seconds. Add the bell pepper, ginger, turmeric, and asafetida and fry for 1 minute. Pour the entire contents over the potatoes and mix thoroughly. Taste and adjust the seasonings and lemon juice. Cover the bowl and let the potato *achaar* stand for 30 minutes at room temperature to absorb the seasonings, stirring occasionally. Transfer the *achaar* to a serving dish and serve.

MOUNTAIN EBONY POTATO SALAD

Makes 4 to 6 servings   *Koiralaa ko Phool re Aloo ko Achaar*

Mountain Ebony is the edible flower of the Bauhinia tree (*see page 34*). The flowers and un-opened buds are collected from the tree and cooked as a delicious vegetable and made into a salad-like dish or a pickle. It is a popular spring flower and has become an integral part of Nepali cuisine, where it has been consumed for centuries.

My memories of homemade *koiralaa ko achaar* are when our family cook, Bajai, used to make a delicious potato-bauhinia salad-like dish when the flowers were in season in the Spring. The flower blooming season only lasted for 2 to 3 weeks. Bajai told us that the raw and uncooked flowers are bitter in taste, so should be cooked properly. Before cooking, she quickly washed the flowers and buds, but did not soak the flowers in the water for extended time as they quickly become waterlogged. The base of *koiralaa ko achaar is*, of course, freshly picked flowers. Wilted, old, dried-up and spotted flowers make a flavorless dish. The first time I tried this recipe, it seemed like I was cooking a beautiful orchid-looking flower, which was too pretty to cook. Now I can't wait until springtime in Nepal to cook this delicious vegetable. Even though I cannot replicate Bajai's recipe, I offer you my version.

4 medium potatoes (any kind red or white)	1 large tomato, finely chopped
6 cups of fresh mountain ebony (Bauhinia tree flowers)	Salt to taste
	2 tablespoons mustard oil
¼ cup brown sesame seeds	¼ teaspoon fenugreek seeds
2 tablespoons fresh lemon or lime juice	⅛ teaspoon jimbu (Nepali aromatic herb; *see page 30*)
½ teaspoon cayenne pepper powder	
⅛ teaspoon timmur (Nepali pepper; *see page 31*), finely ground with a mortar and pestle	¼ teaspoon ground turmeric
	2 or 3 fresh mild green chilies, halved lengthwise
½ cup finely chopped cilantro	
1 medium red onion, finely chopped (about 1 cup)	

Place the potatoes and water to cover in a medium-size pan and bring to boil over high heat. Reduce the heat to low, cover and cook until tender, about 15 minutes. Drain until cool enough to handle, peel, and cut into ½-inch cubes. Set aside.

Bring a pot of salted water to a rolling boil over medium-high heat. Add a few drops of lemon juice and the mountain ebony to the boiling water and boil until tender, about 8 minutes. Drain and run under cold water to halt the cooking further. Squeeze out all the water and transfer to a bowl and set aside.

Heat a small skillet over medium heat and toast the sesame seeds, stirring constantly to prevent them from flying all over, until they give off a

pleasant aroma and darken, about 3 minutes. Pour into a dry container to halt the toasting. When cool transfer to a spice grinder and grind to a fine powder.
In a bowl, place the potatoes, mountain ebony, ground sesame seeds, lemon juice, cayenne pepper powder, timmur, cilantro, onion, tomato and some salt to taste. Mix well and set aside.

Heat mustard oil in a small skillet over medium-high heat until the oil is faintly smoking. Add the fenugreek seeds and jimbu, fry until dark-brown and fully fragrant, less than 5 seconds. Sprinkle in the turmeric and add green chilies and immediately pour the spiced-oil into the mountain ebony mixture. Stir well, cover the bowl, and allow the seasonings to develop for at least 20 minutes. Taste for salt and lemon juice and transfer to serving dish and serve.

BELL PEPPER ACHAAR

Bhede Khursaani Achaar

Makes 4 to 6 servings

Bell-shaped peppers are also known as capsicum, sweet peppers, and *bhede khursaani* in Nepali. These days you can purchase all different colors of bell peppers—red, green, yellow, or orange. They are the same peppers in different stages of ripeness. You can use any variety of bell peppers or mix them to create this colorful *achaar*, but I use green ones here. This green pepper *achaar* is tangy and the toasted sesame seeds add a delicious touch.

¼ cup sesame seeds

2 dried red chilies, seeded and crumbled

⅛ teaspoon timmur (Nepali pepper; *see page 31*)

¼ cup vegetable oil

¼ teaspoon fenugreek seeds

6 medium green bell peppers, tops and seeds removed, halved, cut into strips (about 4 cups)

3 fresh mild green chilies, julienned

½ teaspoon ground turmeric

2 teaspoons cayenne pepper powder, or to taste

3 tablespoons fresh lemon or lime juice, or to taste

Salt, adjust to taste

Heat a small cast-iron skillet over medium heat and toast the sesame seeds, dried red chilies, and timmur, stirring constantly to prevent the seeds from flying all over, until they give off a pleasant aroma and darken, about 2 minutes. Pour them into a dry container to halt the toasting and let them cool. Transfer the cooled spices to a spice grinder, grind to a fine powder, and set aside.

Heat the oil in a large skillet over medium high-heat. When the oil is hot, but not smoking, add the fenugreek seeds and fry until dark brown and fragrant, about 5 seconds. Add the bell peppers, green chilies, and turmeric. Cook, stirring constantly, until the raw taste of the peppers is gone but they are still crunchy, about 4 minutes. With a slotted spoon, remove the bell peppers, draining any excess oil, and transfer them to a bowl to cool.

Combine the cooled bell peppers with the toasted ground spices, cayenne pepper powder, lemon juice, and salt to taste. Taste and adjust the cayenne pepper powder and lemon juice if needed. Let the *achaar* stand for 10 minutes, transfer it to a serving dish, and serve at room temperature.

SAUTÉED SPINACH ACHAAR

Makes 4 to 6 servings

Paalungo ko Achaar

This delicious and easy *achaar* is a simplified adaptation of my mother-in-law's recipe and one of my favorite side dishes to make in short time. The spinach is quickly steamed, drained, and tempered with spices. This *achaar* will perk up any meal.

---

2 tablespoons sesame seeds

1 dried red chili, seeded and broken into several pieces

1 to 2 large bunches spinach (about 2 pounds), stemmed and well washed

1 teaspoon fresh lemon or lime juice

½ teaspoon cayenne pepper powder

¼ teaspoon salt, or adjust to taste

1 tablespoon mustard oil

¼ teaspoon fenugreek seeds

½ teaspoon ground turmeric

Heat a small cast-iron skillet over medium heat and toast the sesame seeds and dried red chili, stirring constantly to prevent the seeds from flying all over, until the seeds give off a pleasant aroma and darken, about 2 minutes. Pour into a dry container to halt the toasting. When cool, transfer them to a spice grinder or a mortar and pestle, and grind into a fine powder.

Place the washed spinach, with only the water clinging to the leaves, in a medium skillet over medium heat. Cover and cook until wilted and soft, about 5 minutes. Remove from the heat and drain off any excess water in a colander by gently pressing on the spinach with the back of a spoon. Transfer to a medium-size bowl and add the sesame seed powder, lemon juice, cayenne pepper powder, and salt. Set aside.

Heat the mustard oil in a small skillet over medium-high heat. When the oil is faintly smoking, add the fenugreek seeds and fry until dark brown and fragrant, about 5 seconds. Remove the skillet from the heat, sprinkle in the turmeric, immediately pour the entire contents over the spinach, and mix well. Cover the bowl and allow the seasonings to develop for about 10 minutes. Transfer the *achaar* to a platter and serve.

Dried Fish Tomato Achaar / *Sukuti Maachaa Achaar*

DRIED FISH TOMATO ACHAAR

Makes 4 to 6 servings

Sukuti Maachaa Achaar

Sidra maachaa are tiny dried fish used in pickles and chutneys. Because they have a strong flavor, they are used sparingly. This recipe can be made with any variety of dehydrated fish (*sukuti* fish). The pungent chutney goes well with fried snacks and adds a spicy tang to any meal. Dried fish are available at Asian food markets or specialty food stores.

2 tablespoons mustard oil
½ teaspoon fenugreek seeds
6 large tomatoes, chopped (about 6 cups)
4 fresh hot green chilies, halved lengthwise
½ teaspoon salt, adjust to taste
½ teaspoon ground turmeric
¼ teaspoon timmur, (Nepali pepper; *see page 31*) finely ground with a mortar and pestle

½ cup finely chopped cilantro
1 cup dried fish (*sidre maachaa*, or any variety of dried fish)
2 tablespoons vegetable oil
3 dried red chilies, stemmed
8 medium cloves garlic, thinly sliced
1½ tablespoons peeled and julienned fresh ginger

Heat the mustard oil in a medium-size saucepan over medium-high heat until faintly smoking. Add the fenugreek seeds and fry until dark brown and fragrant, about 5 seconds. Add the tomatoes, green chilies, salt, and turmeric and cook, covered, until the tomatoes soften, about 10 minutes. Adjust the heat to medium and cook, stirring from time to time, until the liquid has evaporated and the mixture has thickened, about 20 minutes. Remove from the heat, mix in the timmur and cilantro and set aside.

Pinch off and discard the head and tail of each dried fish, along with any visible bones. Break each fish into two to three pieces. Heat the vegetable oil in a small skillet over medium-high heat until hot, but not smoking. Add the dried chilies and fry until dark brown and fragrant, about 5 seconds. Add the garlic and ginger and fry, stirring, until golden and crisp, about 2 minutes. With a slotted spoon, remove the chilies, garlic, and ginger, draining as much oil as possible, and add them to the tomato mixture.

Adjust the heat to medium-low, and add the dried fish to the pan. Cook, stirring constantly, until crisp, about 1 minute. Transfer the fish to the tomato *achaar*, and let it stand for 10 to 15 minutes for the flavors to develop. Transfer the *achaar* to a serving dish.

BITTER MELON ACHAAR

Makes 4 to 6 servings

Tito Karelaa ko Achaar

Bitter melon (*tito karelaa*), also known as bitter gourd, is an acquired taste but is a very popular vegetable in Nepal. The bitter flavor is due to the presence of quinine, which is reduced by soaking in salt and blanching it before cooking. This *achaar* is prepared in such a way that the bitterness is almost nonexistent—and it perks up any meal.

---

4 to 6 medium bitter melons
1 tablespoon plus ½ teaspoon salt
3 tablespoons sesame seeds
1 dried red chili, halved and seeded
2 tablespoons fresh lemon or lime juice
⅛ teaspoon timmur (Nepali pepper; *page 31*), finely ground with a mortar and pestle

2 teaspoons cayenne pepper powder
2 tablespoons mustard oil
6 to 8 strands jimbu (Nepali aromatic herb; *see page 30*)
⅛ teaspoon fenugreek seeds
½ teaspoon ground turmeric

Wash the melons thoroughly, but do not peel them. Slice off 1 inch from the top and bottom. Use the cut-off pieces to rub against the cut surface of the vegetable in a circular motion. A white, foamy substance will be released. Discard the cut-off pieces and wash the melons. This process will extract some of the bitterness. Halve the melons lengthwise, scoop out the seeds and spongy pulp with a spoon and discard. Cut each half into ½-inch pieces (about 7 cups). In a colander, combine the bitter melon and 1 tablespoon of the salt, and set aside in the sink for 30 minutes. With your fingers, squeeze the juice from the melons, rinse with fresh water, and drain.

Heat a small cast-iron skillet over medium heat and toast the sesame seeds and dried red chili, stirring constantly to prevent the seeds from flying all over, until they give off a pleasant aroma and the seeds darken, about 2 minutes. Pour them into a dry container to halt the toasting and let them cool. Transfer the cooled spices to a spice grinder, grind them to a fine powder and set aside.

Bring a medium pot of water to a rolling boil over medium-high heat. Add the bitter melon and boil until tender but crunchy, 3 to 4 minutes. Drain and run under cold water to halt the cooking. Place them in a bowl and toss with the sesame seed mixture, lemon juice, remaining 1 teaspoon of salt, cayenne pepper powder, and timmur.

Heat the mustard oil in a small skillet over medium-high heat. When the oil is
faintly smoking, add the jimbu and fenugreek seeds and fry until dark brown
and fragrant, about 5 seconds. Remove the skillet from the heat, sprinkle in
the turmeric, immediately pour the oil mixture over the bitter melon, and mix
thoroughly. Cover the bowl and let the *achaar* stand for 30 minutes at room
temperature to absorb the seasonings, stirring occasionally. Transfer to a platter
and serve.

SWEET AND SPICY LAPSI/RHUBARB ACHAAR

Guleo Piro Lapsi ko Achaar

Makes 4 cups

Lapsi or *labsi* is a small plum-sized fruit native to Nepal. It is greenish-yellow when ripe, with a single, large seed, and is extremely sour. The fleshy yellow pulp is used to make pickles, candy, and fruit leather. This is among the most popular of all Nepali fruit pickles. Select only ripe, fresh, and smooth-skinned lapsi fruit and wash them carefully. Discard any bruised and discolored fruit. Lapsi fruit is not usually available in the United States and the closest possible substitute flavor wise is rhubarb.

30 to 40 ripe lapsi or 3.5 pounds rhubarb
1½ cups packed brown sugar
3 cassia leaves
8 to 10 green cardamom pods, seeds removed and coarsely crushed with a mortar and pestle
¼ cup vegetable oil
4 dried red chilies, halved and seeded
1 teaspoon fenugreek seeds
⅛ teaspoon jimbu (Nepali aromatic herb; see page 30)
1 teaspoon ground turmeric
Generous pinch ground asafetida

1 cup golden raisins
½ cup raw cashews, coarsely chopped
1 (2-inch) cinnamon stick, halved
2 tablespoons dried coconut chips, coarsely chopped
1½ teaspoons fennel seeds
8 whole cloves
1 tablespoon cayenne pepper powder
1½ teaspoons salt, or as needed
¼ teaspoon timmur (Nepal pepper; see page 31), finely ground with a mortar and pestle

If using lapsi fruit: In a medium-size saucepan, place the lapsi with water to cover and bring them to a boil over medium-high heat. Reduce the heat to low, cover the pan, and cook until the lapsi are tender and the skins are loose, 20 to 25 minutes. Do not overcook. The pulp and seeds should be intact, but the skin should peel off easily. Drain, and when cool enough to handle, peel off the skins. Set aside.

If using rhubarb: Trim the rhubarb stalks, discarding the ends and leaves. Rhubarb stalks are best when used young and peeling is not necessary. If the rhubarb is tough, peel off the outermost stringy covering with a vegetable peeler. Slice the rhubarb into 1-inch pieces and set aside (you should have about 10 cups).

In a small saucepan, combine the brown sugar, 1½ cups of water, and the cassia leaves. Bring the mixture to a boil over medium-high heat, stirring constantly, until the brown sugar is dissolved, about 1 minute. Reduce

the heat to medium-low and simmer until the sugar has slightly thickened into a syrup, about 5 minutes. Mix in the crushed cardamom seeds and set aside.

Heat the oil in a heavy saucepan over medium-high heat. When the oil is hot, but not smoking, add the dried chilies, fenugreek seeds, and jimbu and cook until the spices become dark brown and fully fragrant, about 5 seconds. Sprinkle in the turmeric and asafetida, then add the raisins, cashews, cinnamon stick, coconut chips, fennel seeds, and cloves and fry for 30 seconds. Add the peeled cooked lapsi or raw rhubarb, cayenne pepper powder, salt, and timmur and fry, stirring constantly, for 1 minute. Add the brown sugar syrup and mix well. Reduce the heat to medium-low and cook, stirring occasionally, until the syrup has thickened, about 20 minutes.

Remove the *achaar* from the heat and let it cool completely before placing in a clean 1-quart jar. It will keep for more than 1 year at room temperature.

FERMENTED RADISH PICKLE

Makes 6 cups

Khaadeko Mula Achaar

Radish pickles are commonly served with Nepali meals. The spicy, sharp, refreshing pickle boosts the appetite and is thought to aid in digestion. Any variety of long white or red radishes (such as daikon) can be used as long as they are fresh with smooth skins. Avoid radishes that are limp, woody, or withered. Traditionally, pickles are made on sunny days, which results in faster fermentation. This pickle will keep well for six months if refrigerated.

2 small white or red radishes, peeled and cut into bite-size pieces (about 6 cups)	1 teaspoon ground turmeric
Nylon netting or cheesecloth	¼ teaspoon timmur (Nepali pepper; *see page 31*), finely ground with a mortar and pestle
Kitchen twine	2 tablespoons vegetable oil
3 tablespoons brown mustard seeds, finely ground	2 tablespoons mustard oil
1 tablespoon cayenne pepper powder	½ teaspoon fenugreek seeds
2 teaspoons salt	⅛ teaspoon jimbu (Nepali aromatic herb; *see page 30*)

Place the radishes in a single layer on a wide, large tray. Cover with the netting or cheesecloth and secure with kitchen twine. Place the tray in the sun, and let them dry until slightly wilted, about 4 to 6 hours. If the sun is not present, dry them in the open air for the entire day.

When the moisture from the radishes is completely removed, place them in a large bowl with the mustard seeds, cayenne pepper powder, salt, turmeric, timmur, and vegetable oil. Mix with your hands, making sure the radishes are thoroughly coated with the spices. Cover the bowl and let it stand for 30 minutes before placing the mixture in a jar. Select a clean, wide-mouth jar and pack the radishes into the jar, one by one, pushing firmly until the jar is almost filled. Make sure there is no space between the radishes, but leave a ½ inch of space at the top of the jar.

Heat the mustard oil in a small skillet over medium-high heat. When the oil is faintly smoking, add the fenugreek seeds and jimbu strands and fry until dark brown and fragrant, about 5 seconds. Remove the skillet from the heat and let it cool. Pour the entire contents into the packed radish jar. Cover tightly with a lid, and place the jar outside in the direct sun for several days (bring it indoors in the evenings). If the sun is not present, place the jar in a warm area and leave it to ferment. The fermentation should take 4 to 5 days, depending on the amount of sunlight and the temperature. The formation of gas bubbles indicates that fermentation is taking place. The pickle is ready when the radishes are still crunchy and have a slightly sour taste. If you prefer a stronger and sourer pickle, increase the fermentation time. Store the *achaar* in the refrigerator for up to 6 months. Always use a dry, clean spoon to remove the radishes from the jar.

TOMATO, GREEN CHILI AND GARLIC PICKLE
Paani Achaar

Makes 4 cups

This hot, spicy fermented tomato pickle is called *"fina-taagu achaar"* in Newari and *"paani achaar"* in Nepali. This easy recipe does not require any cooking—instead all ingredients are placed in a jar and the sun does all the pickling. Use only fresh and fully ripened red tomatoes.

4 medium tomatoes	1 teaspoon cayenne pepper powder
3 to 4 hot green chili peppers, cut into long slivers	1½ teaspoon salt, or adjust to taste
4 cloves garlic, thinly sliced	½ teaspoon ground turmeric
1 tablespoon finely julienned fresh ginger	⅛ teaspoon timmur (Nepali pepper; *see page 31*), finely ground with a mortar and pestle
2 tablespoons ground mustard seeds	1 tablespoon mustard or vegetable oil

Cut each tomato into 4 to 6 pieces. Place the tomatoes in a jar with green chilies, garlic, ginger, ground mustard seeds, cayenne pepper powder, salt, turmeric, and timmur. Pour in the oil and shake the jar to mix well.

Cover the jar and place in a warm sunny area. Gently shake the jar every day during the fermentation process. The pickle will be ready when it is slightly soured with a pleasant refreshing taste, 2 to 3 days. Once the pickle is ready, refrigerate it to prevent further souring. Store in the refrigerator for up to 2 weeks.

GREEN CHILI PICKLE

Kudke Khursaani ko Achaar

Makes 4 cups

This is an old-fashioned way to preserve small fresh green chilies. They are sun-dried and skillfully mixed with spices. The pickles keep for more than a year and will become more pungent as they age. This pickle is very hot, so serve only a small quantity and always use a dry, clean spoon to remove the pickles from the jar. In Nepal, bird's eye chilies or bird peppers (*jire khursaani*) are used, but any type of green chili will work.

3 cups fresh green chilies, stemmed
Cheesecloth
Kitchen twine
¼ cup brown mustard seeds
¼ cup cumin seeds
¼ cup coriander seeds
1 tablespoon radish seeds (*mula ko beu*)
1 tablespoon fennel seeds
1½ teaspoons timmur (Nepali pepper; *see page 31*)

1 teaspoon fenugreek seeds
1 cup plus 2 tablespoons mustard oil
8 to 10 medium cloves garlic, thinly sliced
3 tablespoons peeled and finely julienned fresh ginger
1½ cups fresh lemon or lime juice
2 teaspoons salt
1½ teaspoons ground turmeric

If the chilies are long, cut them into 1-inch pieces. Spread them on a large tray lined with a cloth or paper towel. Cover with nylon netting or cheesecloth and secure with kitchen twine. Place the tray outdoors in the full sun or air-dry the chilies in a well-ventilated area, turning them frequently until the moisture is completely removed and they are slightly wilted. This can take from 2 to 12 hours, depending on the weather conditions.

Heat a small cast-iron skillet over medium heat and toast the brown mustard seeds, cumin seeds, coriander seeds, radish seeds, fennel seeds, timmur, and fenugreek seeds, until the mixture darkens and gives off a pleasant aroma, 2 to 3 minutes. Pour them into a dry container to halt the toasting and let them cool. Transfer the spices to a spice grinder and process to a fine powder. Set aside.

Heat 1 cup of the mustard oil in a heavy saucepan over medium-high heat. When the oil is faintly smoking, add the garlic, ginger, and sun-dried green chilies and fry until crisp, 3 to 4 minutes. Mix in the toasted spice mixture, lemon juice, salt, and turmeric and cook for 5 minutes, stirring as needed. Adjust the heat to medium and cook, uncovered, stirring from time to time, until the mixture has thickened and pulls away from the sides of the pan, about 30 minutes. The finished product should be dry, with no liquid.

Remove the pickle from the heat and let it cool completely before putting it in a clean jar, leaving a ½ inch of space at the top. Pour in the remaining 2 tablespoons of mustard oil. Cover tightly with a lid, place the jar in the sun or a warm area for 8 to 10 days. The pickle is then ready to eat and can be stored at room temperature for more than 1 year and tastes better as it ages.

RHUBARB PICKLE

Rhubarb ko Achaar

Makes 4 cups

This spicy, sweet, and tart chutney is prepared from rhubarb and spices. Rhubarb is a perennial plant with juicy red stalks resembling celery stalks, and large, coarse leaves. The leaves of this plant are toxic and not edible; only the red stalks are used. Due to its intense sourness, rhubarb is usually cooked with sugar. Many Nepalese living in the United States have described rhubarb chutney as similar in taste and texture to Nepali lapsi when cooked with the same spices.

3½ pounds rhubarb (10 to 12 cups sliced)	1 cup packed brown sugar, or to taste
2 tablespoons vegetable oil	1½ teaspoons salt
5 whole dried red chilies, halved and seeded	1 teaspoon fennel seeds
1 teaspoon fenugreek seeds	1 teaspoon ground cinnamon
½ teaspoon cumin seeds	½ teaspoon ground nutmeg
½ teaspoon ajowan seeds	½ teaspoon ground cloves

Trim the rhubarb, discarding the ends and leaves. Rhubarb stalks are best when used young and peeling is not necessary. If the rhubarb is tough, peel off the outermost stringy covering with a vegetable peeler. Slice the rhubarb into ¼-inch pieces and set aside.

Heat the oil in a heavy saucepan over medium-high heat. When the oil is hot, but not smoking, add the dried chilies, fenugreek seeds, cumin seeds, and ajowan seeds and fry until dark brown and fully fragrant, about 5 seconds. Add the rhubarb, brown sugar, salt, fennel seeds, cinnamon, nutmeg, and cloves and mix well. Bring the mixture to a boil, stirring constantly. Then reduce the heat to medium-low, cover the pan, and simmer until the rhubarb is tender and the liquid has thickened, about 45 minutes. It should resemble a thick jam.

Remove the pickle from the heat and adjust the seasonings and add more sugar if needed. Serve immediately or cool and transfer to a clean 1-quart jar and refrigerate.

PICKLED CAULIFLOWER

Makes 4 cups

Cauli ko Achaar

To make this spicy, refreshing pickle, use the freshest cauliflower available. The cauliflower is pickled in several toasted aromatic spices, packed in a jar, and placed in the sun to ferment. This pickle keeps at room temperature for more than 6 months and tastes better as it ages. Serve with any bland meal.

1 large head cauliflower, cut into 1-inch florets (about 6 cups)	1½ tablespoons brown mustard seeds
Nylon netting or cheesecloth	1 teaspoon fenugreek seeds
Kitchen twine	¼ teaspoon timmur (Nepali pepper; *see page 31*)
2 dried red chilies, halved, seeded, and crumbled	1½ teaspoons salt, or adjust to taste
	1 teaspoon ground turmeric
	¼ cup vegetable oil

Spread the cauliflower florets in a single layer on a large tray. Cover with the netting or cheesecloth and secure with kitchen twine. Place the tray in the sun, and let the florets dry until all the excess moisture is removed and they are slightly wilted, about 4 to 6 hours. If the sun is not present, dry them in the open air for the entire day.

While the cauliflower is drying, toast the spices. Heat a small cast-iron skillet over medium heat and toast the chilies, mustard seeds, fenugreek seeds, and timmur, stirring constantly, until they are heated through and give off a pleasant aroma, about 2 minutes. Transfer spices to a dry container to halt the toasting and cool. Place the spices in a spice grinder and grind to a fine powder. A mortar and pestle can also be used.

In a bowl, combine the sun-dried cauliflower, toasted spices, salt, turmeric, and 2 tablespoons of the oil, making sure the florets are thoroughly coated with the spices.

Pack the cauliflower florets, one by one, into a clean 1-quart jar, pushing firmly until the jar is almost filled leaving a ½ inch of space at the top of the jar. Try to make it as compact as possible. Pour the remaining 2 tablespoons of oil over the cauliflower.

Cover the jar tightly with a lid, and place it outside in the direct sun for several days (but bring it indoors in the evenings). If the sun is not present, place the jar in a warm area and leave it to ferment. The fermentation should take 4 to 5 days, depending on the amount of sunlight and temperature. The formation of gas bubbles indicates fermentation is taking place. The pickle is ready when it has a slightly sour taste. Store it in a cool, dark place. Always use a clean, dry spoon to remove the pickles from the jar.

PICKLED CUCUMBER

Makes 10 cups

Kaankro ko Achaar (Khalpi)

Nepali cucumbers differ slightly from the varieties available in the United States. They are eaten fresh when the cucumbers are young, but are also left on the vine to mature so they can be made into pickles. Mature Nepali cucumbers are large, oblong, and brown-skinned with a crisp flesh, resembling small watermelons. Pickled cucumber is eaten frequently in Nepal. During the festival of Dashain, when a large amount of meat and rich foods are consumed, pickled cucumbers are served to provide a cooling effect. Traditionally, this pickle is prepared and stored in an old-fashioned clay pot with a wide mouth and a thick interior (*maata ko ghaito*), which helps maintain a cool temperature even during fermentation. The wide mouth facilitates the packing in and pressing of the cucumber pieces.

---

1 large Nepali cucumber or 4 to 6 large
   cucumbers (10 to 12 cups sliced)
Cheesecloth
Kitchen twine
¼ cup brown mustard seeds, finely ground
1½ tablespoons salt, or adjust to taste

1 tablespoon cayenne pepper powder
1 teaspoon ground turmeric
½ teaspoon timmur (Nepali pepper; *see page
   31*), finely ground with a mortar and pestle
5 tablespoons vegetable oil

Halve the cucumbers lengthwise, scoop out and discard the mature seeds. Quarter each cucumber lengthwise and cut the quarters into 1-inch pieces. Place the cucumbers in a single layer (skin-side down) on a tray using two or three trays if needed. Cover with cheesecloth and secure with kitchen twine. Place the trays in the sun and let the cucumbers dry until all the excess moisture is removed and they are slightly wilted, 4 to 6 hours. If the sun is not out, dry them in the open air for the entire day (6 to 8 hours).

In a large bowl, combine the ground mustard seeds, salt, cayenne pepper powder, turmeric, and timmur. Add 3 tablespoons of the oil to create a paste. Add the dried cucumbers and mix with your hands, making sure they are well coated with the spices. Cover the bowl and set aside for 20 minutes.

Pack the cucumbers, one by one, into a clean 2½-quart wide-mouth jar. Push firmly until the jar is almost filled and there is no space between the cucumbers, leaving a ½ inch of space at the top of the jar (if the jar is not packed properly, air pockets will develop leading to spoilage). Pour the remaining 2 tablespoons of oil over the cucumbers.

Cover the jar tightly with a lid, and place it outside in the direct sun for several days (but bring it indoors in the evenings). If the sun is not present, place the jar in a warm area and leave it to ferment. The fermentation should take 4 to 5 days, depending on the temperature. The formation of gas bubbles indicates the fermentation is taking place. The pickle is ready when the cucumbers are still crunchy with a slightly sour taste. Store in the refrigerator to avoid excess souring. Always use a dry, clean spoon to remove the pickles from the jar.

Salads, Chutneys & Pickles

NINETEEN SPICES LEMON PICKLE

Masalaa ko Ledo Achaar

Makes 6 cups

Ledo achaar is a special refreshing pickle made with a number of ground spices and lemon juice and pulp. This is a simplified adaptation of this classic aromatic Nepali preserved pickle from my grandmother's kitchen. Preparing this pickle requires skill and is a time-consuming process, but the result is definitely worthwhile. I can still remember the aroma of spices being pounded in the mortar and pestle. On a sunny day, experienced pickle makers were called to our house to prepare the pickles. They would cut, dry, grind, and cook the vegetables, fruits, nuts, herbs, and spices all day in the sun. At the end of the day, they had made enough pickles for the entire year.

12 large lemons	1 teaspoon ajowan seeds
¾ cup sesame seeds	2 teaspoons fenugreek seeds
½ cup cumin seeds	1 teaspoon freshly ground black pepper
½ cup coriander seeds	4 whole cloves
½ cup brown mustard seeds	1 (2-inch) cinnamon stick, broken into
10 dried red chilies, halved, seeded, and	several pieces
broken into several pieces	1 cup mustard oil
Seeds of 10 green cardamom pods	1 tablespoon jimbu (Nepali aromatic herb;
Seeds of 2 black cardamom pods	see page 30)
1 tablespoon fennel seeds	1½ teaspoons ground turmeric
1 tablespoon yellow mustard seeds	¼ teaspoon ground asafetida
1½ teaspoons timmur (Nepali pepper; see	1 cup fresh lemon or lime juice
page 31)	2 teaspoons salt, adjust to taste
1½ teaspoons radish seeds (mula ko beu)	1 tablespoon vegetable oil

With a sharp paring knife, remove and discard the peel, white piths, membranes, and seeds from the lemons. Reserve the pulp and any juice that has collected.

In a bowl, mix together the sesame seeds, cumin seeds, coriander seeds, brown mustard seeds, dried red chilies, green and black cardamom seeds, fennel seeds, yellow mustard seeds, timmur, radish seeds, ajowan seeds, 1 teaspoon of the fenugreek seeds, the black pepper, cloves, and cinnamon stick pieces. Heat a medium-size cast-iron skillet over medium heat. Toast the spice mixture, stirring constantly, until the spice mixture darkens and gives off a pleasant aroma, 2 to 3 minutes. Pour the spices into a dry container to halt the toasting. When cool, transfer the spices to a spice grinder and grind to a fine powder. (You may have to do this in two or three batches.) Pour the mixture through a sieve and regrind any spices that do not pass through. Set aside.

Heat the mustard oil in a heavy saucepan over medium-high heat. When the oil is faintly smoking, add the remaining 1 teaspoon fenugreek seeds and the jimbu, and fry until dark brown and fragrant, about 5 seconds. Remove the pan from the heat, add the turmeric, asafetida, and toasted spice mixture, and mix thoroughly. Return the pan to the heat, add the reserved lemon pulp and cook, stirring, until the mixture boils. Add the lemon juice and salt and cook, uncovered, for 10 minutes. Adjust the heat to medium-low, cover the pan and cook, stirring from time to time, until the liquid has reduced and thickened and become a rich dark brown, about 45 more minutes. The pickle is done when the oil separates from the spice mixture. Remove the pickle from the heat and cool.

Transfer the cooled pickle into a 2-quart jar. Pour the vegetable oil on top, cover tightly with a lid, and place the jar either in the sun or in a warm, sunny area for 1 month. The pickle is then ready to be eaten. It will keep for more than a year in the refrigerator, and will improve as it ages.

Note: For everyday use, place a small amount of the pickle into a smaller jar and use it from there. Do not use a wet spoon to scoop the pickle from the jar, and never put back pickle that has been taken out of the jar.

Syrup-Filled Sweets / *Jilphi*

Chapter 12

SWEETS & DESSERTS

GULEO KHAANAA & MITHAI

Nepali sweets are usually purchased, but some are prepared at home using time-less old-fashioned methods, especially for religious occasions. They are served throughout the day: with breakfast, with afternoon tea, and with and after dinner. These confections are made from a wide variety of ingredients, including milk, flours, fruits, legumes, vegetables, nuts, and seeds. They are made or sold in sweet shops in all shapes, sizes, colors, flavors and textures. Many sweets are often flavored with green cardamom, saffron, and certain essences. They are decorated with finely chopped or sliced nuts, coconut, melon seeds, and edible varak (silver leaf paper). Some Nepali sweets are super sweet, fried, and soaked in syrup and often paired with yogurt, *swaari* (soft textured bread), or fruits to tone down the sweetness and richness.

One of the best-loved Nepali sweets is *jilphi* or *jeri*, a pretzel-shaped syrup-filled con-fection flavored with cardamom and saffron. They are usually purchased fresh in the morning and eaten with warm milk for breakfast. Other common sweets are *haluwaa* (pudding), *barfi* (a delicious fudge), *laddu* (sweet balls usually made from chickpeas flour), *doodh bari* (made from milk), *peda* (a flat round patty prepared from thickened-reduced milk), and *juju dhau* (sweetened yogurt). Nepalese also enjoy *kheer* (a milk-based rice pudding) and *sikarni* (thick sweetened yogurt).

Some sweets are served for special occasions, such as weddings, religious ceremonies, *Puja ko Thali* (tray offering for gods), and family feasts. These are usually bought from professional sweet makers (*haluwai pasale*), not made at home. During the most impor-tant religious festivals, such as Dashain (a 10-day celebration marking the victory of the goddess Druga over the devil), Laxmi Puja (the celebration of the goddess Laxmi), and Tihaar Festival with the Bhai Tika festival (brother-sister day), many delicately flavored and elaborate sweets are prepared. They are consumed as blessed food or shared and exchanged with family and friends to celebrate the joyous occasion.

RICE PUDDING
Kheer

Makes 4 to 6 servings

Traditionally in Nepal, our family prepares *kheer* with *govindbhog* rice, an aromatic, delicate, medium-grain rice similar in flavor to basmati but with smaller grains. *Kheer* can be made with any variety of white rice of your preference, and each variety will impart its own unique flavor and texture. *Kheer* is associated not only with auspicious occasions and religious ceremonies, but is also enjoyed regularly as a popular sweet dessert.

¾ cup medium-grain white rice
1 tablespoon clarified butter (gheu), melted
⅛ teaspoon saffron threads plus 6 to 8 threads for garnish
8 cups plus 1 tablespoon whole milk
Seeds of 4 to 6 green cardamom pods, finely ground with a mortar and pestle

1 cup sugar, or to taste
2 tablespoons chopped blanched raw almonds
2 tablespoons finely chopped dried unsweetened coconut
2 tablespoons golden raisins
2 tablespoons coarsely chopped raw pistachios

Put the rice in a medium bowl, cover it with plenty of water, and leave to soak for 20 minutes. Drain the water completely. Combine the rice and clarified butter, mix well and set aside. This process will prevent the grains from sticking together while cooking.

Gently crush the saffron with a mortar and pestle. Dissolve in 1 tablespoon of the milk and set aside.

Bring the 8 cups milk and ground cardamom seeds to a boil in a heavy-bottomed saucepan over medium-high heat. Stir occasionally to prevent the milk from burning. Reduce the heat to medium and continue cooking, stirring occasionally, until the milk has slightly thickened, about 15 minutes. Then stir in the rice mixture. Reduce the heat to medium-low and simmer until the rice grains have softened, about 20 minutes. Mix in the sugar, almonds, coconut, and raisins. Continue cooking, stirring, until the mixture has condensed into a thick, smooth pudding. Stir in the saffron-infused milk. Transfer the *kheer* to a serving dish, sprinkle it with the chopped pistachios and saffron threads, and serve immediately.

Note: Refrigeration will thicken the *kheer* and decrease its sweetness.

WHEAT FLOUR PUDDING

Makes 4 to 6 servings

Manbhog Haluwaa

Manbhog or *mana-bhog* is a soft, moist fluffy sweet dessert made from wheat flour, sugar, and clarified butter, and is similar in texture to a thick pudding. In Nepali, *"mana"* translates as "mind" and *"bhog"* is "pure food," so the *mana-bhog* is defined as "an offering to the mind." It is also associated with auspicious occasions and considered one of the purest forms of food to be offered to the deities during religious festivals. This is a popular dessert that is quick and easy to prepare and best served warm. Traditionally, it is paired with *poori*, and this combination is called *haluwaa-puri*, usually served for a delicious breakfast or snack.

---

1 cup sugar
Seeds of 4 to 5 green cardamom pods,
    coarsely ground with a mortar and pestle
¾ cup clarified butter (gheu) or unsalted
    butter

1½ cups all-purpose flour
½ cup golden raisins
¼ cup halved raw cashews
2 tablespoons finely chopped dried coconut
    chips

In a medium-size saucepan, combine the sugar, ground cardamom seeds, and 2 cups of water and bring to a boil over medium heat. Cook until the sugar dissolves and a thin syrup forms, about 5 minutes. Set aside.

Melt the clarified butter in a heavy saucepan over medium-low heat. Add the flour and cook, stirring constantly, until it is light golden brown with a pleasant nutty aroma and starts to release butter in the side of the pan, 15 to 20 minutes. Be careful not to burn the flour.

Stir in the raisins, cashews, and coconut. Slowly add the sugar syrup, stirring constantly—watch carefully as the mixture has a tendency to splutter. Cook until all the syrup is absorbed and the pudding starts to pull away from the sides of the pan. The finished dish should be soft and creamy. Transfer the pudding to a serving dish and serve hot. If not serving immediately, you can refrigerate, but warm it before serving.

CARROT PUDDING
Gaajar ko Haluwaa

Makes 4 to 6 servings

Gaajar ko haluwaa is a favorite family dessert. The recipe is easy to prepare, but requires constant attention and stirring while cooking. It is served hot, warm, or at room temperature, topped with chopped nuts. This dessert can be made ahead of time and stored in the refrigerator for up to one week. When serving, reheat slowly in a saucepan or in the microwave.

⅛ teaspoon saffron threads
8 cups whole milk
¼ cup clarified butter (*gheu*) or unsalted butter
1½ pounds carrots, peeled and coarsely grated
½ cup blanched raw almonds, finely ground

Seeds of 6 green cardamom pods, finely ground with a mortar and pestle
1 cup sugar
2 tablespoons golden raisins
2 tablespoons chopped raw cashews
2 tablespoons raw pistachios, coarsely ground with a mortar and pestle

Rub the saffron threads between your fingers to crush them and place them in a mortar and pestle or small bowl. Add 2 tablespoons of the milk and mix with a pestle or spoon until the saffron is thoroughly dissolved. Set aside.

Heat the clarified butter in a heavy saucepan over medium heat. Add the shredded carrots and any liquid and cook, stirring continuously, until the carrots are soft and the liquid has almost evaporated, about 10 minutes.

Increase the heat to medium-high, add the remaining milk, almonds, and ground cardamom seeds and mix well. Cook, stirring frequently, until the mixture comes to a full boil. Reduce the heat to medium-low, cover, and cook, stirring from time to time, until the milk has thickened and the mixture has reduced by about half, about 30 minutes.

Add the sugar, raisins, cashews, and saffron-infused milk and continue cooking, stirring and scraping the sides of the pan, until the mixture begins to pull away from the sides of the pan to create a thick solid mass, 10 to 15 minutes. Transfer the *haluwa* to a serving dish. Sprinkle with the pistachios and serve.

FRESH CORN PUDDING

Makai ko Tachauera

Makes 4 to 6 servings

Makai ko tachauera is a delicious old-fashioned family recipe. This creamy corn pudding was a culinary treat growing up in Nepal. It was usually prepared during the peak growing season when the corn was freshest.

5 to 6 ears sweet corn	¾ cup sugar
¼ cup clarified butter (gheu) or unsalted butter	2 tablespoons golden raisins
3½ cups whole milk	2 tablespoons blanched slivered raw almonds
Seeds of 4 green cardamom pods, finely ground with a mortar and pestle	

Remove the husks and silks from the corn. With a sharp knife, slice off the kernels. Scrape down the base of the cob with the side of the knife, extracting as much milky juice as possible into a bowl.

Heat the clarified butter in a large skillet over medium-high heat. Add the corn with all its juices and cook, stirring, until all the juice evaporates, about 5 minutes. Add the milk and ground cardamom seeds and cook, stirring occasionally, until the milk boils. Reduce the heat, cover, and continue cooking until the corn is tender, the milk thickens, and the mixture reduces to about half its original volume, 7 to 10 minutes.

Add the sugar, raisins, and almonds, mix well, and cook for 5 more minutes. Serve warm.

Saffron-Pistachio Yogurt / *Sikarni*

FOODS & FLAVORS FROM NEPAL

SAFFRON-PISTACHIO YOGURT

Sikarni

Makes 4 to 6 servings

Simple but elegant, *Sikarni* (pronounced *"see-kar-nee"*) is an exceptionally full-flavored, delicate, and creamy dessert made from drained yogurt, sweetened and flavored with saffron and cardamom. This classic recipe was passed down by my mother years ago, and I have been making it for festive occasions and family get-togethers ever since, especially on Mother's Day (Matha Tirtha Aunsi). *Sikarni* is so delicious, and we savor spoonfuls at a time, sometimes with freshly cut-up tree-ripened mangoes, or just about any other seasonal fruits, or simply chopped nuts. It is definitely worth trying and I hope it becomes a traditional yogurt dessert in your family too! Adjust its sweetness to suit your taste.

8 cups plain whole milk yogurt (two 32-ounce containers)	1 cup sugar, or adjust to taste
⅛ teaspoon saffron threads plus 8 to 10 saffron threads for garnish	Seeds of 8 to 10 green cardamom pods, finely ground with a mortar and pestle
2 tablespoons milk	½ cup raw pistachios, coarsely chopped
	Cheesecloth

Line a large colander with 3 layers of cheesecloth. Place the yogurt in the colander and bring in the corners and tie together to form a bag. Set the colander with the yogurt over a large bowl and drain the whey. (Make sure the bottom of the colander is high enough, so the yogurt does not touch the drained whey.) Place the colander and bowl in the refrigerator and check in a few hours to make sure the whey has not reached the colander. You may need to remove the whey once or twice as the yogurt continues to drain. To facilitate the draining, adjust the bag, shifting it about and turning it upside-down in the colander from time to time. Drain until the yogurt reduces to about half its original volume, or until it resembles soft cream cheese. This will take 10 to 12 hours.

Gently crush the ⅛ teaspoon of saffron with a mortar and pestle. Dissolve in the milk and set aside.

Remove the yogurt from the cheesecloth and transfer to a bowl. Add the saffron-infused milk, sugar, and ground cardamom seeds and beat until it is light and creamy. Stir in ¼ cup of the chopped pistachios.

Transfer the mixture to a decorative platter, sprinkle with the remaining chopped pistachios and saffron threads. Serve it immediately or cover and refrigerate until you are ready to serve. *Sikarni* keeps covered in the refrigerator for up to 4 days. If any whey rises to the surface, stir to incorporate it into the yogurt mixture.

SWEETENED YOGURT

Makes 8 cups

Juju Dhau

Juju dhau is a sweetened, custard-like yogurt that comes from Bhaktapur, Nepal, and is an important component of all feasts and celebrations. Although cow's milk is used to make regular yogurt, buffalo milk (*bhaisi*) is traditionally used for this dessert, resulting in a richer taste and texture. To make *juju dhau*, the milk is boiled, sweetened, mixed with culture, and poured into a decorative red-clay pot called a *kataaro*. It is then placed in a warm spot, on a bed of paddy husks (the papery covering of rice grains), and wrapped in several thick blankets to maintain a warm temperature while the yogurt sets. Because the clay pots are porous, the excess liquid from the yogurt slowly evaporates, leaving a delicious, thick yogurt. The finished yogurt is then served in the *kataaro*. This is my version of *juju dhau*, prepared with cow's milk. Serve it chilled with any meal, by itself, or for dessert.

½ gallon whole milk	¾ cup plain yogurt with active cultures
1 cup sugar	¼ cup raw pistachios, coarsely chopped
¼ cup powdered milk	12 to 15 saffron threads, crushed in a
Seeds of 6 green cardamom pods, finely	mortar and pestle
ground with a mortar and pestle	

Combine the milk, sugar, powdered milk, and ground cardamom seeds in a heavy saucepan over medium-high heat. Bring to a rolling boil, stirring constantly to prevent sticking, and remove any skin that forms on the surface. Reduce the heat to medium-low and simmer, stirring from time to time, until the milk has thickened, about 15 minutes.

Remove the milk from the heat and allow to cool to lukewarm. (You can speed up the cooling process by setting the pan in a bowl of ice and stirring it continuously until the milk has cooled.)

In a small bowl, mix ½ cup of the lukewarm milk mixture with the yogurt. Add the mixture back to the warm milk. To mix thoroughly, pour the milk into another bowl, transfer it back to the pan, and repeat this two to three times. Transfer the mixture to a clay pot or other container, and cover.

Wrap the container with a thick kitchen towel. Place it in a warm spot, such as a pantry or on top of the refrigerator, to allow the culture to grow. It is important that the yogurt is kept warm and undisturbed until it sets, at least 6 hours. To test if the yogurt has set, slowly tilt the container. If it pulls away from the side of the container, it is ready.

Sprinkle the yogurt with the pistachios and saffron. Refrigerate it in the same container for at least 6 hours before using. It will thicken further as it chills. The finished dish should be thick and creamy.

282   FOODS & FLAVORS FROM NEPAL

FRUIT SALAD WITH YOGURT

Makes 4 to 6 servings

Dahi Phal-phul ko Salad

This light fruit salad is a refreshing way to end a spicy meal. This salad is simple to prepare and you can use any combination of seasonal fruits.

8 cups whole milk yogurt
⅛ teaspoon saffron threads
2 tablespoons milk
6 cups chopped assorted fruits (mangoes, pineapple, seedless grapes, strawberries, pears, peaches, bananas)

1 cup sugar
Seeds of 4 to 6 green cardamom pods, finely ground with a mortar and pestle
¼ cup raw pistachios, coarsely ground
Cheesecloth

Line a colander with three layers of cheesecloth. Place the colander over a large bowl. Place the yogurt in the colander and let the whey drain for 2 hours.

Gently crush the saffron with a mortar and pestle. Dissolve in the milk and set aside.

Remove the yogurt and place it in a medium-size bowl. Stir in the fruits, sugar, ground cardamom seeds, and saffron-infused milk. Transfer the salad to a serving dish and garnish it with the pistachios. Chill for at least 1 hour and then serve.

MILK DESSERT WITH CARDAMOM AND PISTACHIOS

Makes 6 to 8 servings

Doodh ko Kurauni

Kurauni is a delicate sweet dish that is prepared by slowly boiling milk until it has reduced to a cream-like consistency. You can serve *kurauni* plain or with chopped fruits and nuts. This recipe is time-consuming, but is well worth the effort for its cool, creamy, and delectable taste.

---

1 gallon whole milk
2 green cardamom pods, crushed
⅓ cup sugar
2 tablespoons coarsely chopped raw
   pistachios

Seeds of 4 green cardamom pods, finely
   ground with a mortar and pestle
6 to 8 saffron threads, crushed

Bring the milk and 2 crushed cardamom pods to a rolling boil in a heavy saucepan over medium-high heat, stirring constantly. Reduce the heat to medium-low and simmer, stirring from time to time, until the milk has thickened and reduced to half its original volume. As the milk thickens, stir it often to prevent scorching. This process may take 45 minutes to 1 hour.

Remove the pan from the heat, add the sugar and mix well. Discard the cardamom pods. Transfer the mixture to a serving dish and sprinkle it with the pistachios, ground cardamom seeds, and crushed saffron. Cover and refrigerate the *kurauni* for several hours before serving.

SWEET CHICKPEA FLOUR BALLS

Makes 20 pieces

Besan ko Laddu

Laddus are traditional sweet, round balls that can be made from any type of flour such as chickpea, wheat, semolina, or a blend of these. No Nepali festivals are complete without *laddus*. In the morning hours, many devotees head to temples with a small tray of *laddus* to offer to deities and later distribute as blessed sweets. It is a popular confection, eaten any time of the day with various beverages.

---

1 cup clarified butter (*gheu*) or unsalted butter
2 cups chickpea flour (besan)
1½ cups shredded unsweetened coconut
½ cup blanched raw almonds, finely chopped

½ cup raw pistachio nuts, finely chopped
2 tablespoons walnuts, chopped
Seeds from 8 to10 green cardamom pods, finely ground with a mortar and pestle
1 cup sugar

Melt the butter in a heavy saucepan over medium-low heat. Gradually add the chickpea flour, stirring constantly, until the flour becomes rich golden brown and has a pleasant nutty aroma, about 15 to 20 minutes. Be careful not to burn the flour, for this may produce a bitter taste.

Add the coconut, almonds, pistachio nuts, walnuts, and ground cardamom seeds and mix well. Remove the pan from the heat and allow the mixture to cool slightly.

Stir the sugar into the cooled mixture. With your hands, form 1-inch balls of the chickpea flour mixture. Carefully place the balls on a tray to harden for 15 to 20 minutes. Transfer the balls to a platter and serve. *Laddu* keeps in a well-sealed container, refrigerated, for 4 to 5 weeks.

SYRUP-FILLED SWEETS

Jilphi

Makes 20 pieces

Jilphi, also known as *jalebi* or *jeri*, are one of the most common sweets in Nepal. They are deep-fried, pretzel-shaped yellow-orange loops dipped in saffron syrup. *Jilphi* taste best when freshly made as they are crisp and the filling is succulent and aromatic. When they cool, they lose their crispiness and the filling crystallizes—but they are still delicious. Traditionally, *jilphi* are paired with a soft Nepali bread called *swaari*. This sweet dish is very rich, so I usually serve them with fruit, yogurt, or pressed rice flakes (*cheuraa*) to tone down their sweetness.

2¾ cups all-purpose flour	4 cups sugar
3½ tablespoons rice flour	6 to 8 green cardamom pods, crushed
2 tablespoons plain yogurt	2 to 3 cups vegetable oil
⅛ teaspoon saffron threads	

In a large bowl, combine both flours. In a separate bowl, mix together the yogurt and 2 cups of water. Gradually add the yogurt mixture to the flour and mix until the batter has a creamy consistency without lumps. Cover the bowl and let it stand in a warm place (such as a pantry or an oven with a pilot light) to ferment for 12 to 16 hours. Once fermented, the mixture will double in volume and bubbles will form on the surface. The batter should have a pleasant faintly sour aroma.

When fermented, mix the batter again for 2 minutes with a whisk or fork. If necessary, add 1 to 2 tablespoons of water to make a smooth, pourable batter.

Gently crush the saffron with a mortar and pestle. Dissolve it in 2 tablespoons water and set aside.

In a wide saucepan, combine the sugar, 3 cups of water, and the crushed cardamom pods and mix well. Bring the mixture to a boil over medium-high heat, stirring constantly, until the sugar has dissolved, about 2 minutes. Reduce the heat to medium-low and simmer until slightly thickened about 5 minutes. Remove the pan from the heat, stir in the saffron-infused water and set it aside, covered.

Heat the oil in a heavy wide skillet over medium-high heat until it reaches 350 to 375 degrees F. Test the readiness of the oil by placing a little batter into the hot oil. If it bubbles and rises to the surface immediately, it is ready. Place some of the batter in a pastry bag or a heavy plastic bag with one corner snipped off. (Do not overfill the bag—there should be enough space to twist the top of the bag.) Squeeze the batter directly into

the hot oil in a circular motion to make a spiral loop about 4 inches in diameter that somewhat resembles a pretzel. Fry four to five *jilphi* at a time, turning them a few times, until crisp and golden brown on both sides. With a slotted spoon, remove the *jilphi*, draining as much oil as possible, and immediately submerge in the warm syrup until it has filled the coils. With a slotted spoon, immediately remove the *jilphi*, draining the excess syrup, and transfer it to a platter. Repeat the procedure for the remaining batter. If the syrup thickens, add 1 tablespoon of water and reheat it slowly. Serve the *jilphi* at room temperature.

FRESH CHEESE BALLS IN CARDAMOM SYRUP
Rasbari

Makes 20 to 25 balls

Rasbari is a popular sweet dish made for special occasions. In Nepali, *"ras"* is "juice" and *"bari"* is "balls," so *rasbari* translates to "savory balls in juice." To make *rasbari*, the fresh cheese is shaped into small balls and then simmered in a delicately flavored syrup until they double in size and become light and spongy, with a delicious dairy-rich taste. *Rasbari* are best served at room temperature, right after they are made. Once they have been refrigerated their texture and flavor begin to change, and they lose their spongy texture.

> 1 recipe freshly made paneer cheese (*chhana*) (*see directions page 313*)
> 5 cups sugar
>
> 4 to 5 green cardamom pods, crushed
> ½ teaspoon rose essence (optional)

Place the paneer on a work surface and knead it with the heel of your hand until it becomes a soft and pliable dough, 3 to 5 minutes. Scoop up about 2 tablespoons of the cheese dough and roll it into a smooth ball. Repeat the process with the remaining cheese. Set the balls aside and cover them with a damp kitchen towel.

In a large wide saucepan, combine the sugar, cardamom pods, and 8 cups of water. Bring the mixture to a boil over medium-high heat, stirring from time to time, for 5 minutes. Gently add the cheese balls, one at a time, adding as many as the pan can hold in a single layer. Do not crowd the pan, there needs to be enough room between the balls to allow for swelling. Reduce the heat to medium, cover the pan, and continue cooking until the balls double in size, about 20 minutes.

With a slotted spoon, remove the cheese balls and place them in a bowl and add ½ cup of syrup from the pan and set aside while you make the second batch. If the syrup has thickened, add ¼ cup of water. Repeat the process with the remaining cheese balls.

Transfer all the *rasbari* to a large bowl and pour on any of the remaining syrup. Add the rose essence if using, cover, and set aside for at least 2 hours at room temperature. Once the *rasbari* have cooled, they will shrink and firm up slightly. Serve at room temperature or refrigerate them for up to a week in an airtight container.

SAFFRON COCONUT-ALMOND FUDGE

Makes 25 to 30 pieces

Kesar-Naribal-Badaam Barfi

Barfi is a traditional fudge made from any combination of flours, lentils, nuts, fruits, vegetables, and thickened milk (*khuwaa*). It can be eaten any time of the day (like candy) as a snack or as an after-dinner dessert.

⅛ teaspoon saffron threads
½ cup clarified butter (ghee) or unsalted butter
1 cup sugar
1½ cups whole milk
3 cups non-fat powdered dry milk

¼ cup blanched raw almonds, finely ground
¼ cup shredded unsweetened coconut
Seeds of 8 to 10 green cardamom pods, finely ground with a mortar and pestle
½ cup raw pistachios, coarsely ground with a mortar and pestle

Grease a 9 x 13-inch pan and set aside.

Rub the saffron threads between your fingers to crush them, and place them in a mortar and pestle or small bowl with 1 tablespoon of water. Continue mixing with a pestle or spoon until the saffron is thoroughly dissolved. Set aside.

Heat the clarified butter in a medium-size saucepan over medium-low heat. Gradually add the sugar and mix well, stirring constantly. Increase the heat to medium-high, add the milk, and bring it to a boil. Stir in the powdered milk, almonds, coconut, and ground cardamom seeds and cook until the liquid evaporates and the mixture starts to pull away from the sides of the pan forming a thick, solid mass, about 10 minutes. Stir in the saffron-infused water and mix well. At this stage, the mixture will stick to the bottom of the pan, so stir constantly.

Transfer the mixture to the prepared pan and spread it evenly. Sprinkle the *barfi* with the pistachios and gently press into the surface. Set the pan aside for 1 hour until the fudge sets. Then cut into 1-inch diamond-shapes or small squares. Carefully remove the pieces from the pan, arrange them on a decorative platter, and serve. If not serving them immediately, refrigerate the *barfi* in an airtight container for up to 2 weeks, but bring it to room temperature before serving.

DUMPLINGS IN SAFFRON-CARDAMOM SYRUP
Gulaab Jaamun

Makes 25 dumplings

A very popular dessert, *gulaab jaamun*, also called *gup-chup*, are round fried dumplings soaked in saffron-cardamom syrup. They resemble small reddish-brown plums and have a soft, spongy texture. *Gulaab jaamun* are made for special occasions, holidays, religious festivals, and wedding ceremonies. Traditionally, they are made from *khuwaa* (thickened milk), but this is a simplified recipe. They are served warm or at room temperature, and can be served alone or with beverages, fruit, or yogurt to tone down the sweetness and richness.

⅛ teaspoon saffron threads
4 cups sugar
6 green cardamom pods, crushed
2½ cups nonfat powdered milk
½ cup all-purpose white flour
1 teaspoon baking soda
¼ cup unsalted butter, melted

¾ cup whole milk, or as needed
¼ cup raw pistachios, coarsely chopped
¼ cup raw almonds, coarsely chopped
Seeds of 4 green cardamom pods, coarsely
   ground with a mortar and pestle
3 to 4 cups vegetable oil

Gently crush the saffron with a mortar and pestle. Dissolve it in 1 tablespoon of water and set aside.

In a wide saucepan, combine the sugar, 6 whole crushed cardamom pods, and 4 cups of water and bring to a boil over medium-high heat, stirring constantly, until the sugar has dissolved, about 2 minutes. Reduce the heat to medium-low and simmer until the mixture has slightly thickened, about 5 minutes. Remove the pan from the heat, stir in the saffron-infused water, and set the syrup aside, covered.

In a medium-size bowl, combine the powdered milk, flour, and baking soda and mix well by hand. Stir in the butter and mix thoroughly. Gradually add the milk, a little at a time, to form a dough that holds together. Knead the dough until it is soft and pliable and can be easily molded into small balls.

If the dough is too sticky, add some flour; if it feels too firm, add a little water, and knead it some more. Cover the bowl and set aside at room temperature for 20 to 25 minutes.

To make the filling, combine the pistachios, almonds, and ground cardamom seeds in a small bowl and mix well. Set aside.

When the dough is well rested, remove it from the bowl, place on a flat surface, and knead again for 1 minute. Divide the dough into 25 equal pieces. Roll each piece into a small ball. Make an indentation in the ball, place a pinch of the filling in the center, close the dough around the filling and reroll to smooth it. If there are cracks, seal them and reroll into a smooth ball. Cover the balls with a damp kitchen towel and set aside until ready to fry.

Heat the oil in a medium heavy skillet over medium-high heat until it reaches 350 to 375 degrees F. Test the readiness of the oil by placing a small piece of dough into the hot oil. If it bubbles and slowly rises to the surface, it is ready. (Do not cook the *gulaab jaamun* over high heat or the outside will burn before the inside cooks.) Drop four or five balls at a time into the hot oil. They will first sink to the bottom and then will rise to the surface slowly. Fry them gently, turning, until they are reddish-brown on all sides, 3 to 5 minutes.

Remove the fried balls from the pan with a slotted spoon and drain the excess oil. Gently submerge the balls in the warm syrup and let them soak for at least 2 hours, until they are soft and spongy. Serve the *gulaab jaamun* warm or at room temperature. Store them (in the syrup) in the refrigerator for up to 1 week, but bring them back to room temperature or warm them before serving.

Chapter 13 BEVERAGES

CHEESO-TAATO PEEUNE

f you have ever traveled to Nepal or are familiar with Nepali customs, you know that Nepali hospitality is expressed by offering all guests some kind of beverage, whether It Is just a glass of water or one of many hot and cold drinks.

Among the most beloved beverages is hot tea. Tea drinking is an important part of Nepali culture and it is served throughout the day, most commonly prepared with milk and sugar and/or with spices. One can see tea stalls on most of the streets or roadside shops where people stop for a quick tea break.

Another popular beverage served during the warmer months is fruit *sharbat*, which is a non-alcoholic drink made from fresh lemons or fruit juice and sugar. Mint leaves are also sometimes added depending on individual taste. *Kagati-paani* (lemonade) is a traditional and very common drink prepared with lemon juice, ginger, ice water, salt, and crushed cumin.

Another popular cooling and refreshing drink, called *lassi*, is made from yogurt, water, and sugar. Some yogurt drinks are flavored with crushed mango pulp, banana, and other fruits and flavorings and then topped with nuts. Many of the beverages are filling and nourishing and served at any time of the day. Healthy, refreshing buttermilk drinks with salt and spices are also popular during hot summer days.

MILKY TEA
Doodh Haaleko Chiya

Makes 4 servings

Chai, or *chiya* in Nepali (pronounced *chee-yah*), milky tea is the most widely consumed hot beverage in Nepal, where it is enjoyed throughout the day, starting in the early morning. Many people drink several cups of milky tea instead of breakfast, followed by an early lunch. These days, tea bags have become more popular in Nepal, but loose black tea is still preferred for its richer flavor, color, and usually, lower price. Tea is grown mainly in the eastern parts of Nepal and Nepali tea is now exported all over the world. The *chiya* I grew up with was made with loose black tea leaves, boiled with water, milk, and sugar, sometimes flavored with spices (cardamom, cloves, cinnamon, and fresh ginger).

> 1½ to 2 tablespoons good quality loose black tea leaves
> 1 cup whole milk
> Sugar to taste

In a medium-size saucepan, bring 6 cups of water to a rolling boil over medium-high heat. Add the tea leaves and continue boiling until the water has become dark reddish-brown, about 1 minute. Reduce the heat to medium-low. Add the milk and sugar, and simmer until the tea becomes light brown. Make sure the tea is not too watery or mild. Strain into individual cups and serve immediately.

Variations
CARDAMOM MILKY TEA
Add 2 cracked green cardamom pods while boiling the water.

FRESH GINGER MILKY TEA
Add 1 teaspoon minced fresh ginger while boiling the water.

MILKY TEA WITH WHOLE SPICES

Makes 4 servings

Singo Masalaa ko Chiya

Masalaa ko chiya is a sweet milky tea prepared with an aromatic blend of fresh whole spices. The whole spices are gently boiled with loose tea leaves so that they swell and double in size and subtly release their flavor into the tea. The tea is refreshing, mildly spicy and has a soothing effect after a long hard day. This recipe is for those who do not like ground spice mixtures in their tea and the best way to enjoy it is serving it steaming hot and sipping slowly.

1 (1-inch) cinnamon stick, divided lengthwise into 2 pieces	3 to 4 whole cloves
1 small piece fresh ginger, peeled and cut into 1-inch-thick slices	5 black peppercorns
	1½ to 2 tablespoons loose black tea leaves
3 green cardamom pods, slightly crushed to break pods	3 cups whole milk
	Sugar to taste

In a medium-size saucepan, bring 4½ cups of water to a full boil. Add the cinnamon stick, ginger, cardamom pods, cloves, peppercorns, and tea leaves and return to a boil over medium-high heat and continue boiling until the water has become reddish brown.

Reduce the heat to medium and add the milk. Bring to a boil stirring continuously to prevent it from boiling over. Boil until the tea becomes light brown. Add sugar according to your own taste. Strain the tea directly into individual cups and serve immediately.

TEA TIPS

- As a rule, for each cup of tea, you will need 1½ cups of water, because the water evaporates during the continued boiling and simmering
- Always boil the water vigorously before adding the tea leaves and spices. This helps bring out the color and aroma of the tea
- Too many loose tea leaves may make the tea bitter and too strong, so adjust the measurements to suit your taste
- Too much milk makes the tea flavorless
- As it sits around, tea loses its flavor so it should be served immediately after brewing

MILKY MIXED SPICES TEA
Masalaa ko Chiya

Makes 4 servings

Masalaa is a strong, aromatic, refreshing tea prepared with milk, sugar, and a combination of freshly ground spices. Ready-made spice mixtures are easily available at Nepali and Indian grocery stores, but I recommend making your own (*see below*) because it will be fresher and will taste better.

4 cups whole or low-fat milk	½ to 1 teaspoon Masala Tea Mixture (*recipe below*)
1 tablespoon good quality loose black tea leaves	Sugar to taste

In a medium-size saucepan, combine the milk, tea leaves, spice mixture, and 2 cups of water and bring to a rapid boil over medium-high heat. Reduce the heat to medium-low and simmer until the tea becomes light brown, stirring continuously to prevent it from boiling over. Add the sugar according to taste. Strain the tea directly into individual cups and serve immediately.

HOMEMADE MASALA TEA MIXTURE
Chiya ko Masala

Makes ¾ cup

4 tablespoons green cardamom seeds	1 (2-inch) cinnamon stick, broken into several pieces
Seeds from 5 black cardamom pods (about 2¼ teaspoons)	⅛ teaspoon whole black peppercorns
1 tablespoon whole cloves	¾ teaspoon ground ginger
1 teaspoon fennel seeds	

Heat a small cast-iron skillet over medium-high heat. When it is hot, add the green and black cardamom seeds, cloves, fennel seeds, cinnamon stick, and peppercorns and toast them, stirring constantly, until they give off a pleasant aroma, about 2 minutes. Pour into a dry container to halt the toasting. Once they are cooled, grind them in a spice grinder or mortar and pestle until finely ground. Add the ginger and mix well. Transfer to an airtight glass jar to store. When making tea, use ⅛ to ¼ teaspoon per cup of boiling water, or according to personal preference.

NEPALI HERBAL TEA

Sittal Chiya

Makes 6 servings

This relaxing, easy-to-make herbal tea is prepared with several whole spices, dried gooseberries, and goddess basil leaves. I usually prepare a large pot of this tea and drink it throughout the day. Most of the ingredients are readily available through mail order online or at local Nepali markets or Indian grocery stores.

3 tablespoons dried green gooseberries (*amalaa*)
1 (1-inch) cinnamon stick
1 (¼-inch) piece fresh ginger, peeled and halved
4 green cardamom pods, crushed

2 black cardamom pods, crushed
1 teaspoon whole cloves
1 teaspoon dried goddess basil leaves (*tulasi*)
2 small cassia leaves
¼ cup sugar, or to taste
2 tablespoons fresh lemon or lime juice

In a large saucepan, combine 8 cups of water, the gooseberries, cinnamon stick, ginger, green and black cardamom pods, cloves, basil, and cassia leaves and bring them to a rapid boil over medium-high heat. Reduce the heat to low and simmer until the flavors of the spices are released, about 25 minutes. If the tea becomes too strong, add some water to adjust the taste. Stir in the sugar and lemon juice. Strain and serve.

HOT GINGER AND LEMON TEA

Makes 4 servings

Taato Kaagati ra Aduwaa

This refreshing drink is served any time of the day throughout the year. It is prepared by boiling fresh ginger, lemon juice, and water.

> ¼ cup fresh lemon or lime juice
> 1 (½-inch) piece fresh ginger, peeled and halved
> 2 tablespoons sugar, or to taste

In a saucepan, bring 6 cups of water to a rolling boil over high heat. Add the lemon juice, ginger, and sugar, and reduce the heat to low. Simmer until the ginger releases its flavor, about 5 minutes. Pour the entire contents into a teapot. There is no need to remove the ginger, as it will sink to the bottom and continue flavoring the beverage. Serve hot.

BUTTERMILK DRINK

Makes 4 servings

Mohi

Mohi is an old-fashioned drink, prepared from the liquid leftover after churning butter. I remember drinking it at my husband's maternal grandparents' home in Dhading, Nepal, where a meal without yogurt and *mohi* is unthinkable. A tall glass was always served to visitors as a gesture of hospitality. This is my version of *mohi* prepared from ready-made cultured buttermilk.

> ¼ teaspoon cumin seeds
> 2 cups cultured buttermilk
> ½ cup crushed ice
>
> Salt to taste (some buttermilk contains salt)

Heat a small skillet over medium heat and toast cumin seeds, stirring constantly, until they give off a pleasant aroma, about 1 minute. Transfer to a mortar and pestle and grind coarsely.

Combine the ground cumin seeds, buttermilk, ice, and 1 cup of cold water in a blender and process at high speed until well blended. Taste and add salt if needed. Pour the mixture into tall glasses and serve.

LASSI

Lassi, a delicious sweet beverage made with yogurt, is a refreshing drink served during hot summer days.

---

4 cups plain yogurt
½ cup sugar, or to taste
Seeds of 2 green cardamom pods, finely
  ground with a mortar and pestle

⅛ teaspoon saffron threads, lightly crushed
  with a mortar and pestle
1 cup ice cubes or crushed ice

Combine the yogurt, sugar, ground cardamom seeds, saffron, and 2 cups of cold water in a blender and process at high speed until well blended. With the blender running, add the ice cubes one at a time through the feeder hole. Continue to process until the ice is finely ground. Pour the *lassi* into tall glasses and serve chilled.

MANGO LASSI

To make mango *lassi*, omit the saffron and add 2 peeled and chopped ripe mangoes or 2 cups canned mango pulp and 1 teaspoon rosewater (optional) with the ice and process as directed above. Garnish each glass with a sprinkling of coarsely chopped raw pistachios.

FRUIT LASSI

Other fruits, such as strawberries, bananas, peaches, pears, or grapes can be used to make *lassi* as well, following the directions for Mango Lassi, but reduce the water to ½ cup. You may also use honey or maple syrup instead of sugar.

ALMOND-PISTACHIO LASSI

Add ¼ cup blanched raw almonds, ¼ cup raw pistachios, and ½ cup honey diluted with 1 tablespoon warm water with the ice and process as directed above.

NEPALI LEMONADE
Kaagati ko Sharbat

Makes 4 servings

This refreshing lemonade is often served to welcome guests on hot days. Serve the lemonade chilled, garnished with lemon or lime slices.

1 cup fresh lemon or lime juice	6 to 8 fresh mint leaves, crushed
1 cup sugar, or to taste	Ice cubes or crushed ice
1 lemon or lime, sliced	

In a large pitcher, combine the lemon juice, sugar, and 6 cups of cold water and mix thoroughly to dissolve the sugar. Add the lemon slices and mint, and chill. When you are ready to serve, pour the lemonade into glasses of crushed ice.

MINT-GINGER LEMONADE
Kaagati Aduha ko Sharbat

Makes 5 servings

1 (¼-inch) piece ginger	1 cup fresh lemon juice
1½ cups sugar	6 to 8 mint leaves

In a saucepan, combine ginger, sugar, and 7 cups of water and bring them to a quick rolling boil over high heat. Reduce the heat to low, cover, and simmer gently for 10 minutes. Uncover and allow the mixture to cool to room temperature. Pour the entire contents into a pitcher with the fresh lemon juice. Gently bruise the mint leaves and add them to the pitcher. Garnish with additional mint leaves.

Chapter 14

AFTER-MEAL REFRESHERS

BAASNA-AUNE-MASALAA HARU

Nepali meals are always finished off with a special selection of fragrant whole spices, dried fruits and nuts, sweet or salted *titauraa* (fruit nuggets), *supaari* (betel or areca nut), or ready-made digestive powders. A mixture of whole cloves, green or black cardamom seeds, and cinnamon sticks are often chewed and sucked to cleanse and refresh the palate. Some people find betel nuts the most satisfying and they chew them by themselves or with cloves and cardamom throughout the day. A mixture made of fennel seeds, finely shredded betel nuts, and aromatic flavorings is also chewed to cleanse the mouth.

Nepalese also enjoy a popular digestive chew prepared from green betel leaves, locally known as *paan*. The leaves are neatly rolled and folded into a triangular pouch that is filled with different combinations of ingredients, such as betel nuts, cardamom seeds, cloves, dried fruits, fennel seeds, and coconut chips. The combination is usually chewed slowly to refresh the palate. When habitually chewed, betel leaves stain the teeth and turn the mouth a deep red color. Betel leaf chewing is an acquired taste and some people find it too strong.

Cloves are the most common mouth freshener. Nepalese chew cloves throughout the day, alone or with green or black cardamom or cinnamon sticks and betel nuts. Chewing cloves is certainly a cultivated taste, and at first they can be biting sharp, hot, and leave a numb sensation in the mouth, but once you get used to it you enjoy the taste. Cloves act as a quick home remedy for relieving toothaches by simply tucking them in the affected corner of the mouth and chewing slowly to release the oil. This also helps to minimize tooth decay and eliminates halitosis. Cloves are also used to cure nausea and flatulence and to promote digestion, especially when eating fatty and spicy food.

BASIC AFTER-MEAL REFRESHER

Makes 4 cups *Baasna Aune Masala Haru*

The following recipe uses the most common combination of refreshing ingredients that are typically served in a Nepali *paan batta*. They act as digestive aids as well as mouth refreshers. Nepalese believe that chewing cardamom and cloves slowly helps to cure bloating, helps digestion, and removes bad breath. The volatile oil in the spices prevent toothaches.

---

1 cup green cardamom pods
½ cup black cardamom pods
½ cup areca or betel nuts, chopped
1 cup whole cloves

½ cup cinnamon sticks, broken into
  1-inch pieces
½ cup *churpi* (yak cheese chew), optional

Place each ingredient in a compartment of a *paan batta* or other divided container and serve.

PAAN BATTA

Many Nepali households own a traditional container, called a *paan batta* or *panbatta*, an elaborate box with beautiful carvings. The boxes are usually made of silver, but can also be made from anything, from wood to precious metals. The bigger boxes have compartments to hold different ingredients. It is customary at the end of a meal for the host or hostess to bring out the *paan batta* filled with fragrant whole spices, betel nuts, and/or dried fruits and offer them to the guests, whether the occasion is formal or informal. There is a custom in Nepal of presenting a silver *paan batta* to the bride as a wedding present so that she may serve and impress her guests once she goes to her husband's house.

A Nepali *paan batta* is usually carved with *Astamangala*, which is eight sacred auspicious signs. They are: a white parasol (protects from evil desire), two fishes (symbolizing rescue from ocean of misery and existence), conch *sankha* (melodious-sound), *dhvja* (protection from harmful forces), endless knot *srivatsa* (wisdom and compassion), *kalasa* (spiritual wealth), lotus flower (purity), and *chamaru* (tantric manifestations). Each sign symbolizes auspiciousness. They appear grouped together as a decorative motif in metal, stone, wood, and painting. These are believed to represent the gifts given by Sakyamuni on his attainment of Enlightenment of Buddha.

DRIED FRUIT AND NUT REFRESHER

Makes 8 cups

Masalaa Haru

A combination of different dried fruits and nuts, chopped into bite-size pieces, is another after-meal refresher in Nepal. Sugar or rock candy are available through online retailers or in Indian or Nepali markets. This popular snack is a natural energy booster and a cure for sweet cravings. They are healthy, tasty, and packed with nutrition. Nepalese eat them as snacks before or in-between meals any time of the day.

1 cup raw almonds	1 cup shelled raw pistachios
1 cup raw cashews	1 cup dark or golden raisins
1 cup walnuts	1 cup puffed lotus seeds (*makhanaa*)
1 cup pitted dried dates	½ cup rock candy (*misri*)
1 cup chopped dried coconut	

Chop the almonds, cashews, walnuts, and dates into uniform-size pieces. Combine with the coconut, pistachios, raisins, lotus seeds, and rock candy. Transfer the mixture to a decorative serving dish (or *paan batta*) and serve.

FENNEL SEED AND COCONUT REFRESHER

Saunp, Misri, Naribal

Makes 2¼ cups

Fennel seeds are used extensively as an after-meal digestive or palate cleanser after a spicy Nepali meal. A small quantity is chewed slowly just like an after-dinner mint. They are served toasted by themselves or with a combination of shredded coconut, tiny candy balls, roasted melon seeds, and tiny pieces of rock candy. Sometimes the fennel seeds are coated with multi-colored candy coatings, which are available through online retailers or at Indian stores.

1½ cups fennel seeds
½ cup finely chopped dried coconut
¼ cup old-fashioned rock candy (*misri*)

Heat a small cast-iron skillet over medium heat, and toast the fennel seeds, stirring constantly, until they give off a pleasant aroma, 2 to 3 minutes. Pour them into a dry bowl to halt the toasting.

In the same skillet, toast the coconut, stirring and shaking the skillet, until crispy and light brown, about 1 minute. Mix it with the fennel seeds. Let the mixture cool completely, then stir in the rock candy. Store in an airtight container and serve as needed.

COLORFUL AFTER-MEAL MUNCH

Makes 3 cups

Ayurvedic Masalaa

This refreshing combination of crunchy and colorful seeds, nuts, and spices is generally chewed after a meal. The fragrant and mildly sweet mixture helps with digestion and serves as a mouth freshener after a spicy meal. This recipe is versatile, and you can alter the blend according to your personal preferences. All ingredients are available from online retailers or at Indian stores.

1 cup fennel seeds
½ cup sesame seeds
½ cup melon seeds
½ cup candy-coated fennel seeds
¼ cup thinly shredded betel nuts

Seeds of 12 green cardamom pods
Seeds of 8 black cardamom pods
2 tablespoons sweetened dried shredded
  coconut

Heat a small cast-iron skillet over medium heat and toast the fennel seeds, stirring constantly until they give off a pleasant aroma, 2 to 3 minutes. Pour them into a dry bowl to halt the toasting.

In the same skillet, toast the sesame seeds, stirring constantly with a wooden spoon to prevent the seeds from flying all over, until they give off a pleasant aroma and darken, 2 to 3 minutes. Mix them with the fennel seeds. Toast the melon seeds in the same skillet for 1 minute. Add them to the fennel-sesame mixture.

Let the mixture cool completely, and then stir in the candy-coated fennel seeds, betel nuts, green and black cardamom seeds, and coconut. Transfer the mixture to an airtight container and serve as needed.

GREEN GOOSEBERRY NUGGETS

Makes 2½ cups

Amalaa ko Titauraa

Amalaa is the Nepali name for the Indian gooseberry, which is a small, round, light yellow fruit that has a sour taste. The fruit is one of the richest known natural sources of vitamin C. It is known as a medicinal fruit used for healing and rejuvenation in Ayurvedic medicine. Upon chewing, the fruit is initially quite sour, but when followed by water it produces a very sweet and refreshing aftertaste. In this recipe, the gooseberries are boiled until the seeds separate from the pulp. The fruit is then lightly spiced, formed into nuggets, and dried. Chew these any time of the day or after meals. Gooseberries are available in the US at some supermarkets and online.

10 cups fresh green gooseberries, washed and stemmed	½ teaspoon ground turmeric
	½ teaspoon ground cumin
1 tablespoon minced fresh ginger	Small pinch ground asafetida
1 teaspoon salt	1 tablespoon vegetable oil
1 teaspoon cayenne pepper powder	Cheesecloth

Place the gooseberries and water to cover in a medium-size saucepan, and bring to a boil over medium-high heat. Reduce the heat to low, cover the pan, and cook until the fruit is tender and the seeds are easily removable, 25 to 30 minutes. Drain and when cool enough to handle, separate the seeds from the pulp and discard the seeds.

Place the gooseberry pulp in a bowl and mash it well. Stir in the ginger, salt, cayenne pepper powder, turmeric, cumin, and asafetida. Before making the nuggets, grease one or two wicker trays (*naanglo*) with a little oil. Shape the gooseberry mixture into grape-size nuggets, and place them on the prepared tray close together, but not touching.

Place the tray outside in the full sun, cover with cheesecloth, and let the nuggets dry slowly. Always bring the tray indoors after the sun has set. Once the nuggets are slightly firm on top, gently turn them over to allow the bottom sides to dry evenly. The nuggets should be dried in 2 to 3 days, depending upon the amount of sunlight. Alternatively, you can dry the nuggets in a food dehydrator according to the manufacturer's instructions. When the nuggets are fully dried, they will shrink and become light brown. The nuggets can be stored in an airtight container for up to 6 months.

GOOSEBERRY CHIPS

Instead of mashing the boiled pulp, separate it into segments. Mix the segments with the spices and dry as directed above.

DRIED LEMON CHEWS
Kaagati ko Sankhatro

Makes 4 cups

Popular *sankhatro* chews are very refreshing, with a tart and fruity flavor. They are slowly chewed any time of the day or after meals. They are also used as a home remedy to aid digestion and to cure stomach disorders and nausea. *Sankhatro* are traditionally prepared from Nepali lemons (*nibuwa*), a large, oblong fruit with a thick yellow and rough skin. They are extremely sour and are used for making pickles and chutneys. The juice extracted from the *nibuwa* is made into a concentrated dark brown liquid (*chook amilo*), which is used as a souring agent in many pickles. For this recipe, I use large regular lemons, which are equally delicious.

15 large lemons	Cheesecloth
¼ cup salt	Kitchen twine

Wash the lemons thoroughly and wipe them with a clean cloth or paper towel. With a sharp knife, cut off a small piece from the top end of each lemon, then make two cuts, cutting halfway through the lemons as if you were making 4 wedges, making sure the bottom is still attached. Pick out any visible seeds and discard. Rub the salt on the lemons and into the cuts.

Select a clean jar, big enough to fit all the lemons, and place them inside. Close the lid tightly and shake the jar vigorously. Place the jar outside in the direct sun (but bring it indoors in the evenings). If the sun is not present, place the jar in a warm area. Shake the jar once a day until the lemons soften, the skins become tender, and the color lightens. This process may take 3 to 4 weeks.

Remove the lemons from the jar and place them on a flat tray in a single layer. Cover with cheesecloth and secure with kitchen twine. Situate the tray in the full sun and let the lemons dry slowly. Always bring the tray indoors after the sun has set. (Alternatively, use a food dehydrator, following the manufacturer's instructions.) Dry the lemons until all the moisture evaporates and the pulp has a chewy texture. Cut the lemons into bite-size pieces. Store in airtight containers for up to a year at room temperature.

SPICY-SWEET LAPSI CHEWS

Makes 60 to 65 lapsi chews

Guleo Lapsi ko Titauraa

Lapsi ko titauraa is one of the most favorite and delicious Nepali fruit chews made from the native lapsi fruit (Nepalese hog plums). The fruit is greenish-yellow when ripe, and has a large hard seed that is almost the size of the whole fruit itself. The plum-sized fruit has a pleasant flavor, but is extremely sour even when completely ripe. The pulp is firmly attached to the seed and difficult to separate, so it must be boiled first. The pulp is then mixed with sugar and spices, made into nuggets, and sun-dried. Lapsi may not be available outside Nepal, but if you do manage to get hold of this fruit, this recipe is a must!

75 to 80 medium lapsi fruits	Small pinch ground asafetida
2½ to 3 cups sugar, or to taste	1 tablespoon vegetable oil
1 tablespoon cayenne pepper powder	Cheesecloth
2 teaspoons salt	Kitchen twine
Seeds of 10 to 12 green cardamom pods, finely ground with a mortar and pestle	

Place the fruit with water to cover in a medium-size saucepan and bring to a boil over medium-high heat. Reduce the heat to medium-low, cover the pan, and cook until the lapsi are tender, the skins loosen, and the seeds easily separate from the pulp, 25 to 30 minutes. Drain, and when cool enough to handle, peel off the skins and separate the pulp and discard the seeds and skins.

In a bowl, combine the lapsi pulp, sugar, cayenne pepper powder, salt, ground cardamom seeds, and asafetida. Knead the mixture vigorously by hand, making sure the spices are well incorporated. The pulp will be sticky and slippery. Before making the fruit chews, grease one or two wicker trays (*naanglo*) with oil. Form pulp mixture into grape-size nuggets and drop them onto the prepared tray, placing them close together, but not touching.

Cover the tray with cheesecloth and secure with kitchen twine. Place it in the full sun, but always bring the tray indoors after the sun has set. Once the chews are slightly firm on top, gently turn them over to allow the bottom sides to dry evenly. The chews should be completely dried in 4 to 5 days, depending upon the temperature, humidity, and amount of sunlight. Take care to completely dry them, or they may mold. (Alternatively, you can use a food dehydrator, following the manufacturer's instructions.) Once they are dry, roll the chews in sugar. The lapsi chews keep stored in an airtight container for up to 6 months.

Chapter 15

SPICE BLENDS & BASIC RECIPES

NEPALI GARAM MASALAA

Garam masalaa is an aromatic combination of several toasted and ground spices. There are many variations of this spice blend and each family has their own version according to their preference and taste. The most common and basic components of the mixture are cumin, coriander, black pepper, nutmeg, green cardamom, cinnamon, and cloves. Premixed and ground garam masalaa or curry powders are also readily available at Indian markets and in the spice section of some supermarkets. They are also available through online retailers or some local Nepali markets outside Nepal. But they bear little resemblance in flavor and taste to freshly ground homemade blends—if not bought from reputable stores, the mixture may be stale and/or include cheap fillers. If you use a ready-made garam masalaa, use less than the amount mentioned in my recipes because they may overpower the dish. Try to experiment with a small amount to get familiar with the results.

Making your own garam masalaa is easy and assures a fresher and more intensely flavored spice mix. The trick to making successful spice blends is to purchase whole spices, gently toast them until they give off a pleasant aroma, cool them, and grind them to a powder. The ground spices should be stored in a cool, dry place in an airtight container. Whole spices have a longer shelf life than ground spices because they have seed coatings and bark to protect the flavors, which are released once they are crushed. Therefore, it is always best to make spice blends in small quantities. Nepali garam masalaa may be added at the beginning, halfway, or toward the end of the cooking process. It can also be used as a marinade or a dry rub, and a small amount of garam masalaa sprinkled on prepared food also gives the dish more flavor.

Here is my recipe for homemade garam masalaa that has been passed down to me from older family members.

½ cup cumin seeds	8 green cardamom pods, crushed
½ cup coriander seeds	2 black cardamom pods, crushed
1 tablespoon whole black peppercorns	1 tablespoon whole cloves
3 to 4 small cassia leaves	1 small whole nutmeg, broken into several
3 (1-inch) cinnamon sticks, broken into several pieces	pieces

Heat a cast-iron skillet over medium-low heat. When it is hot, add all of the spices and toast them, stirring constantly and swirling the pan, until they give off a pleasant aroma and darken, 3 to 4 minutes. The heat will draw out the natural oils of the spices and mellow the flavors. Pour the spices into a dry container to halt the toasting and let them cool.

Remove the seeds from the green and black cardamom pods. Discard the pods and return the seeds to the spice mixture. Working in small batches, grind the spice mixture to a fine powder in a spice grinder, blender, or mortar and pestle. Sieve, and regrind any bits of the mixture that do not pass through the sieve. Store the garam masalaa in a sealed container with a tight-fitting lid. It can be stored for up to several months without losing much of its flavor, but make sure to keep the container tightly closed after each use.

FRAGRANT GARAM MASALAA

Makes ¾ cup

When I was in Nepal recently, I went to several spice shops in the Kathmandu area searching for a recipe for the most authentic Nepali *garam masalaa* mixture. There are many versions of spice blends and the ingredients and proportions vary. Finally, I found an ancient herbal medicine spice shop called "*Baidya Ausadi Pasal*" in the Kilaagal area of Kathmandu. Mr. Manik Kazi Shakya jotted down the most popular combination of spices that is widely used all over Nepal and handed it to me. He told me his combination has the right flavor, texture, and aroma. While reading his list, I noticed that he uses dried ginger (*sutho*) and mace (*javitri*) for his combination of spices. Personally, I have never used these two spices in my homemade spice mixtures. I decided to make a fresh batch of *garam masalaa* with dried ginger and mace along with other ingredients and was very satisfied with the taste and aroma. I am so glad that I went on this quest since I ended up finding an incredibly aromatic combination for this spice blend.

This spice blend is more aromatic and milder than basic Nepali *garam masalaa*, where cumin and coriander dominate. Just a pinch of this fragrant mixture lends a wonderful aroma to any dish. It is usually added towards the end of the cooking process or sprinkled over cooked dishes as a last-minute garnish.

Seeds of 20 to 22 green cardamom pods (about 2½ tablespoons)
Seeds of 3 to 4 black cardamom pods (about 2 teaspoons)
1 tablespoon whole cloves
1 (3-inch) cinnamon stick, broken into several pieces

3 small cassia leaves, crumbled
1 tablespoon whole black peppercorns
½ whole nutmeg, broken into several pieces
2 tablespoons coriander seeds
1 tablespoon cumin seeds

Heat a small cast-iron skillet over medium-low heat. When it is hot, add all the spices and toast them, stirring constantly and swirling the pan, until they give off a pleasant aroma, 2 to 3 minutes. Pour them into a dry container to halt the toasting and let cool.

Transfer the cooled toasted spices to a spice grinder or mortar and pestle and grind to a fine powder. Sieve the spice mixture and regrind any bits that do not pass through the sieve. Store the mixture in a container with a tight-fitting lid. It can be stored for up to several months without losing much of its flavor, but make sure to keep the container tightly closed after each use.

NEPALI SEASONED SALT

Noon-Khursani ko Dhulo

Makes 1¼ cups

Nepali seasoned salt is a tasty combination of salt and many other spices that are usually found in your kitchen. It is a quick and convenient way to add flavor to a variety of Nepali dishes. It is sprinkled over boiled potatoes, roasted meats, eggs, fruits and vegetables, snacks, yogurt dishes, salads, and drinks. If you do not like the heat of cayenne pepper, you can customize the mixture to suit your own taste by adding more or decreasing it. For best results, make sure the spices are finely ground, so that they will not separate from the mixture while sprinkling.

¼ cup cumin seeds
1 tablespoon ajowan seeds
2 tablespoons timmur (Nepali pepper; *see page 31*)
½ cup salt

¼ cup Himalayan black salt powder
¼ cup cayenne pepper powder
1 tablespoon ground black pepper
¼ teaspoon asafetida powder

Heat a small cast-iron skillet over medium heat and toast the cumin seeds, ajowan seeds, and timmur, stirring constantly, until they give off a pleasant aroma and darken, about 2 minutes. Pour into a dry container to halt the toasting. When cool, transfer them to a spice grinder or a mortar and pestle, and grind into a fine powder.

Mix the dry-roasted ground seeds with the salt, black salt, cayenne pepper powder, black pepper, and asafetida powder. Transfer to a glass container with tight seal and store in a cool, dry place for up to 6 months.

HOMEMADE PANEER CHEESE

Makes 4 to 4½ cups

Chhanaa

Homemade cheese, called *chhanaa* in Nepali, is a versatile ingredient that absorbs the flavors of the food it is cooked with. It can be cubed and fried and added to almost any vegetable dish with a sauce. It can also be coated with chickpea flour and fried, or used in sweet dishes. If properly refrigerated, *chhanaa* keeps for four to five days, but it is best used within a day or two of making it.

> 1 gallon whole milk
> 1 to 1¼ cups fresh lemon or lime juice, strained*
> Cheesecloth

Pour the milk into a heavy saucepan and bring it to a rolling boil over high heat, stirring constantly. Be careful not to let it burn. When the milk threatens to boil over, quickly stir in the lemon juice. It will immediately separate into soft curds and whey. Stir gently. Remove the pan from the heat and allow the curdled milk to sit undisturbed for 2 minutes.

Line a strainer or colander with three layers of cheesecloth. Place the colander over a large bowl. Pour the curdled milk into the colander and let the whey drain. The whey can be used for the next batch of *chhanaa* (*see Note below*) or as a base for soup, vegetable dishes, or to cook rice.

Pull the corners of the cheesecloth together and tie them into a bundle. Twist the bundle and squeeze out as much liquid as possible from the curds. Hang the cheesecloth bundle on the kitchen faucet for at least 45 minutes to allow the whey to drain further. When it has stopped dripping, remove the bundle and wrap it in paper towels or a clean dry kitchen towel. Place the bundle on a flat surface and squeeze and roll it to extract any additional moisture. Unwrap it, remove the cheese, place it in a bowl, and knead it until smooth, 2 to 3 minutes. Use as directed in recipes or transfer the cheese to a baking sheet and spread 1 inch thick. Cut it into cubes or other shapes. If not using the *chhanaa* immediately, refrigerate it in an airtight container for 3 to 4 days.

*Note: You can use any of the following ingredients as coagulating agents for 1 gallon milk instead of lemon juice: 2 cups plain yogurt; ¾ cup white vinegar, diluted with a little water; 6 cups cultured buttermilk; or 3 cups *chhanaa* whey saved from a previous batch.

CLARIFIED BUTTER

Gheu

Makes 2¾ to 3 cups

Clarified butter is simply butter that has been simmered until it separates. The clear golden liquid that remains is called *gheu* in Nepal. It adds a unique buttery flavor to food that it is cooked with. It also has a higher smoking point than regular butter and therefore may even be used in deep-frying without burning. *Gheu* is used extensively in Nepali cuisine and is considered the secret ingredient in sweets. It has a pure, clean flavor and will remain fresh even stored at room temperature. I prefer to use *gheu* as a cooking medium in many of my recipes, and usually make it at home. It is also available ready-made at Nepali and Indian food stores or some well-stocked larger supermarkets, only in US it is called *ghee*.

> 2 pounds unsalted butter
> 2 large bay leaves

Cut the butter into small chunks and place it in a heavy saucepan with the bay leaves. Heat over low heat, stirring from time to time, until completely melted. Then raise the temperature to medium and cook, stirring occasionally, until the butter crackles and bubbles, 4 to 5 minutes. Reduce the heat to medium-low and simmer until it separates into three layers—a top layer of white foam, clear liquid in the middle, and a bottom layer of golden brown milky solids—35 to 40 minutes. Do not stir, but check the butter frequently to make sure it is not burning. Carefully skim off any white foam without disturbing the bottom.

Remove the pan from the heat and set aside for 10 minutes to allow the milk solids to further settle to the bottom. When the liquid has slightly cooled and it is easy to handle, pour or spoon the clear golden liquid into a wide-mouth container, leaving as much of the sediment in the pan as you can. You may also strain the liquid through a cheesecloth-lined strainer or a paper towel. Discard the bay leaves and milky solids. Cover the *gheu* and store it either in the refrigerator or at room temperature. Once cooled, the *gheu* will have a rich golden color, buttery aroma, and will solidify, but not harden.

Note: When making *gheu*, I prefer to use unsalted butter. Make sure that the milk solids that separate are not allowed to brown too much or the *gheu* will turn bitter. Do not use a wet spoon to scoop out the *gheu* from the jar while using it for a recipe, because when heated and it may splatter.

SPICED CLARIFIED BUTTER

Simmer cinnamon sticks, cardamom pods, or a combination of whole spices and herbs to make spice-infused *gheu*, but remove them before pouring the *gheu* into a storage container.

HOMEMADE YOGURT

Dahi

Makes 16 cups

Yogurt (*dahi*) is considered one of the most important dairy products in Nepal. Making it at home is simple and most of the equipment needed is already in your kitchen. You can also use reduced fat milk (2% fat), low-fat (1% fat), or skim (no fat), whatever you prefer. The fat content of the milk you use will dictate the consistency of your yogurt: the higher the fat content, the creamier the yogurt will be.

> 1 gallon whole milk
> ¾ cup plain yogurt with live and active cultures

Heat the milk in a heavy saucepan over medium-high heat. Stir constantly to prevent sticking and remove any skin that forms on the surface. Once it has come to a boil, remove from heat and let cool to lukewarm. You can speed up the cooling process by setting the pan in a bowl of ice and stirring continuously.

In a small bowl, mix ¼ cup of the lukewarm milk with the yogurt. Return the mixture to the warm milk. To mix thoroughly, pour the milk into another bowl then transfer it back to the pan, and then pour it back and forth two to three times. Transfer the mixture to a clean container and cover it with a lid. Wrap the container in a kitchen towel and place it in a warm spot, such as a pantry or on top of the refrigerator (see Helpful Hints below). It is important that the yogurt is kept warm and not disturbed until it is set, at least 6 hours. Do not shake or stir the milk during this process.

To test if the yogurt has set, slowly tilt the container, but do not stir. If the yogurt pulls away from the side of the container, then it is ready. Once the yogurt has set, transfer the pot to the refrigerator and chill for 5 hours. The yogurt will continue to thicken as it chills. The longer yogurt is left at room temperature, the tarter it becomes.

Helpful Hints:
If there is a large amount of whey floating on top of the set yogurt, your incubation period was too long. If your yogurt is too watery, there may have been insufficient starter culture, the culture may not have been properly mixed with the milk, or the mixture may have been disturbed during incubation period.

Alternative methods for incubation of yogurt:
Preheat the oven to its lowest setting for 10 minutes. Turn it off and place the yogurt mixture in the oven. To maintain the temperature, turn the oven on again every few hours. If your oven has a pilot light, there is no need to turn it on as the yogurt will set from just the heat of the pilot light. You may also place the bowl of yogurt in a cardboard box lined with a clean kitchen towel or on a rack on top of a food warmer set to the lowest setting.

NEPALI-ENGLISH GLOSSARY

aaashirbaad blessings
aalu potato
aamp mango
aandra-bhudi tripe
achaar pickle or chutney
aduwaa fresh ginger
ailaa home-made alcohol
aipan an auspicious religious design made with thin rice paste
akshataa uncooked, unbroken white rice used for ritualistic worship
akshataa/acheetaa ko tikaa paste made from vermillion powder, rice grains, and yogurt, applied on the center of forehead symbolizing good luck
alainchi black cardamom pods
amalaa green gooseberries
amchoor powdered dried mangoes
amilo dahi sour yogurt
anarsaa-roti sweet rice bread flavored with white poppy seeds
anna grain or food
Annaprashana rice feeding ceremony (page 16)
Annapurna goddess of grains and prosperity (page 26)
arsaa-roti rice molasses bread
atta flour durum wheat flour
aushedi medicine
Ayurveda ancient natural medicine

baabari mint
baara deep-fried spongy doughnut-shaped patties prepared from beans
baasi khanaa leftover, old, stale food
badaam almond; peanuts; also other multiple meaning
badian Indian lentil nuggets
bael wood apple
bajee pressed rice flakes or pounded rice
bakulla simi fava beans
banda ko paat cabbage leaves
bandaa govi cabbage
banel boar
bangoor pork
ban-kukhuraa turkey
barelaa balsam apple
barfi fudge-like sweet made from flour, thickened milk, nuts, fruits, and vegetables
bari small, round, Nepali-style meatballs/patties made from seasoned ground meat
Basmati long-grain fragrant white rice
battain quail
battisaa powder medicinal plant mixture
besaar turmeric
besan chickpea flour
betel nuts seed of areca palm
bhaadaa-kuda kitchen equipment
bhaat-bhujaa cooked rice

bhaat-ko-maad milky-starchy water obtained from boiling rice
bhaisi water buffalo
Bhai-Tikaa Brother-Sister Day (page 13)
bhantaa eggplant
bhatmaas fresh or dried soybeans
bhedaa lamb
bhedaa-ko-maasu lamb meat
bhitryaas tripe
bhogate pomelo
bhujaa cooked rice
bhujuri scrambled
bhus rice husks
bhuttan boiled-fried organ meat
bhutuwaa fried
biraulaa mixed sprouted beans
bire-noon black salt
bodi black-eyed peas
bokaa goat
bokaa ko maasu goat meat
boso fat
botaa leaf bowl made from saal leaves
bungo banana blossom

chaaku re-treated molasses unrefined sugar made into dark brown firm chunks
chaalaa skin
chaamal uncooked rice
chaamal ko pitho rice flour
chakati woven mat
chamari-gai yak
chamenaa appetizer or snacks
chamkera sprinkle
chamsoor garden cress
chanaa ko daal yellow split chickpeas or split Bengal gram
chapatti durum whole wheat flour
chataamari rice flower bread
chaukaa-belanaa dough rolling pins and platform
Chaurasi Benjan 84 varieties of dishes
cheuraa/chewraa pressed rice flakes or pounded rice
chhanaa paneer cheese
chhang white liquor from fermented rice
chhataa ko daal split white urad beans without skins
chhaype green onions
chhope dry-powdered pickle usually made from sesame seeds
chimta metal tong
chiplo daal slippery textured daal
chiya tea
chiya-pasal teahouse or roadside tea shop (page 24)
chokho pure and fresh
chook-amilo souring agent for pickles
chop oval or round patties made from vegetables, meat, or fish
chowelaa grilled-spiced meat salad
chuche karelaa balsam apple
chukar/chyakhura partridge

chulo wood-fed stove
chyau mushroom

daal all dried legumes, lentils, beans, and peas
daal-badi sun-dried lentil nuggets made with spicy lentil paste
daal-bhaat rice and lentils together
daal-bhaat-power-24-hour rice-lentil giving energy 24 hours
daal-bhaat-tarkaari lentils, rice, and vegetables
daalchini cinnamon
daal mahaaraani daal dish fit to serve a queen
dahi plain yogurt
dahi-cheuraa mixture of yogurt and pressed rice flakes
Dahi-cheuraa-khane-din Paddy Plantation Day, when you eat yogurt/pressed rice **dahi kadi** yogurt soup
dahi ko beu yogurt starter culture
Dashain Nepali religious festival (page 11)
Dhan Diwas Paddy Plantation Day (page 8)
dhaniya/dhania cilantro or fresh coriander
dhaniya/dhania ko geda coriander seeds
dhau pusa Newari word for yogurt starter cultures
dhauka triangle wood stand to hold yogurt in clay pot
dhindo millet, barley, buckwheat, cornmeal thick porridge
doodh milk
doodh-bari dessert cheese patties soaked in thickened milk
dubo holy grass
due maanaa two cups measurements
dum-alu potato dish
dunaa leaf bowl made from saal leaves

ek rate dahi yogurt made overnight

falaam ko taapke iron pot or pan
farsi ko phool squash blossom
furindaanaa popular savory snack mixture made from nuts, seeds, pressed rice flakes

gaaba young stalks of taro plant
gaajar carrot
garam masalaa blend of ground spices
Ghatasthaapanaa sowing barley seed day – Dashain festival
gheeraula smooth luffa gourd
gheu clarified butter
golbheda tomato
gulaab-jaamun popular dessert dumpling in fragrant syrup
guleo sweet

gundruk fermented greens
gyanth govi kohlrabi

haad-maasu bone-in meat
haaku chowelaa broiled meat with spices
haas duck
haluwaa sweet dish made with flour, vegetables, and fruits
Haluwai ko Pasal sweet shop
Haluwai Pasale sweet maker
hariyo bhatmaas fresh soybeans
hariyo dhania ko paat cilantro or fresh coriander
hariyo pharsi green squash
hariyo-bhatmaas-kosa soybeans in the pod
hariyo-chana fresh green chickpeas
heeng asafetida

imili tamarind
Indra Jatra Festival religious festival honoring Indra, the god of rain *(page 15)*
ishkush chayote squash

jaad local beer
jaato circular milling or grinding stone on a pivot
jaiphal nutmeg
jamaraa barley shoots
Janai/Kwaanti Purnima Day Nepali Sacred Thread Festival when a special sprouted bean soup (*Kwaanti*) is eaten *(page 10)*
jaulo rice porridge with lentils and vegetables
jeera cumin seeds
jesthalangwagi-churna medicinal plant mixture
jhaajar large slotted spoon
jhanne tempering spice to enhance the flavor of any dish
jhanne-masalaa spices for tempering food
jhol maasu soupy meat dish
jhol tarkaari curried vegetable dish
jilphi/jalebi/jeri deep-fried, pretzel-shaped confection in syrup
jimbu Nepali aromatic herb
jinge maachaa shrimp
jire-khursaani bird's eye chili pepper
jjaipatri mace
juju dhau sweetened yogurt
jutho impure, polluted or inedible food
jwaano/ajowan/ajwain bishop's weed, omum, or carom seeds
jwaano ko ras ajowan soup

kaagati lemon or lime
kaaju cashew nuts
kaaleej/kaaliz pheasant
kaalo chana dried, dark brown chickpeas
kaalo daal black urad beans
kaalo jeera black cumin seeds
kaalo maas ko daal split black urad beans with skin
kaalo noon black salt

kaankro cucumber
kachilaa marinated, spiced, raw ground meat
kadi smooth and creamy soup-like dish of yogurt and chickpea flour
kalejo liver
karaahi wok-shaped round-bottomed pot
karkalo taro root; **karkalo ko paat** taro leaves
kasaudi traditional rice cooking pot with round bottom and narrow neck
kataaro clay pot
kauli ko paat cauliflower leaves
keraa banana
kerau green peas
kerau ko daal split pea daal
kerau ko munta pea shoots
kesar saffron
khaajaa snacks
khaanaa food
khal mortar and pestle
khande thaal compartmentalized platter or divided plates
khasi castrated goat
khasi ko maasu castrated goat meat
kheer rice pudding
khichadi/khichari soft cooked rice and daal combination dish
khoste moong daal split green mung beans with skins
khudo molasses
khursaani chili
khus-khus poppy seeds
khuwaa concentrated thickened milk; base for many sweets
kodo ko pitho millet flour
koiralaa ko phool mountain ebony (flower of Bauhania trees)
kokyaoone irritating sensation to the throat when taro is eaten raw
kubhindo ash gourd
kukhuraa chicken
kurelo asparagus
kwaanti ko ras sprouted 8 bean soup
Kwaanti Purnima Nepali Sacred Thread Festival when a special sprouted bean soup (*Kwaanti*) is eaten *(page 10)*
kwaanti mixed sprouted bean soup

laabaa unhusked and puffed rice used during marriage ceremony
laakhaa-mari Newari ceremonial sweet bread
laddu sweet dessert balls
lapsi native fruit of Nepal, hog plum
lapsi ko bokraa lapsi fruit peels
lapsi ko gedaa seed of lapsi fruit
lapsi ko titaura fruit candy or nuggets or fruit rolls
lasoon ko poti garlic
lassi yogurt drink
lauka bottle gourd, opo squash
ledo achaar ground spice pickle
lwaang cloves

maachaa fish
maachaa ko sukuti dehydrated fish

maachaa-maasu fish-meat
maadaa fruit leather, roll-ups made from lapsi fruit
Maaghe Winter Festival *(page 9)*
maalpuwa sweetened batter-fried pancakes flavored with fennel seeds
maamuri golden brown, crusty, thin rice cake
maas ko daal urad beans or black gram daal
maas ko phulaura deep-fried lentil balls
maas ko pitho urad flour
maasu meat
maata ko ghaito earthen pots with wide necks for making pickles
maida ko pitho all-purpose white flour
makai corn
makhanaa puffed lotus seed
makkal small portable clay pot with charcoal fire
mana-bhog fluffy wheat haluwaa
marich peppercorn
marsi chaamal medium to short-grain white rice
masalaa spices
masalaa-dani spice box
maseura sun-dried nuggets made with lentils and vegetables
masino chaamal long-grain white rice
maskaune stir vigorously
matar green peas
methi ko geda fenugreek seeds
mirga venison
mirga ko maasu deer meat
mismaas mixed
misri rock candy
mithai sweets
mohi buttermilk
momochaa filled dumpling
momos meat or vegetable stuffed dumplings
moong/mugi ko daal split yellow mung beans without skin
mulaa radish
mulaa ko beu radish seeds
mulaa ko paat radish leaves used as greens
mung/moong mung beans
mung/moong ko roti bread prepared from mung bean batter
mung/moong ko titaura sun-dried split yellow mung bean nuggets
mungrelo nigella seeds
musuro ko daal red or pink lentils

naan Indian leavened bread baked in tandoor ovens
naanglo round wicker tray
namkeen salted crackers
naribal coconut
nauni homemade butter
neuro fiddlehead ferns
nibuwaa Nepali lemon
nimki snack crackers

paakeko pharsi yellow pumpkin
paakyo cooked
paalungo ko saag spinach

paan betel leaf chew
paan-batta traditional container filled with fragrant whole spices, betel nuts, dried fruits
paani water
paani chamkhera pakaune sprinkling water while cooking
Paasne Rice Feeding Ceremony *(page 16)*
paaun fruit leather
pahelo moong ko daal split yellow mung beans without skins
pakaaune cooking
pakaudaa chickpea batter-fried savory fritters
pakku cooked food
panyu iron spoon / large flat or round spoon with long handle
parvar/parwar pointed gourd
Pasne rice feeding ceremony
pate gheeraula angled luffa gourd
patre-roti flaky flatbread with multiple layers
paun fruit leather made from lapsi fruit
paun kwaa lapsi fruit soup
peda flat, round, sweet thickened milk patty
phaapar buckwheat
phaapar ko pitho buckwheat flour
phaapar ko roti buckwheat bread
pharsi ko muntaa pumpkin vine shoots
phaune whisk
phool eggs
phool-govi cauliflower
phulauraa deep-fried croquette
phulka-roti whole wheat light flatbread
pidaalu taro tubers
piro spicy
pista pistachio
pitho flour
pooja ko saamaan small tray filled with offerings to the gods
poori deep-fried puffed bread
prashaad food offered to gods and blessed
Prashaad ko maasu blessed meat
pulaau flavorful and festive rice dish
pyaj onion

quaanti/kwaanti mixed sprouted beans

raajmaa daal dried kidney beans
raam-toriya okra
raango ko maasu water buffalo meat
raato bodi dried kidney beans
raayo ko gedaa mustard seeds or sarsyun
raayo ko saag mustard greens
rabadi sweets made from thickened milk
rahar ko daal yellow split pigeon peas or toor daal
rakshee local liquor
rango ko Maasu water buffalo meat
ras soup

rasbari sweet dish made from fresh *chhana* cheese in fragrant syrup
raseelo juicy
roti bread
rukh-katahar green jackfruit

saada bhaat plain rice
saag green leaves
saal ko paat saal leaves
saandheko method of cooking marinated and spice tempered food
saano kerau small field peas
sagun food served to bring luck, success, and good fortune
sakhar-khanda sweet potatoes
samay baji ritual food tower consisting of pressed rice flakes with meat, beans, and fried-boiled eggs *(page 15)*
samosaa deep-fried triangular turnover
sanduke spice box
sankhatro lemon chew
saptarangi tikaa seven-colored tikaa
sattu toasted corn, wheat, millet, and barley flour
saunp fennel seeds
sel-roti crisp, sweet rice bread resembling a large, thin, puffed-up doughnut
shalgam ko paat turnip leaves
sharbat beverage
Shraadh yearly ceremony for ancestors *(page 17)*
sidraa maachhaa dried small dried fish
sikarni yogurt dessert flavored with cardamom and saffron
silauto-bachhaa heavy rectangular stone slab and roller-grinding stone
simi green beans
singo maas ko daal whole black urad beans with skins
singo moong ko daal whole green mung beans with skins
singo musuro ko daal brownish-green whole lentils
sinkaa bamboo stick
sinki pickled radish
sishnu nettle greens
sit lae khaeko tenderized by frost
sukeko chanaa dried chickpeas
sukeko hariyo kerau dried whole green peas
sukeko maachaa sun-dried fish
sukeko pahelo kerau dried yellow peas
sukumel green cardamom pods
sukuti dried fish or meat, jerky, dehydrated meat
supaari betel nuts
suruwaa maasu soupy boiled meat
Sutkeri ko Ausedhi postpartum super confectionery *(page 20)*
swaari soft deep-fried wheat bread
swan-puka batter fried lungs, boiled and fried

swaya baji puffed rice

taabaa/taawaa heavy cast-iron griddle
taamaa bamboo shoots, fermented or plain
taapke cast-iron pot with long handle and rounded bottom
taareko fried
tachauera corn pudding
tai-taapke frying pan
takhaa jellied meat
tane-bodi long beans
tapari woven, curved leaf plate made from multiple saal leaves
taraaju hand-help measuring scale
tarbujaa watermelon
tarikaa method
tarkaari vegetable
tarkaari bazaar vegetable market
tarul Nepali yam
tasalaa brass pot
teen maanaa 3 cups measurements
tejpaat cassia leaves
thaal-kachaura round tray with bowl
tharak marne completely cooked rice
thukpaa noodle soup
thulo chanaa dried whole yellow chickpeas
thulo kerau whole dried peas, both green and yellow
thwon homemade alcohol
Tihaar Festival five-day-long Nepali festival *(page 12)*
tikaa rice and yogurt ceremonial paste
til sesame seeds
til ko laddu sesame seed balls
tilauri chewy sesame candy
timmur Nepal pepper
tin-kune roti triangular-shaped bread
titauraa fruit nuggets made from lapsi fruit
tito karelaa bitter melon or bitter gourd
tori ko saag mustard greens
tori ko tel mustard oil
tsaampaa roasted flour made from corn, wheat, millet, barley
tulasi goddess basil
tyaamatar tamarillo or tree tomato

umaaleko boiled
usineko chaamal parboiled rice

woh lentil patties

yohmari stuffed steamed rice flour bread

INDEX

(*var.* = variation)